Toni Schindler Zimmerman, PhD
Editor

Integrating Gender and Culture in Family Therapy Training

Integrating Gender and Culture in Family Therapy Training has been co-published simultaneously as *Journal of Feminist Family Therapy,* Volume 12, Numbers 2/3 and 4 2001.

Pre-publication
REVIEWS,
COMMENTARIES,
EVALUATIONS . . .

"**F**ASCINATING. . . explores real families and family therapy through the overlapping lenses of culture, gender, power, sexual orientation, and social justice. RICH IN INSIGHT, WISDOM, AND DEPTH."

Fred P. Piercy, PhD
Professor and Head,
Department of Human Development,
Virginia Polytechnic Institute
and State University, Blacksburg

The Haworth Press, Inc.

Integrating Gender
and Culture
in Family Therapy Training

Integrating Gender and Culture in Family Therapy Training has been co-published simultaneously as *Journal of Feminist Family Therapy,* Volume 12, Numbers 2/3 and 4 2001.

The *Journal of Feminist Family Therapy (An International Forum)* Monographic "Separates"

Below is a list of "separates," which in serials librarianship means a special issue simultaneously published as a special journal issue or double-issue *and* as a "separate" hardbound monograph. (This is a format which we also call a "DocuSerial.")

"Separates" are published because specialized libraries or professionals may wish to purchase a specific thematic issue by itself in a format which can be separately cataloged and shelved, as opposed to purchasing the journal on an on-going basis. Faculty members may also more easily consider a "separate" for classroom adoption.

"Separates" are carefully classified separately with the major book jobbers so that the journal tie-in can be noted on new book order slips to avoid duplicate purchasing.

You may wish to visit Haworth's website at . . .

http://www.HaworthPress.com

. . . to search our online catalog for complete tables of contents of these separates and related publications.

You may also call 1-800-HAWORTH (outside US/Canada: 607-722-5857), or Fax 1-800-895-0582 (outside US/Canada: 607-771-0012), or e-mail at:

getinfo@haworthpressinc.com

Integrating Gender and Culture in Family Therapy Training, edited by Toni Schindler Zimmerman, PhD (Vol. 12, No. 2/3 and 4, 2001). *"ENGAGING. . . . THE PREDOMINANT THEME IS INFUSION, NOT JUST INCLUSION. In a time when trainers, supervisors, trainees, supervisees, and clients are increasingly likely to come from diverse cultural backgrounds, this book will serve to keep us engaged in dialogue that addresses our own sexism, racism, and homophobia, and broadens our own cultural and gender lenses." (Janie Long, PhD, MFT Faculty, Purdue University, Indiana)*

Feminism, Community, and Communication, edited by Mary W. Olson, PhD, LICSW (Vol. 11, No. 4, 2000). *This important book rethinks therapy, research, teaching, and community work with a renewed emphasis on collaboration, intersubjectivity, and the process of communication as a world-making and identity-making activity. The issues of gender, culture, religion, race, and class figure prominently in this valuable book.*

Transformations of Gender and Race: Family and Developmental Perspectives, edited by Rhea V. Almeida, LCSW, DVS (Vol. 10, No. 1, 1998/99). *Offers superb contemporary thinking in cultural studies, post-colonial theory, gender theory, queer theory, and clinical and research work with numerous populations who have been overlooked and undertheorized.*

Reflections on Feminist Family Therapy Training, edited by Kathy Weingarten, PhD, and Michele Bograd, PhD (Vol. 8, No. 2, 1996). *"Those new to a feminist perspective on family therapy will find their eyes widened; experienced trainers will become immersed in the subjective dialogue." (Kathleen McGuire, PhD, Center for the Study of Women in Society, University of Oregon)*

Cultural Resistance: Challenging Beliefs About Men, Women, and Therapy, edited by Kathy Weingarten, PhD (Vol. 7, No. 1/2, 1995). *"It explores the possibilities for therapy to act in resistance to culturally contructed and dominant narratives that constrain therapists and our clients." (Australian New Zealand Journal of Family Therapy)*

Ethical Issues in Feminist Family Therapy, edited by Maryhelen Snyder, PhD (Vol. 6, No. 3, 1995). *"These deeply felt and tightly reasoned chapters . . . illuminate therapist positions that are more likely to foster just relations." (Kathy Weingarten, PhD, Co-Director, Program in Narrative Therapies, Family Institute of Cambridge, MA)*

Expansions of Feminist Family Theory Through Diversity, edited by Rhea V. Almeida, LCSW, DVS (Vol. 5, No. 3/4, 1994). *"Represents an important turning point in the history of family therapy. The authors explicitly address fundamental power differentials–based on race, gender, social class, and sexual orientation–that organize life for all families in America." (Robert-Jay Green, PhD, Professor and Coordinator of Family/Child Psychology Training, California School of Professional Psychology, Berkeley)*

Feminism and Addiction, edited by Claudia Bepko, MSW (Vol. 3, No. 3/4, 1992). *"Provides valuable clinical information for therapists working with alcohol- and drug-addicted women. It describes methods of therapeutic training and intervention based on an integration of feminist theory and other major theories that expand the boundaries of treatment for addicted women." (Contemporary Psychology)*

Feminist Approaches for Men in Family Therapy, edited by Michele Bograd, PhD (Vol. 2, No. 3/4, 1991). *"A new offering that marriage and family therapists will find to be a valuable addition and resource." (Journal of Family Psychotherapy)*

Integrating Gender and Culture in Family Therapy Training

Toni Schindler Zimmerman
Editor

Integrating Gender and Culture in Family Therapy Training has been co-published simultaneously as *Journal of Feminist Family Therapy,* Volume 12, Numbers 2/3 and 4 2001.

The Haworth Press, Inc.
New York • London • Oxford

Integrating Gender and Culture in Family Therapy Training has been co-published simultaneously as *Journal of Feminist Family Therapy*™, Volume 12, Numbers 2/3 and 4 2001.

The development, preparation, and publication of this work has been undertaken with great care. However, the publisher, employees, editors, and agents of The Haworth Press and all imprints of The Haworth Press, Inc., including The Haworth Medical Press® and Pharmaceutical Products Press®, are not responsible for any errors contained herein or for consequences that may ensue from use of materials or information contained in this work. Opinions expressed by the author(s) are not necessarily those of The Haworth Press, Inc.

The Haworth Press, Inc., 10 Alice Street, Binghamton, NY 13904-1580 USA

Cover design by Thomas J. Mayshock Jr.

Library of Congress Cataloging-in-Publication Data

Integrating gender and culture in family therapy training / Toni Schindler Zimmerman, editor.
      p. cm.
      "Co-published simultaneously as Journal of feminist family therapy, volume 12, numbers 2/3 and 4, 2001."
      Includes bibliographical references and index.
      ISBN 0-7890-1353-3 (alk. paper) – ISBN 0-7890-1354-1 (alk. paper)
      1. Family psychotherapy. 2. Feminist therapy. 3. Psychiatry, Transcultural. 4. Cultural psychiatry. I. Zimmerman, Toni Schindler.
RC488.5. .I4975 2001
616.89'156–dc21
                                                2001026452

Indexing, Abstracting & Website/Internet Coverage

This section provides you with a list of major indexing & abstracting services. That is to say, each service began covering this periodical during the year noted in the right column. Most Websites which are listed below have indicated that they will either post, disseminate, compile, archive, cite or alert their own Website users with research-based content from this work. (This list is as current as the copyright date of this publication.)

Abstracting, Website/Indexing Coverage .... Year When Coverage Began

- *Alternative Press Index (online & CD-ROM from NISC) <www.nisc.com>* **1995**

- *Applied Social Sciences Index & Abstracts (ASSIA) (Online: ASSI via Data-Star) (CDRom: ASSIA Plus) <www.bowker-saur.co.uk>* **1996**

- *CNPIEC Reference Guide: Chinese National Directory of Foreign Periodicals* **1995**

- *Contemporary Women's Issues* **1998**

- *e-psyche, LLC <www.e-psyche.net>* **2001**

- *Family Studies Database (online and CD/ROM) <www.nisc.com>* **1996**

- *Family Violence & Sexual Assault Bulletin* **1992**

- *Feminist Periodicals: A Current Listing of Contents* **1992**

- *FINDEX <www.publist.com>* **1999**

- *Gay & Lesbian Abstracts <www.nisc.com>* **1997**

- *GenderWatch <www.slinfo.com>* **1998**

- *IBZ International Bibliography of Periodical Literature* **1996**

(continued)

Special Bibliographic Notes related to special journal issues (separates) and indexing/abstracting:

- indexing/abstracting services in this list will also cover material in any "separate" that is co-published simultaneously with Haworth's special thematic journal issue or DocuSerial. Indexing/abstracting usually covers material at the article/chapter level.
- monographic co-editions are intended for either non-subscribers or libraries which intend to purchase a second copy for their circulating collections.
- monographic co-editions are reported to all jobbers/wholesalers/approval plans. The source journal is listed as the "series" to assist the prevention of duplicate purchasing in the same manner utilized for books-in-series.
- to facilitate user/access services all indexing/abstracting services are encouraged to utilize the co-indexing entry note indicated at the bottom of the first page of each article/chapter/contribution.
- this is intended to assist a library user of any reference tool (whether print, electronic, online, or CD-ROM) to locate the monographic version if the library has purchased this version but not a subscription to the source journal.
- individual articles/chapters in any Haworth publication are also available through the Haworth Document Delivery Service (HDDS).

Integrating Gender and Culture in Family Therapy Training

CONTENTS

ABOUT THE EDITOR

Toni Schindler Zimmerman, PhD, is Associate Professor at Colorado State University. She has been the Director of the Marriage and Family Therapy Program at CSU for ten years. This program is strong in both research training and clinical skill training. The CSU MFT Program has been widely recognized for its tremendous efforts for integrating gender and culture in family therapy training. Toni Schindler Zimmerman has been a leader in gender and family therapy integration. In 1999, the MFT Program that she directs was given the AAMFT National Training Award. In 1997, she was awarded the Ruth Strang Research Award by the National Association for Women in Education. Also, in 1997, she was honored as the Colorado Marriage and Family Therapist of the Year by the CAMFT. Currently, she is editor for *Journal of Feminist Family Therapy* and has over 50 publications in the area of Marriage and Family Therapy. Her research, teaching and outreach efforts are in the areas of gender and culture integration in marriage and family therapy, work and family balance issues in family therapy, and gender and parenting. She currently has a grant from the Alfred P. Sloan Foundation for $206,000.00 studying successful balance of work and family. She is considered an outstanding teacher and trainer by her students and colleagues.

Preface:
Integrating Gender and Culture in Family Therapy Training

In the past twenty-five years or so, the field of family therapy has undergone significant changes. Prior to this time, therapists and trainers did not consider gender, race, ethnicity, class, sexual orientation, and spirituality as relevant to their work with clients. Today, many trainers and therapists consider these constructs to be organizing principles of society, people's lives and relationships. Rather than treating these principles as peripheral or "special topics," many family therapists fully integrate gender and culture into every therapy and supervision session, course, and interaction with students and colleagues. Although a full integration has not been realized by all trainers and therapists, we have much to celebrate.

These accomplishments have been realized through meaningful and difficult dialogue, in which persons in the field began to recognize and bring themselves and one another through the fog of sexism, racism, homophobia, and classism. As the fog continues to lift for each of us (e.g., clients, trainees, and ourselves), we are able to not only see the dynamics of power and oppression; we can also see how our own privilege and fear blind us. Our own transformation and effectiveness as trainers and therapists are realized when–in the face of our own blind spots–we take responsibility, are humbled, and continue to participate in this profound and often difficult dialogue. We continue to change.

Although there are many reasons to be optimistic, there is still much work to be done. This work will require all of our voices and a

---

[Haworth co-indexing entry note]: "Preface." Zimmerman, Toni Schindler. Co-published simultaneously in *Journal of Feminist Family Therapy* (The Haworth Press, Inc.) Vol. 12, No. 2/3, 2001, pp. xv-xvi; and: *Integrating Gender and Culture in Family Therapy Training* (ed: Toni Schindler Zimmerman) The Haworth Press, Inc., 2001, pp. xiii-xiv. Single or multiple copies of this article are available for a fee from The Haworth Document Delivery Service [1-800-342-9678, 9:00 a.m. - 5:00 p.m. (EST). E-mail address: getinfo@haworthpressinc.com].

xiii

commitment to remain in this necessary conversation. Each of these contributions attempts to continue this dialogue as it pertains to training and the socialization of the next generation of family therapists. This collection is dedicated to the many courageous and wise women and allied men–the lighthouses in the fog–who have been the beacons in our search for social justice.

Toni Schindler Zimmerman

The Weave of Gender and Culture in the Tapestry of a Family Therapy Training Program: Promoting Social Justice in the Practice of Family Therapy

Toni Schindler Zimmerman
Shelley A. Haddock

SUMMARY. Family therapy training programs are being challenged to ensure that future generations of family therapists are proficient in addressing gender, culture, and social justice issues in their practice of therapy. To address this challenge, MFT program faculty must fully integrate the organizing principles of gender and culture throughout every aspect of the curricula. This article describes specific ways that the faculty members in a marriage and family therapy training program weave gender and culture throughout the tapestry of a training program. It provides specific, concrete, and transferable strategies, activities,

Toni Schindler Zimmerman, PhD, is Associate Professor in Human Development & Family Studies, and Director of the Marriage & Family Therapy Program at Colorado State University. Shelley A. Haddock, MS, is Lecturer and Clinical Supervisor in the Marriage & Family Therapy Program, and Interim Director of the Marriage & Family Therapy Clinic at Colorado State University. The CSU Marriage & Family Therapy Program received the 1999 Training Award from the American Association for Marriage & Family Therapy in recognition of its strengths in training which include integrating gender and culture throughout the program.

This article is dedicated to the students and alumni of CSU's HDFS Department who are the best teachers and inspiration of the HDFS faculty.

[Haworth co-indexing entry note]: "The Weave of Gender and Culture in the Tapestry of a Family Therapy Training Program: Promoting Social Justice in the Practice of Family Therapy." Zimmerman, Toni Schindler, and Shelley A. Haddock. Co-published simultaneously in *Journal of Feminist Family Therapy* (The Haworth Press, Inc.) Vol. 12, No. 2/3, 2001, pp. 1-31; and: *Integrating Gender and Culture in Family Therapy Training* (ed: Toni Schindler Zimmerman) The Haworth Press, Inc., 2001, pp. 1-31. Single or multiple copies of this article are available for a fee from The Haworth Document Delivery Service [1-800-342-9678, 9:00 a.m. - 5:00 p.m. (EST). E-mail address: getinfo@haworthpressinc.com].

ideas, and resources for integrating gender and culture in family therapy courses, supervision, research, service, and clinical environments. *[Article copies available for a fee from The Haworth Document Delivery Service: 1-800-342-9678. E-mail address: <getinfo@haworthpressinc.com> Website: <http://www.HaworthPress.com> © 2001 by The Haworth Press, Inc. All rights reserved.]*

KEYWORDS. MFT training, gender, culture, graduate training, instruction, therapy

In response to the feminist critique, the field of family therapy is in the process of widening its systemic lens to more accurately reflect the fundamental organizing principles of gender and culture on relationships and families. Although several studies (e.g., Gilbert, 1995; Haddock, 1995; Leslie & Clossick, 1996; Werner-Wilson, Price, Zimmerman, & Murphy, 1998) have revealed that many practitioners and trainers have yet to fully adopt and/or apply this more systemic perspective (Taggart, 1985), there is evidence that this widening lens is gaining currency. For instance, there has been a proliferation of articles related to incorporating gender and culture in the practice of family therapy, and the Commission on Marriage and Family Therapy Education (COAMFTE) now requires that gender and culture are addressed in the curricula of accredited training programs.

It is incumbent upon training programs to ensure that future generations of family therapists are proficient in addressing gender, culture, and social justice in their practice of therapy for several reasons. First, as several scholars have argued, it is unethical not to do so (e.g., Avis, 1989; Weiner & Boss, 1985). Because we are all products of a racist, sexist, classist, and homophobic society, we must directly challenge these attitudes and behaviors in ourselves. Failing to do so will result in therapists providing less effective treatment, and most likely, even unwittingly causing harm to clients. For instance, in Gilbert's (1995) study, 53% of a sample of AAMFT clinical members did not address safety in their treatment plan for a situation involving wife abuse. Second, given the growing diversity of our society coupled with professional standards calling for therapists to be skilled in working with a diverse clientele, therapist without such training will be at a distinct professional disadvantage. And, third, a multicultural and gender emphasis enriches the theories and practice of family therapy in general.

For instance, as stated by Green (1998a), "the multicultural lens will bring into clearer focus the uniqueness of each race's normative family experience . . . . In addition, the study of therapist-client interracial differentness will help illuminate the more general process of negotiating differentness between therapist and client, regardless of race" (p. 95).

Although a burgeoning literature exists related to the practice of gender and culturally sensitive therapy, less has been written about addressing these fundamental categories of human experience in our training programs. When addressing gender in training and supervision, there are several excellent resources available. For instance, Avis (1989) and Leslie and Clossick (1992) outlined key assumptions and general guidelines for teaching a feminist perspective to family therapy trainees. Helmeke (1994) elaborated on specific ways to foster a safe atmosphere for discussing gender in family therapy training programs. Wheeler, Avis, Miller, and Chaney (1986) proposed a model that delineates the perceptual, conceptual, and executive skills that trainees must obtain to practice from a feminist perspective. Other authors have described specific activities for integrating gender in a family therapy course (Haddock, Zimmerman, & MacPhee, in press; McGill Roberts; 1991; Sirles, 1994; Storm, 1991), supervision (Ault-Riche, 1988; Haddock et al., in press; Nelson, 1991; Wheeler et al., 1986), or program curriculum (Storm, York, & Keller, 1997). Finally, there also have been articles related to special considerations when training women and men in the practice of feminist-informed family therapy (Nutt, 1991; Reid, McDaniel, Donaldson, & Tollers, 1987).

Although resources exist related to the incorporation of cultural variables in the practice of therapy (e.g., McGoldrick, 1998; McGoldrick, Pearce, & Giordano, 1996), less has been written in the family therapy literature on methods for providing trainees with the skills to address the organizing principles of race, ethnicity, socioeconomic status, and sexual orientation in their work with clients. Hardy and Laszloffy (1995) proposed the use of cultural genograms in training, and Falicov (1988; 1995) introduced a multidimensional, comparative framework for integrating culture in therapy and training. Four chapters in *Re-Envisioning Family Therapy* (McGoldrick, 1998) provide guidelines for transforming our theory and training to overcome the dominant culture's blinders to racism (Green, 1998b; Hardy & Laszloffy, 1998; Akamatsu, 1998).

With this article, we hope to contribute to the dynamic and necessary dialogue related to effective methods for training therapists to incorporate gender and culture in their practice. Although we describe training philosophies and assumptions, our primary contribution will be to provide specific and concrete activities, strategies, ideas, and resources for integrating gender and culture as a critical overlay in a Marriage and Family Therapy (MFT) Program. Our intention is to highlight activities and strategies that would be easily adopted by other family therapy trainers. These activities and strategies, however, cannot fully portray the importance and nature of the daily intricacies of interaction and environment that are foundational to creating a gender and culturally sensitive program. Specifically, we will describe the specific ways that faculty members in the Marriage and Family Therapy (MFT) Program at Colorado State University (CSU) integrate gender and culture throughout the major components of the program, including teaching, supervision, research, and service. This program was awarded the 1999 AAMFT Training Award in recognition of its integration of gender and culture in its curriculum.

TRAINING PHILOSOPHY AND ASSUMPTIONS

As many writers have persuasively argued (e.g., Avis, 1989; Falicov, 1995; Green, 1998; Hardy & Laszloffy, 1998; Storm et al., 1997), widening students' lenses to include gender, race, ethnicity, and sexual orientation requires much more than adding readings or devoting a few class sessions to these "special topics." We agree with Storm et al. (1997) that a complete "transformation" of the program and curriculum is required. The curriculum of the CSU MFT Program is based on the premise that gender and culture–like age–are organizing principles of relationships and families (Falicov, 1995; Goldner, 1988). Likewise, we believe that gender and culture necessarily must be central organizing principles of the entire program. Considerations of gender and culture provide the framework from which theories are taught and applied, research is conducted and critiqued, clinical supervision and therapy are conducted, programmatic decisions are made and implemented, and perhaps most importantly, from which the daily intricacies of interaction between faculty, students, and clients are enacted. Metaphorically speaking, in the tapestry of the training program, gender and culture are woven through all other areas or topics. It is our experience that this truly integrated approach produces a stronger, richer, and more colorful tapestry. When these philosophies are realized within a training program, trainers' and students' lives are "transformed" (Storm et al., 1997) personally and professionally, allowing them to be more conscious and effective in both arenas.

Foundational Assumptions of the Program

The curriculum is based on four basic assumptions about how to best integrate gender, culture, and social justice issues in training methods.

1. *Consistency of process and content.* The process of training is ideally consistent with the content (Avis, 1989). Rather than addressing gender and multicultural topics simply through dissemination of information, it is best for trainers to provide students with opportunities to experience feminist and multicultural principles in the every day interactions of the program. This can be accomplished by attending to power dynamics among students, between students and faculty, and among the faculty. For example, relationships between faculty and students need not be characterized by rigid hierarchy in order to create respect; maintaining "human, flexible" (Avis, 1989) relationships is more consistent with feminist and multicultural principles.

2. *Atmosphere of humility.* It is important to cultivate an atmosphere of humility and safety around feminist and multicultural topics. This can be accomplished through maintaining a shared conviction that because we are all influenced by the sexist, racist, and homophobic messages of our society (Avis, 1989), we will all have "blind spots" and will continually need to challenge ourselves in these areas (Lerman, 1994).

3. *Attention to theory and application.* Feminist and multicultural principles are taught ideally on a theoretical and applied level. Trainers should facilitate students' rethinking of the societal and familial relationships through extensive reading, theoretical discussion, and personal exploration (Avis, 1989; Goodrich, Rampage, Ellman, & Halstead, 1988; Storm, 1991; Wheeler et al., 1989). However, training must go beyond theoretical issues to stress practical application (Haddock et al., in press). In other words, training should address the intricacies and practicalities

of specific ways that therapists can attend to gender and culture in interactions with clients.

4. *Attention to the interlocking nature of gender and culture.* Rather than addressing gender and culture as separate dimensions (e.g., a section in a course on gender, another section on race, and a third on sexual orientation), faculty should assist students in understanding the intersections of gender and culture. Trainees ideally recognize that experiences of power, oppression, and socialization vary according to an individual's "ecological niche" and position vis-à-vis the dominant culture (Falicov, 1995).

Having described the primary assumptions that inform our approach to training, we will provide specific examples of how we operationalize these assumptions in teaching, supervision, research, and service.

TEACHING

Within our curriculum, we have chosen not to include a separate course on gender and culture. Rather, these topics are infused throughout virtually all courses in the curriculum. The majority of faculty members in the Human Development and Family Studies Department (within which the Marriage and Family Therapy Program is housed) have participated in two university-sponsored programs on methods for integrating gender and culture in their courses (MacPhee, Kreutzer, & Fritz, 1994; MacPhee, Oltjenbruns, Fritz, & Kreutzer, 1994). Therefore, in family therapy courses, for instance, all theories (e.g., solution focused, strategic, structural) and presenting problems (e.g., domestic violence, eating disorders, substance abuse, sexual and communication difficulties) are viewed through a feminist and multicultural lens. In developmental courses, each phase of the life span is examined with regard to gender, ethnicity, race, and sexual orientation. Because of space limitations, we are unable to describe the way in which each course in the curriculum infuses these topics. Instead, we will showcase three of the therapy courses–an introductory marriage and family therapy theories course (HD534: Marriage and Family Therapy Theories), an ethics course (HD677: Legal and Ethical Issues in Marriage and Family Therapy), and an introductory course on basic skills in family therapy (HD686: Professional Skills Development). The first two courses are taught by the first author, and the third by the second author.

HD534: Marriage and Family Therapy Theories

Students enroll in this course during their first semester of the program. The goals of the course are to: (a) introduce students to four metaframeworks–systemic, constructivist, feminist, and multicultural–and the integration of these metaframeworks, (b) introduce students to six family therapy theories (e.g., solution focused, narrative), (c) critique and apply these therapy theories using the feminist and multicultural frameworks, and (d) encourage application and integration of the metaframeworks and family therapy theories in the practice of therapy.

As recommended by Avis (1989), students read a great deal of material on gender and culture in the course. In addition to reading a basic marriage and family therapy text (e.g., Schwartz & Nichols, 1998), students also read *Ethnicity and Family Therapy* by McGoldrick, Giordano, and Pearce (1996), and *Equal Partners, Good Friends* by Rabin (1996). Additionally, students read a collection of selected articles that includes additional material on gender and culture. As described below, the instructor provides both lecture material and opportunities for experiential activities in the course.

Introduction to metaframeworks. The first half of the course is devoted to introducing students to the metaframeworks. These metaframeworks form the foundation of the remainder of the course and are applied consistently to all other materials in the course. Before addressing each metaframework in depth, the instructor introduces the concept of metaframeworks in general, using a metaphor of an umbrella. The instructor conceptualizes the MFT theories as the handle of an umbrella, while the metaframeworks provide the "cover" (i.e., umbrella fabric). Students learn that–when they walk into the therapy room–regardless of which family therapy theory they have "in hand," they should open their umbrella so they are "covered" by the metaframeworks. The metaframeworks are conceptualized as "safety" from "bad weather" (e.g., racism, sexism, classism, and homophobia).

The instructor describes therapists' use of the metaframeworks as lying on a continuum from "1" to "5." For instance, if a therapist fails to fully open their systemic umbrella (and therefore stays on the low end of the continuum), they will conceptualize problems and solutions from a linear perspective. If they fully open their umbrella (moving to the upper end of the continuum), they will operate from the "safety" of a systemic perspective. Similarly, if they fail to open their constructivist umbrella, they will take an expert stance with clients; whereas the coverage of this umbrella will provide them the "safety" of considering multiple realities in their work with clients.

It is important to discuss the application of metaframeworks as falling on a continuum for several reasons. First, it is more reflective of what typically occurs in therapy. As Haddock et al. (in press) argued, it is typically not accurate to label any one session–or even an intervention–as "feminist" or "not feminist." Typically, a therapist incorporates some principles from feminist and multicultural meta-theories in a session while neglecting others; further, an intervention may have had a feminist-informed *intention,* but be *delivered* in a less feminist-informed manner. Using a continuum emphasizes the fluidity of and progression in therapists' behaviors and skills. In conceptualizing the application of metaframeworks on a continuum, the instructor can challenge students to "open their umbrella" more fully (or move towards the upper end of the continuum) while also recognizing that this is a challenging process–one that none of us do perfectly in every session. For instance, metaphorically speaking, sometimes the wind catches our umbrella; sometimes we forget to carry it with us; some-times our umbrella gets holes in it that we may not at first notice. Regardless, it is our responsibility to keep our umbrella in good shape, hold it against the wind, and use it for the "safety" of our clients. Following this general introduction, the instructor describes each me-taframework in depth. In this article, we will only address how the instructor introduces the feminist and multicultural metaframeworks. Although these metaframeworks are initially introduced separately, the instructor emphasizes the interlocking nature of gender and culture throughout classroom discussions and assignments.

The feminist metaframework. To introduce the topic of gender, the instructor uses two primary methods to facilitate her lecture material. The first, a modified version of "In-the-Box, Out-of-the-Box" (Creighton & Kivel, 1992), invites students to examine the socializa-tion process for women and men and how this process influences their relationships. See Appendix A for a brief description of this model and ideas for presentation. Following a full discussion of this model, the instructor transitions to a theoretical discussion of the feminist critique of family therapy, and the importance of conceptualizing gender as an organizing principle of relationships. Students are given an opportunity to discuss the assigned readings in this context. The film *Tough Guise* (Bailey, 1999), a powerful portrayal of the construction of masculinity in American society, is shown. Students also view *Still Killing Us Softly* (1987; a new version is due in year 2000), which illustrates issues central to female socialization through images in advertising.

As mentioned above, given our experience that students typically have more difficulty with *enactment* rather than *assimilation* of feminist principles, the instructor uses the *Power Equity Guide* (Haddock et al., in press) to facilitate a discussion of how gender can *specifically* be addressed by therapists in their work with clients. Rabin (1996) and Whipple (1996) are excellent resources in this context because each includes theoretical and practical guidance to therapists. Following a detailed review of the *Power Equity Guide,* students are shown clips from two AAMFT Master's Series tapes–one that depicts a therapist working on the upper end of the feminist continuum, and one that depicts several interventions that are at the lower end of this continuum. Students use the *Power Equity Guide* to critique the therapists' work at various points in the tapes according to feminist principles, and brainstorm specific ways that the therapist could have moved further up the feminist continuum. The instructor also provides therapy for a client of the CSU Marriage and Family Therapy Clinic so students may observe the case from behind the one-way mirror. Students are directed to focus their observations on application of the metaframeworks and integration of family therapy theories reviewed in the course.

The multicultural framework. In introducing the multicultural framework, the instructor has four primary goals: (a) providing students with a safe and supportive environment where they can develop the skills, emotional capacity, and desire to acknowledge their own racism, classism, and homophobia in an ongoing manner; (b) inviting students to take responsibility for developing multicultural sensitivity while encouraging them to be comfortable with "not knowing everything" and enthusiastic about learning more (Green, 1998); (c) facilitating students to develop intracultural sensitivity (e.g., an awareness of cultural differences and their importance); (d) assisting students to develop intercultural sensitivity (e.g., an awareness of the institutionalized privilege and power of some groups relative to others); and

(e) assisting students in understanding the intersections of culture and gender.

To introduce a discussion of racism, the instructor begins by showing and facilitating a discussion of two powerful films, *The Color of Fear* (Mun Wah & Foo, 1994) and *The Way Home* (Butler, 1998). The instructor encourages students to apply the content of these films to the practice of therapy (e.g., How will the content of these films influence your work as a therapist? What did you learn about how to address power differentials between clients? What did you notice about the invisibility of power differentials to those group members who belonged to the majority group? How might this invisibility affect the therapeutic process and families in general? What did you learn about the way in which gender socialization varies for individuals of diverse racial backgrounds?)

To promote intracultural sensitivity, the instructor leads discussions based on the students' reading of *Ethnicity and Family Therapy* by McGoldrick, Giordano, and Pearce (1996). This book allows students to learn culturally specific information, such as family relationships, class structures, and help-seeking behaviors. This culturally specific information is discussed with the recognition that families are acculturated at different levels, and therefore will reflect this general information to varying degrees.

To encourage synthesis of the material covered thus far in the course, the instructor assigns a metaframeworks synthesis paper, which requires students to develop a short case scenario. For this case, they are to describe how they would provide therapy if they were working from the low end of the continuum (with their umbrella down) versus if they were working from underneath a fully opened umbrella. For each end of the continuum, students are asked to address the following questions: What are the specific questions you would ask? What kinds of interventions would you use? What kinds of homework assignments would you give? For instance, in discussing the feminist and multicultural metaframework, one student wrote, "If I had my metaframeworks umbrella up, I would openly encourage an egalitarian relationship between this couple by . . . . " Another student wrote, "If I had my umbrella up, I would investigate in what ways does acculturation, racism, and gender socialization affect the client's depression."

Application of the metaframeworks to MFT theories. In the second half of the course, six family therapy theories are introduced. For each therapy theory, two students are assigned to create a videotaped role play of a therapist applying the family therapy theory (e.g., solution focused, narrative). This videotape is shown to the class when that particular family therapy theory is introduced by the instructor. "Clients" in the role play represent a marginalized group (e.g., a gay or lesbian couple, a family from a marginalized ethnic or racial group, or a family living in poverty), allowing students an opportunity to operationalize multicultural competencies. Students are also expected to incorporate feminist principles in their role played therapy session, addressing specific ways that gender socialization interacts with culture for this particular client.

For this assignment, it is helpful to have a teaching assistant–a more advanced student in the program–to act as a mentor or coach to the students in developing their videotape. Typically, the assistant will provide specific suggestions on additional ways to include the concepts and techniques of the therapy theory and to move their work further along the metaframework continuums (e.g., maintaining a nonhierarchical stance with clients, empowering clients to explore nontraditional gender choices, or actively assessing the influence of racism or homophobia on the presenting problem). After receiving this feedback, students typically conduct and videotape the role play again; this improved version is shown to the class. Again, in a safe environment, the class and instructor provide feedback on the videotape with regard to application of the particular family therapy theory and their incorporation of the metaframeworks.

Another course assignment is used to encourage students to apply the feminist and multicultural metaframeworks to particular family therapy theories and techniques. For each family therapy theory covered in the course, students complete an "Application of Feminist and Multicultural Metatheories to Family Therapy Theories" worksheet (see Figure 1). On this worksheet, the "metaframeworks umbrella" is depicted. Directions on the worksheet ask students to brainstorm ideas for applying these principles to a particular family therapy theory (e.g., narrative). Space for their ideas is provided on the worksheet underneath the "metaframework umbrellas." For instance, a student may write: "When you consider a client's problem-saturated dominant story, ask them in what ways their gender and culture have influenced or participated in the problem saturation. In what ways does your culture or gender influence your ability to participate in an alternative story?"

The final examination is held during the second to the last class period. For this exam, students are shown a clip of a therapy session.

FIGURE 1. Application of Feminist and Multicultural Metaframeworks to Family Therapy Theories

DIRECTIONS: Brainstorm Ideas for Applying Feminist and Multicultural Principles in the Application of the Therapy Theory Indicated

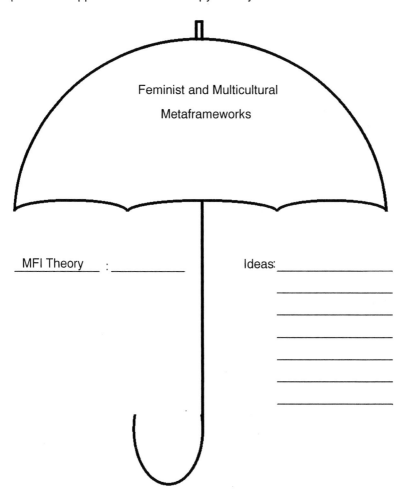

They randomly select a therapy theory and develop a detailed treatment plan for the case based on this theory. Additionally, the students randomly select a societally marginalized status (e.g., gay or lesbian, African American, Jewish), and discuss potential special considerations in working with the family on the videotape if one or more of the members were from this marginalized group. It is an expectation that treatment plans incorporate feminist principles.

During the last session of class, the instructor returns the students' graded exams. The students take turns briefly describing their treatment plan for the case. This activity is beneficial for several reasons. First, it allows students the opportunity to see how a case can be approached from a variety of family therapy theories. Second, it provides students with an opportunity to see how a case would be handled differently based on the clients' "ecological niche" (Falicov, 1995), e.g., their ethnicity, socioeconomic status, or sexual orientation. For instance, if the case involved a family with a truant adolescent, the student who selected "gay or lesbian client," may emphasize the influence of the "coming out" process and societal homophobia on the adolescent's behavior. One of the therapist's interventions might involve referring the young man to a group for gay youth and his parents to P-FLAG (a national organization for Parents and Friends of Lesbians and Gays). The student who selected "African American client" may emphasize that the young man is one of five African-American students in a predominantly Caucasian school. The treatment plan might include initiating a conversation between the young man and his parents about racism and ways they have dealt with it in their own lives, facilitating dialogue with school staff to address racism, and empowering the adolescent by encouraging peer relationships and acknowledging his experience.

Student feedback on this course has been consistently positive. Students report experiencing a paradigm shift, allowing them to recognize the influences of gender and culture on individuals and their relationships and the importance of integrating these issues in therapy.

HD686: Professional Skills Development

Students enroll in this course concurrently with HD534: Marriage and Family Therapy Theories during their first semester in the program. The goal of this course is to provide students with basic therapy skills (e.g., joining, assessment, goal setting), and to transition them into their practicum experience in the Marriage and Family Therapy Clinic as therapists (by teaching them the policies and procedures of the clinic). Additionally, opportunities are presented to students to begin the ongoing process of self-examination in terms of their own "ecological niche" (Falicov, 1995). Excellent resources exist for these training purposes (e.g., Hardy & Lazsloffly, 1995; Falicov, 1995; Papp & Imber-Black, 1996; Storm, 1991). Because it is taken concurrently with HD534, the course is also designed to provide students with additional opportunities to apply family therapy theories and metaframeworks in the practice of therapy. The following three assignments in this course are particularly relevant with regards to integration of gender and culture.

Application of the metaframeworks during therapy observation. The first assignment requires students to observe from behind the one-way mirror fifteen hours of therapy conducted by second-year students in the program's Marriage and Family Therapy Clinic. To encourage students to focus their observation on those aspects central to the course, they are required to address several questions related to (a) basic skills (e.g., "Specifically, how is the therapist joining with the client? Specifically, how is the therapist structuring the session–e.g., initiating closure to the session, interrupting problematic interactions?"); (b) the systemic metatheory (e.g., What are one linear and two systemic hypotheses about the case?); and (c) feminist and multicultural metatheories (e.g., How did the therapist include gender as a topic? How did the therapist manage the hierarchy in the therapist-client relationship?) Students also indicate what they might have asked or done in the session to further integrate the metaframeworks.

Therapy simulations with theater students acting as clients. For the second assignment, students are required to conduct a three-session therapy simulation with theater students acting as clients, an activity developed by Werner-Wilson (2000). To facilitate this assignment, the instructor requests assistance from the theater department on campus in recruiting and preparing theater students to act as therapy clients for this activity. Each pair of theater students is provided with a scenario from which to further develop characters and a situation. The scenarios depict clients of diverse backgrounds and involve presenting problems that are clearly influenced by gender and culture. For instance, one scenario involves a heterosexual couple who recently had their first child. The couple is struggling with topics that are typically gender-laden, such as division of housework and parenting responsibility, and breadwinning pressures.

Presentations of therapy simulations. The third assignment requires students to present their simulated therapy case to the class–after the first or second session has been conducted. As part of the presentation, they show a videotape clip of their session and present their emerging treatment plan. During their case presentation, among other topics, students are required to discuss the possible influences of gender and culture on the presenting problem. Students have reported that the simulated therapy sessions and case presentation are very beneficial by allowing them to practice (a) clinic protocols (e.g., turning on the taping equipment, reviewing intake paperwork, administering assessments, and taking case notes), (b) basic therapy skills covered in the course, (c) case presentation, and (d) application of the metaframeworks and therapy theories introduced in HD534. The assignment generally leads students to experience heightened confidence in their abilities prior to beginning to work as therapists in the clinic with "real" clients.

HD677: Legal and Ethical Issues in Marriage and Family Therapy

The goals of this course are to provide students with (a) a thorough understanding of the AAMFT Code of Ethics, and national and state laws governing therapist behavior, (b) skills for recognizing and resolving ethical situations or dilemmas, (c) skills for interpreting and applying ethical standards within the context of feminist and multicultural metaframeworks, and (d) information and skills related to various professional issues, such as operating a private practice, obtaining licensure, and conducting research. Three books are required reading: *Ethical, Legal, and Professional Issues in the Practice of Family Therapy* (Huber, 1994), *Feminist Ethics in Psychotherapy* (Lerman & Porter, 1990), and *Soul Searching* (Doherty, 1995). Additionally, a reading packet on ethics with many readings related to gender and culture is assigned.

The course begins with a review of ethics in general and the importance of interpreting ethical codes within the context of the organizing principles of gender, race, class, and sexual orientation. Students are encouraged to apply the feminist and multicultural metatheories to the topic of ethics. One of the primary considerations when applying feminist and multicultural principles to ethics is the management of power differentials between therapists and clients (Haddock et al., in press; Whipple, 1996). It has been argued that minimizing and managing power differentials facilitates the healing potential of therapy, and reduces therapists' risk of violating ethical principles or harming clients (either intentionally or unintentionally). To illustrate this important principle, the instructor shows excerpts from the movie, *The Doctor*. This film is an excellent illustration of how taking an expert or power position with clients tends to lead to objectification of clients (and therefore an increased risk of committing ethical violations). Through his own personal experience with cancer, the doctor portrayed in this film reevaluates his approach to patients. Through this process, he learns to more effectively manage the power differentials between himself and his patients. The film also depicts the violation of several ethical principles, including situations of sexual harrassment, professional dishonesty, and inappropriate uses of humor with patients, which provide additional material for class discussion.

The instructor then leads discussions based on Lerman and Porter (1990) and articles included in the reading packet to illustrate the importance of considering contextual issues in the application of ethical principles. For instance, ethical principles related to dual relationships are analyzed from the perspective of special populations, such as rural community members or gay and lesbian individuals. A discussion is facilitated on the way in which therapists handle confidentiality between the members of a couple where violence is an issue. Students also discuss the ethics of diagnosis from a feminist and multicultural lens. For instance, students learn that cultural biases lead to some diagnoses being disproportionately given to particular groups by therapists (e.g., women are disproportionally diagnosed as having borderline or dependent personality disorder, and African American men are disproportionally diagnosed as paranoid personality disorder) (Soloman, 1992; Cook, Warnke, & Dupoy, 1993).

As part of the course assignments, groups of students provide presentations to the class on topics that were selected from a list of possible topics at the beginning of the course, such as child abuse, suicide, homicide, adult violence, court testimony, licensure and certifications, and research ethics. These topics are those commonly addressed in graduate professional ethics courses. However, to fulfill the goal of fully infusing gender and culture, students are required to fully integrate the topics of gender and culture in their presentation.

Another relevant course assignment requires that students write a personal disclosure statement that they can use upon graduation. The assignment requires students to include a description of their theoretical orientation and methods and to be explicit about their personal value system on important and controversial topics, such as abortion, homosexuality, and divorce. As argued by many feminist writers (e.g., Haddock et al., in press), therapists should be overt about their personal values so that clients can make an informed choice about their selection of a therapist. For instance, a gay or lesbian adolescent who is coming out should know the therapist's beliefs about homosexuality. Similarly, a woman considering her options for a crisis pregnancy should know the therapist's stance regarding abortion, adoption, and parenting.

For the final examination, students are provided with actual cases in which ethical violations occurred. These cases are from Brock (1994) and clippings from local and national newspapers. For each case, students discuss or write short papers on the following: the particular ethical and/or legal violation, what actions the therapist could have taken to avoid the violation, what actions the therapist could take now that the violation has occurred, and what feminist and cultural considerations are relevant to the case. The final examination is discussed the final week of the course to enhance further learning.

SUPERVISION

As in all accredited programs, students receive both group and individual supervision. Supervision offers many opportunities to teach students to apply the feminist and multicultural frameworks in the assessment and intervention of each case. Below, specific strategies for integrating gender and culture throughout group and individual supervision will be provided.

Group Supervision

Group supervision is co-taught by all of the MFT faculty members. Students enroll in this weekly course during every semester of the program. Two basic components–case presentation and reading–comprise the assignments and expectations for the group supervision experience.

Case presentation. For the first component of the course, students are provided the opportunity to present their cases and receive feedback in a group setting. In this and other settings, the influences of gender and culture are central to the discussion of virtually every case. These discussions typically arise spontaneously because of the emphasis given to the feminist and multicultural metaframeworks in the program. However, attention to these topics is also formally integrated through inclusion on a required group staffing form. For each case presentation, students are required to complete a presentation form that outlines relevant case material (e.g., age, race, ethnicity, gender, and relationship status of the client, the presenting problem, and the treatment goals and plan). This form also includes a separate section that invites the therapist to examine and comment on the influences of the societal organizing principles of gender and culture on the client and presenting problem.

Popular press books. With regards to the reading component of the course, students are required to read ten books per year (20 books total in the two-year program) that are valuable resources to which to refer clients in particular situations. Students select these books from among many included in a bibliography designed for the course (Zimmerman, Haddock, McGeorge, & Holm, 1999). Most of the books included in this bibliography are popular press books that would be useful supplements to therapy. The selection criteria for inclusion on the bibliography are that the books are based on or consistent with current research and are consistent with the feminist and multicultural metaframeworks. Examples of books that are included are: *Seven Principles for Making Marriage Work* (Gottman & Silver, 1999); *Reviving Ophelia* (Pipher, 1994); *Not Guilty* (Holcomb, 1998); *Real Boys* (Pollack, 1998); and *Love Between Equals: How Peer Marriage Really Works* (Schwartz, 1994).

For each book, students are required to write a paper based on one of the following assignment options: (a) an application of the book's material to one of their cases; (b) a Cliff Note summary of the major aspects of the book; or (c) a collection of handouts and/or activities based on the book to be used with clients. For all papers, students are required to critique the book from a feminist and multicultural lens.

When students write a paper based on one of the latter two options, these papers are compiled in a notebook for use by therapists of the program's Marriage and Family Therapy Clinic. This notebook allows therapists to determine which books they would like to read, to quickly select appropriate books for which to refer their clients, or to use the handouts or activities developed from this book.

At the beginning of this course, students are introduced to the power of the self-help industry. They learn the prevalence of the self-help industry, and how this industry may influence their work with clients both positively and negatively. To introduce this topic, course instructors review the results of a thematic analysis of the ten best-selling self-help books (Zimmerman, Holm, & Starrels, 1999). Students learn the prevalent themes in these books–many of which are not consistent with research or feminist and multicultural perspectives. As an experiential activity, students watch a videotape of the author of the leading self-help book, *Men Are from Mars, Women Are from Venus* (Gray, 1992), and critique his suggestions from a feminist and multicultural perspective, using the *Power Equity Guide.* This activity helps students become critical consumers of popular press books.

Individual Supervision

In individual supervision, faculty members integrate gender and culture in a variety of ways, including providing students with opportunities to work with both male and female supervisors and co-therapists, managing the hierarchy in the supervisor-supervisee relationship, and discussing gender and culture with every case.

Providing opportunities to work with various supervisors and classmates. For each of three semesters of practicum, students are assigned a different supervisor, allowing them to work with supervisors of both genders. Students also have the opportunity to participate in a supervision team with a different classmate each semester, again enhancing their opportunities to obtain multiple perspectives on their cases. Furthermore, students are encouraged to do co-therapy on some cases and observe one another's cases as another means to obtain multiple perspectives.

Minimizing the hierarchy in the supervisor-supervisee relationship. Supervisors attempt to minimize the hierarchy in the supervision relationship, creating safe and respectful relationships with supervisees. As suggested by Wheeler et al. (1989), we attempt to accomplish this goal through contracting, which underscores the shared responsibility for change and learning; evaluation, in which both supervisor and supervisee share responsibility for evaluating each other's successes and limitations in reaching the intended goals; and through the use of clear, uncomplicated, and nonsexist language and suggestions, which reduces power and status differentials and facilitates learning. Below, we provide specific examples of how these three goals may be operationalized during supervision.

Supervisors elicit supervisees' goals at the beginning of each semester, and together, they develop a plan for accomplishing these goals during the semester. The supervisor is attentive to integrating attention to gender and culture in this plan. For instance, a supervisee may indicate the goals of becoming (a) more adept with MRI, (b) more comfortable working with adolescent clients, and (c) appropriately directive in sessions. The following plan may be developed. With regard to the first goal, one or two cases may be selected (based on their fit with the model) for which the supervisor and supervisee can develop and implement treatment plans based on MRI theory. The supervisor will provide clear guidance in this process, including how the therapist can operationalize this theory with their "metaframeworks umbrella" fully open. For instance, in teaching a supervisee how to map a cycle, the supervisor may teach the supervisee to also map a "societal influence cycle" outside of (but connected to) the original cycle. Clients, then, could be helped to see how gender and culture influence their patterns of interaction. Based on the feminist critique of the concept of circularity, the supervisor may help the supervisee find alternative ways to create cycles that attend to power dynamics. For instance, in mapping an argument cycle with clients, if abusive behaviors are reported, these behaviors would be depicted as "outside" of an argument cycle, indicating personal responsibility of the perpetrator. The therapist could underscore this depiction by overtly stating that there is nothing that anyone can do that warrants abusive behaviors by another person, and developing a treatment plan that addresses the violence and safety concerns. In other situations, some "turns" in the cycle may be drawn in bold to reflect an action based on power.

With regard to a goal of becoming more comfortable with and skilled in working with adolescent clients, the supervisor may recommend that the supervisee select related books for group supervision, such as *Reviving Ophelia* (Pipher, 1994) or *Real Boys* (Pollock, 1998). These books address ways in which gender socialization can negatively influence adolescent females and males.

Finally, with regard to the supervisee's goal of becoming appropriately directive, the supervisor may ask questions to help the supervisee understand their inclination to use a more or less directive approach, and the benefits and drawbacks of these approaches. These questions might include the influence of gender and culture on the supervisee's comfort with being directive. For instance, a supervisee of color may discover that this aspect of her style is partly influenced by concerns about being perceived as less credible by Caucasian and/or male clients. A male supervisee may recognize that this aspect of his style is influenced by socialization that encourages men to "have the answers" and "take the lead."

At the end of the semester, supervisors and supervisees engage in a mutual evaluation process. Although supervisors are committed to providing ongoing verbal feedback, a written evaluation form is also provided to students. This evaluation typically will include feedback regarding the students' attention to gender and culture in their work. Students also provide written feedback to supervisors, including comments about the supervisors' attention to gender and culture during supervision.

Including gender and culture as a topic. Congruent with our expectation that students include gender and culture in their assessment of and interventions on each case, supervisors attempt to include these topics during each supervision session. Because students are encouraged to address these topics each time they complete case notes, they are often aware of the influences of gender and culture on the case. Typically, then, conversations include practical suggestions for bringing these topics into the therapy room. In this regard, supervisors will often use the *Power Equity Guide* (Haddock et al., in press) to facilitate discussion and ideas for intervention. The *Guide* can be used in a variety of ways in supervision. For instance, it can be completed for each case and kept in the clients' files, used to record intervention strategies across cases, or used as an evaluation tool of a therapist's overall development.

RESEARCH

Program faculty use four primary methods for infusing gender and culture throughout the research component of the program: (a) providing a workshop on feminist and multicultural critiques of and methods for research, (b) communicating an expectation that gender and multicultural issues are integrated in thesis research, (c) highlighting and critiquing particular research studies in classes and supervision, and (d) integrating gender and culture in their own research.

Feminist and multicultural research workshop. A faculty member provides a workshop for graduate students that introduces them to the feminist critique of quantitative and qualitative research methods, and reviews feminist and multicultural proposals for research methods. Students are encouraged to apply the material learned in this workshop to their thesis projects.

Thesis requirement. A thesis is required for students of the program for several reasons, three of which are relevant to this article. First, gaining the skills for conducting original research allows students to become better consumers of research, for instance, they are able to critique articles for gender or cultural bias. Second, conducting thesis research allows students to gain in-depth knowledge of a particular topic. Because of the emphasis on gender and culture in our program, many students choose projects directly or indirectly related to these topics. In fact, between 1995 and 1998, approximately 75 percent of students conducted thesis research on a topic directly related to gender or culture. There is a departmental expectation that all students will integrate gender and culture in their thesis research. Students are asked to address considerations of gender and culture related to their thesis topic at their oral examination.

Critique of research in classes and supervision. One of the methods used by faculty members for infusing gender and culture in their courses is to encourage students to critique research presented in the course from a feminist and multicultural lens. For instance, students might be asked, "What population is left out in terms of sampling? What population is typically used in the development of psychometric measures? What biases might be informing the research questions or hypotheses of the study?"

Incorporating gender and culture in faculty research. Because of the strong commitment to integrating gender and culture in our conceptualizations and treatment of families, faculty members' research is often directly related to these topics. When not directly related, gender and culture are routinely infused in faculty research.

SERVICE

In addition to integrating gender and culture in their teaching, supervision, and research, faculty members also attempt to use this expertise in their service activities as well. Such a commitment benefits the community, allows the faculty member to further develop their own awareness and skills, and provides additional opportunities for students. Faculty members have integrated gender and culture in their service responsibilities in two primary ways. First, individual faculty members select service activities, such as committee membership and community involvement, that reflect their commitment to promoting gender and culture awareness. Second, they centralize the organizing principles of gender and culture in the operation of the CSU Marriage and Family Therapy Clinic.

Faculty service activities. There are many ways that faculty members have integrated gender and culture in their individual service activities. For instance, the HDFS Department has a strong relationship with CSU Women's Program and Studies. HDFS faculty members have served both as the chair of the board and as committee members, and the staff of Women's Programs and Studies provide our faculty with significant support, excellent training resources, and opportunities for community involvement. The Program director currently serves as the editor of the *Journal of Feminist Family Therapy*, and other faculty members serve on the advisory board. The Program director also has served as chair of the CSU President's Commission on Women and Gender Equity. Faculty members and students have been very involved in community and university educational opportunities by providing seminars on the integration of gender and culture in school environments, parenting, work environments, and intimate partner relationships.

Clinic Services

The CSU MFT Program maintains the CSU Marriage and Family Therapy (MFT) Clinic that provides low-fee therapy services to CSU students and community members. Similar to the Program, the clinic's mission is to maintain gender and culture as organizing principles in its operation. Below, we provide several specific examples of ways that we integrate gender and culture in the operation and environment of the clinic, specifically in (a) how the clinic is represented to the community, (b) special services offered, and (c) the environment of the clinic for clients and student therapists.

Clinic representation. We attempt to communicate our mission in our representation of the clinic to the community. For instance, we are currently in the process of changing the name of the clinic to be more inclusive of non-married and gay and lesbian individuals. The clinic's marketing materials (e.g., brochure and fliers) overtly communicate our mission by including the statement: "We are dedicated to empowering families, couples, and individuals to strengthen their relationships, resolve troubling issues, and achieve personal well being. We are committed to creating a safe environment that honors diverse backgrounds, family forms, and experiences. We do not discriminate or refuse services to anyone on the basis of age, culture, ethnicity, gender, physical disability, race, religion, or sexual orientation."

Additionally, the clinic's director attempts to personally meet with representatives of various groups and agencies that serve societally marginalized clients (e.g., the gay lesbian community center and campus advocacy groups) to discuss ways that the clinic can better meet the needs of the members of these organizations.

Special programs. The clinic sponsors special programs that are consistent with its mission. Students in the program are encouraged and supported in designing and/or implementing special programs in particular areas of interests. Below are some examples of special programs that have recently been offered by the clinic, several of which were designed and initiated by students in the program. The clinic's premarital program highlights the importance of shared power in relationships, and provides couples with the information and skills necessary to strive for shared power in their relationships. The clinic also offers a Couple's Ropes Course experience (that is open to all couples). This past year, we offered a Ropes Course experience specifically for lesbian couples, and will continue to offer this experience for both gay and lesbian couples. Additionally, the clinic–in partnership with the Lambda Community Center–offered a solution-focused couple's group for gay and lesbian couples.

As described by Green (1998a), many individuals from marginalized groups are wary of therapeutic services because of cultural perceptions and/or negative experiences. To meet the needs of these individuals, Green (1998a) challenged therapists to offer community-based prevention and intervention programs that have an educational or preventative orientation. Consistent with this recommendation, the clinic (with the HDFS department) is hosting "Families at Five"–a free monthly lecture series for community members, with an accompanying children's program. Each month, a faculty member in the Human Development and Family Studies department presents on a topic of interest to families, such as "Raising strong and sensitive boys and girls," "Preventing adolescent substance abuse," and "Caring for aging parents." These topics are designed to incorporate gender and culture and to be inclusive of and relevant to community members of diverse backgrounds.

Clinical environment for clients. For clients, we attempt to communicate our mission primarily through therapist behaviors, but also through environmental cues. For instance, the first form that clients see when they come to the clinic, the Client Information Form, includes the statement listed above that appears on all marketing materials. Furthermore, this form does not assume that clients have a heterosexual orientation by inquiring about "marital status." Instead, it asks clients to indicate their relationship configuration–male-female, male-male, or female-female. Each of the therapy rooms is decorated with artwork that depicts various family forms (e.g., single-parent families, gay and lesbian couples) and individuals of diverse racial backgrounds. The toys and books in the children's therapy room reflect families of diverse backgrounds. For instance, toys include dolls of various ethnicities, pretend foods from various ethnic backgrounds, and books that depict culturally diverse families.

Clinical environment for students. We also are attentive that the therapists' environment reflects our commitment to integrating gender and culture. We designed posters for the therapists' office for each of the four metaframeworks emphasized in the program (e.g., systemic, constructivist, feminist, and multicultural). For instance, the "feminist metaframework" poster outlines Whipple's (1996) five principles that characterize a feminist-informed approach to therapy. The "multicultural metaframeworks" poster outlines the principles of this metaframework as outlined in *Ethnicity and Family Therapy* (McGoldrick et al., 1996). We also maintain a corkboard for faculty members and students to post newspaper clippings, quotes, or other materials that would be of interest to family therapists. Often, this corkboard contains materials that reflect faculty members' and students' critical evaluation of society from a feminist and multicultural perspective. Other ways that we shape our environment to reflect our mission are (a) including a section on the case note form for therapists' hypotheses about the influences of gender and culture on their cases, and (b) including a section on the case note form that requires students to select the metaframeworks and family therapy theories that informed their work in each session. Students also attend to maintaining a fair and equitable environment among themselves, for instance, by ensuring that female students do not disproportionately take responsibility for cleaning the microwave or office environment.

CONCLUSION

In closing, it is important to note that this paper has not provided a formal or systematic report of students' experiences of the various aspects of the program. Such a report is outside the scope of this paper. However, student feedback about all aspects of the program is of primary concern to the faculty. This feedback is regularly sought through formal means, such as course and supervision evaluations, candidacy reviews, and exit interviews; further, informal feedback is encouraged on a regular basis. This feedback is consistently used to improve various aspects of the program.

The most prominent theme in students overall feedback of the program relates to the integration of gender and culture throughout the program. Students routinely cite this integration as the most pronounced aspect of their learning and their success as a therapist. For instance, some representative statements from students are:

> What is amazing about this program is not that issues of diversity are formally included in the curriculum–for that can be implemented easily and does not necessarily imply a personal commitment to these issues on the part of the faculty. Rather, what had the greatest impact on me is that the environment in general and the faculty in particular are committed to equity and reducing power differentials (due to race, ethnicity, gender, sexual orientation, and SES). This personal commitment on the part of the faculty is exhibited in their research and, most meaningfully, in every day conversations.

> Feminism has changed my life.

> Gender and diversity at CSU has changed my worldview so that I

understand how women and minorities are oppressed within the mainstream culture. Benefits to my clients are tremendous because, as their therapist, I am more able to reflect the experiences of their every day life and reduce the blame for their life circumstances.

We experience very little resistance from students–both male and female–regarding the emphasis on gender and culture in the program, which we believe is primarily due to three aspects of the training experience. First, program advertisements clearly state the program's emphasis on these topics, which allows students that are interested in and/or open to these topics to self-select into the program. Second, it is our perception that the emphasis placed on humility around social justice topics provides students with a safe environment for effective learning. Third, because students are provided with concrete guidance in applying feminist and multicultural principles in their work with clients, they quickly experience the power of integrating these ideas in the process of therapy with their clients. This experience typically results in students wanting to learn more about these topics.

Providing therapist trainees with the necessary skills for integrating gender and culture in their practice of therapy is challenging for most trainers. However, it is an effort with high dividends. As Storm et al. (1997) related, the process is transformational for program faculty, students, and clients. It is our hope that family therapy trainers will continue to experiment with and share ideas for weaving gender and culture throughout the rich tapestry of family therapy training programs.

REFERENCES

Akamatsu, N. N. (1998). The talking oppression blues: Including the experience of power/powerlessness in the teaching of "cultural sensitivity." In M. McGoldrick (ed.) *Re-visioning family therapy: Race, culture, and gender in clinical practice* (pp. 129-143). New York: Guilford.

Ault-Riche, M. (1988). Teaching an integrated model of family therapy: Women as students, women as supervisors.

Avis, J. M. (1989). Integrating gender into the family therapy curriculum. *Journal of Feminist Family Therapy, 1*(2), 3-26.

Bailey, S. M. (1999). *Tough guise: Violence, media, and the crisis of masculinity.* Northampton, MA: Media Education Foundation.

Brock, G. W. (1994). *Ethics casebook.* Washington, DC: American Association for Marriage and Family Therapy.

Butler, S. (1998). *The way home.* Oakland, CA: World Trust.

Cook, E., Warnke, M., & Dupoy, P. (1993). Gender bias and the DSMIII-R. *Counselor Education and Supervision, 32,* 311-321.

Creighton, A., & Kivel, P. (1992). *Helping teens stop violence: A practical guide for educators, counselors, and parents.* Alameda, CA: Hunter House.

Doherty, W. J. (1995). *Soul searching: Why psychotherapy must promote moral responsibility.* New York: Basic Books.

Falicov, C. J. (1995). Training to think culturally: A multidimensional comparative framework. *Family Process,* 373-388.

Falicov, C.J. (1988). *Family transitions: Continuity and change over the life cycle.* New York: Guilford Press.

Gilbert, K. (1995). *Marriage and family therapists' use of feminist theory in their clinical practices.* Unpublished master's thesis, Colorado State University.

Goldner, V. (1988). Generation and gender: Normative and covert hierarchies. *Family Process, 27,* 17-31.

Goodrich, T. J., Rampage, C., Ellman, B., & Halstead, K. (1988). *Feminist family therapy: A casebook.* New York: Norton.

Gottman, J. M., & Silver, N. (1999). *The seven principles for making marriage work.* New York: Random House.

Gray, J. (1992). *Men Are from Mars, Women Are from Venus.* New York: HarperCollins.

Green, R. J. (1998a). Race and the field of family therapy. In M. McGoldrick (ed.) *Re-visioning family therapy: Race, culture, and gender in clinical practice* (pp. 93-110). New York: Guilford.

Green, R. J. (1998b). Training programs: Guidelines for multicultural transformation. In M. McGoldrick (ed.) *Re-visioning family therapy: Race, culture, and gender in clinical practice* (pp. 111-128). New York: Guilford.

Haddock, S. A. (1995). *A content analysis of AAMFT Master Series tapes: A feminist perspective.* Unpublished master's thesis, Colorado State University, Fort Collins.

Haddock, S. A., Zimmerman, T. S., & MacPhee, D. (April 2000). The power equity guide: Attending to gender in family therapy. *Journal of Marital and Family Therapy, 26* (2), pp. 153-170.

Hardy, K. V. & Laszloffy, T. A. (1998). The dynamics of a pro-racist ideology: Implications for family therapists. In M. McGoldrick (ed.) *Re-visioning family therapy: Race, culture, and gender in clinical practice* (pp. 118-128). New York: Guilford.

Hardy, K. V., & Laszloffy, T. A. (1995). The cultural genogram: Key to training culturally competent family therapists. *Journal of Marital and Family Therapy, 21,* 227-238.

Helmeke, K. L. (1994). Fostering a safe atmosphere: A first step in discussing gender in family therapy training programs. *Contemporary Family Therapy, 18,* 503-519.

Holcomb, B. (1998). *Not Guilty: The Good News About Working Mothers.* New York: Scribner.

Huber, C. H. (1994). *Ethical, legal, and professional issues in the practice of marriage and family therapy.* New Jersey: Prentice Hall.

Kilbourne (1987). *Still killing us softly.* Cambridge, MA: Cambridge Documentary Films.

Lerman, H. (1994). The practice of ethics within feminist therapy. *Women & Therapy, 8,* 85-92.

Lerman, H., & Porter, N. (1990). *Feminist ethics in psychotherapy.* New York: Springer Publishing Company.

Leslie, L. A., & Clossick, M. L. (1992). Changing set: Teaching family therapy from a feminist perspective. *Family Relations, 41,* 256-263.

Leslie, L. A., & Clossick, M. L. (1996). Sexism in family therapy: Does training in gender make a difference? *Journal of Marital and Family Therapy, 22*(2), 253-269.

MacPhee, D., Kreutzer, J. C., & Fritz, J. J. (1994). Infusing a diversity perspective into human development courses. *Child Development, 65,* 699-715.

MacPhee, D., Oltjenbruns, K. A., Fritz, J. J., & Kreutzer, J. C. (1994). Strategies for infusing curricula with a multicultural perspective. *Innovative Higher Education, 18,* 289-309.

McGill Roberts, J. (1991). Sugar and spice, toad and mice: Gender issues in family therapy training. *Journal of Marital and Family Therapy, 17*(2), 121-132.

McGoldrick, M. (1998) *Re-visioning family therapy: Race, culture, and gender in clinical practice.* New York: Guilford.

McGoldrick, M., Giordano, J., & Pearce, J. K. (1996). *Ethnicity and family therapy.* New York: Guilford.

Mun Wah, L., & Foo, A. (1994). *The Color of Fear.* Oakland, CA: Stir-Fry Seminars.

Nelson, T. S. (1991). Gender in family therapy supervision. *Contemporary Family Therapy, 13,* 357-369.

Nichols, M. P. & Schwartz, R. C. (1998). *Family therapy: Concepts and methods.* Boston: Allyn & Bacon.

Nutt, R. L. (1991). Family therapy training issues of male students in a gender-sensitive doctoral program. In M. Bograd (Ed.), *Feminist approaches for men in family therapy* (261-266). New York: Haworth Press.

Papp, P., & Imber-Black, E. (1996). Family themes: Transmission and transformation. *Family Process, 35*(1), 5-20.

Pipher, M. (1994). *Reviving Ophelia: Saving the selves of adolescent girls.* New York: Ballantine Books.

Pollack, W. (1998). *Real Boys: Rescuing our sons from the myths of boyhood.* New York: Random House.

Rabin, C. (1996). *Equal partners, good friends: Empowering couples through therapy.* New York: Routledge.

Reid, E., McDaniel, S., Donaldson, C., & Tollers, M. (1987). Taking it personally: Issues of personal authority and competence for the female in family therapy training. *Journal of Marital and Family Therapy, 13,* 157-165.

Schwartz, P. (1994). *Love between equals: How peer marriage really works.* New York: Free Press.

Sirles, E. A. (1994). Teaching feminist family therapy: Practicing what we preach. *Journal of Feminist Family Therapy, 6*(1), 1-18.

Soloman, A. (1992). Clinical diagnosis among diverse populations: A multicultural perspective. *Families in Society, 73*(6), 371-377.

Storm, C. L. (1991). Placing gender in the heart of MFT masters programs: Teaching a gender sensitive systemic view. *Journal of Marital and Family Therapy, 17,* 45-52.

Storm, C. L., York, C. D., & Keller, J. G. (1997). A genderist philosophy transforms an MFT program. *The American Journal of Family Therapy, 25,* 151-168.

Taggart, M. (1985). The feminist critique in epistemological perspective: Questions of context in family therapy. *Journal of Marital and Family Therapy, 11,* 113-126.

Weiner, J. P., & Boss, P. (1985). Exploring gender bias against women: Ethics for marriage and family therapy. *Counseling and Values, 30,* 9-23.

Werner-Wilson, R. (2000). *Simulated therapy experience: An experiential exercise to facilitate transition to clinical work and sensitivity to gender, power, and diversity.* Manuscript submitted for publication.

Werner-Wilson, R., Price, S., Zimmerman, T. S., & Murphy, M. (1997). Client gender as a process variable in marriage and family therapy: Are women clients interrupted more than men clients? *Journal of Family Psychology, 11*(3), 373-377.

Wheeler, D., Avis, J. M., Miller, L. A., & Chaney, S. (1986). Rethinking family therapy education and supervision: A feminist model. In M. McGoldrick, C. Anderson, & F. Walsh (Eds.), *Women in families: A framework for family therapy* (pp. 135-151). New York: Norton.

Whipple, V. (1996). Developing an identity as a feminist family therapist: Implications for training. *Journal of Marital and Family Therapy, 22,* 381-396.

Zimmerman, T. S., Haddock, S. A., McGeorge, C., & Holm, K. (October, 1999). Beyond Mars and Venus: Analyzing self-help books from a feminist perspective. Annual American Association for Marriage and Family Therapy Conference. Chicago, Illinois.

Zimmerman, T. S., Holm, K, & Starrels, M. (1999). *A feminist analysis of self-help bestsellers for improving relationships: A decade review.* Manuscript submitted for publication.

APPENDIX A
"In-the-Box/Out-of-the-Box": Presentation Ideas

In presenting the modified version of "In-the-box/Out-of-the-box" (Creighton & Kivel, 1992), the instructor introduces the topic of gender socialization and gender-based power differentials. She draws two boxes on the board– one is labeled "female" and the other "male." Students are invited to brainstorm the traits, characteristics, attitudes, or behaviors that society encourages for each gender (e.g., "in-the-box" behaviors), and these descriptors are written in the appropriate box. For instance, "in-the-box" traits for women might include nurturing, emotional, passive, dependent, thin, pretty, "homemaker." "In-the-box" traits for males might include aggressive, rational, strong, independent, breadwinner, muscular. The instructor then asks students to describe what consequences women and men experience for stepping "out-of-the-box." For instance, if a woman behaves out of the box, she might be perceived as unloving, as a "bitch," or as "wearing the pants in the family." Men might be labeled as "gay," "wimps," or "weak." This leads to an in-depth discussion of the power and effects of gender socialization. Students are invited to consider the benefits and consequences of "in-the-box" versus "out-of-the-box" behavior for couples and families. The instructor then introduces the way in which this gender socialization reinforces power differentials between men and women. For instance, the instructor describes how her "in-the-box" behaviors encourage her to have less say about major aspects of her life (e.g., finances and career) and encourages him to feel overly responsible for breadwinning and under-involved in fathering and housework. Students are encouraged to help couples in therapy find the "common gender box" where they can interact with less gender constraint and conflict. Examples of "common box" behaviors include interdependence, assertiveness, and a sharing of major life responsibilities (e.g., housework, childcare).

Therapists' Gender Assumptions and How These Assumptions Influence Therapy

Tal Harris
Laurie B. Moret
Jerry Gale
Karen L. Kampmeyer

SUMMARY. The purpose of this study is to investigate therapists' construction of gender through an examination of clinicians' attributions of expressiveness and instrumentality. Ninety-nine therapists participated in this study by watching a 25 minute videotaped vignette of a clinician interviewing a Caucasian female-male couple. Half of the participants viewed a female actor performing an expressive role with a male actor performing an instrumental role, while the other half watched a tape where the roles were reversed. After viewing the video-

Tal Harris, MA, is affiliated with Child Family Studies. Laurie B. Moret, PhD, is an Independent Consultant and Private Practitioner. Jerry Gale, PhD, is affiliated with the Department of Child and Family Development and Marriage and Family Therapy and Director, Marriage and Family Therapy Program. Karen L. Kampmeyer is a PhD.

Acknowledgments should be given to Rita Slavich, Steve Kogan, and Hilary Rose for their contributions to this article. A special thanks to Anna Durden, Lachele Folley, and Scott Bowers, the actors who volunteered their time to this project.

A portion of this paper was presented at the American Family Therapy Association Annual Conference in San Francisco California, 1996.

Address correspondence to: Jerry Gale, The University of Georgia, Department of Child and Family Development, Dawson Hall, Athens, GA 30602-3622 (E-mail: <jgale@hestia.fcs.uga.edu>).

[Haworth co-indexing entry note]: "Therapists' Gender Assumptions and How These Assumptions Influence Therapy." Harris et al. Co-published simultaneously in *Journal of Feminist Family Therapy* (The Haworth Press, Inc.) Vol. 12, No. 2/3, 2001, pp. 33-59; and: *Integrating Gender and Culture in Family Therapy Training* (ed: Toni Schindler Zimmerman) The Haworth Press, Inc., 2001, pp. 33-59. Single or multiple copies of this article are available for a fee from The Haworth Document Delivery Service [1-800-342-9678, 9:00 a.m. - 5:00 p.m. (EST). E-mail address: getinfo@haworthpressinc.com].

tape, the participants completed the Bem Sex Role Inventory for the husband and wife and two one-item measures of power and gender. The results indicated that the sex of the actor organized therapists' construction of expressiveness and instrumentality. For example, when the woman was performing the expressive role she was rated higher on expressiveness than the man when the man was performing the same role. These findings suggest that the dominant discourse on gender may have infiltrated therapists' empirical assessments of their clients' behavior. The relevance of this study to training is also discussed. *[Article copies available for a fee from The Haworth Document Delivery Service: 1-800-342-9678. E-mail address: <getinfo@haworthpressinc.com> Website: <http://www.HaworthPress.com> © 2001 by The Haworth Press, Inc. All rights reserved.]*

KEYWORDS. Gender, therapy, sex role

PURPOSE

Over the past 20 years, feminists have challenged marriage and family therapists to examine the impact of gender on the process of therapy (Goodrich, 1991; Hare-Mustin, 1978, 1987; Libow, Raskin, & Caust, 1982; Luepnitz, 1988; McGoldrick, Anderson, & Walsh, 1989). These authors have criticized the field of family therapy for not taking into consideration the role that gender plays in organizing conversations between therapists and clients. It has been argued that when therapists do not consider gender they are implicitly accepting definitions of women and men that are determined by the dominant discourse (Hare-Mustin, 1994). The danger in not considering gender is that therapists then ignore the power differentials that exist between women and men in a patriarchal society (Knudson-Martin & Mahoney, 1996).

HISTORY OF GENDER IN COUPLES THERAPY

Gender and Power

The discrediting of power in relation to gender by family therapists is often connected to the influence of general systems theory on the field of marriage and family therapy. One example of the impact of systems thinking on therapy can be seen in Bateson's (1972) work where patterns of interaction were understood to be the result of homeostatic mechanisms. From the perspective of his cybernetic epistemology, Bateson described power as a "myth which, if everybody believes in it, becomes to that extent self-validating. But it is still epistemological lunacy and leads inevitably to various sorts of disaster" (pp. 494-495). Cybernetic explanations for behavior assert that women and men are equal participants in problematic interactions. These explanations imply that there is a constant flow of feedback within a couple where the woman's actions cannot be explained without considering the man's actions, and then the man's actions cannot be understood separate from the woman's actions in an ongoing and recursive process (Keeney, 1983). Therefore, from a cybernetic perspective, responsibility for the problem rests in the interactional pattern between the couple, not within either of the two individuals.

These systemic explanations were widely criticized by feminist theorists for implying that women may be equally responsible for the physical abuse they have received from their male partners (Kaufman, 1992; Luepnitz, 1988; Dell, 1989). Feminists pointed out how systemic therapies had traditionally failed to consider the repercussions of assuming equality from within a socio-cultural context where men and women are not equal (Avis, 1992; Bograd, 1992). These observations have subsequently led to some changes in how clinicians address gender in the process of therapy and have demonstrated the importance of feminist critiques within the field of marriage and family therapy.

CURRENT STATUS OF GENDER IN THERAPY

The current thinking on the role of gender in therapy is also a response to critics who have accused the feminist movement of imposing gender on the process of therapy. In the past, feminist-informed approaches have been described as overemphasizing the relevance of gender in the study of therapy (Lichtenberg & Heck, 1981). The argument was that feminist-oriented clinicians inserted their own political agenda into the therapeutic process by asserting that all therapists make gendered assumptions about their clients. This agenda was then said to bias feminist researchers by predisposing them to slant their research to support a pre-established point of view (Barak & Fischer, 1989). What is lacking in Barak and Fischer's critique is an interrogation of the role of gendered assumptions among clinicians that led these researchers to discredit the evidence indicating the presence of gender bias. The question then becomes why did Barak and Fischer find it important to state that it was too early to say whether therapists discriminate against female clients despite their own assertion that a review of the literature had "yielded remarkably contradictory findings" (Barak & Fischer, 1989, p. 377). Given the amount of research that indicated the existence of gender bias, why did these authors contend that it was not enough?

THE CULTURE OF GENDER ASSUMPTIONS AND STEREOTYPES

When clinicians and researchers suggest that gender does not affect therapists' conceptualization and treatment of their clients they are falling victim to what Hare-Mustin (1987) termed Beta bias. In short, Beta bias is the tendency to minimize gender inequities when they exist by ignoring the role that the social context plays in the construction of gender (Hare-Mustin, 1988). Therapists are guilty of Beta bias when they believe that they can make judgements about a particular case free of assumptions about gender. Some feminists have argued that such assessments of clients are not possible because we are all immersed in a culture that is sexist, ergo, we are all sexist to some degree (Avis, 1989). As Hare-Mustin (1991) said, "we construct the world around us, not from an idiosyncratic view, but from within the meaning community in which we live" (p. 65). In short, it is not possible to not make gendered assumptions about clients (Weiner & Boss, 1985).

Initially, most of the discussions of gender in family therapy were conducted at the theoretical level. In the past several years, however, researchers have turned increasing attention to empirical investigations of clinicians' differential treatment of men and women in therapy (Fischer, 1989; Hardy & Johnson, 1992; Stabb, Cox, & Harber, 1997; Werner-Wilson, Zimmmerman & Price, 1999). The hope is that through these quantitative studies, more evidence will be presented that recognizes the influence that cultural norms have on the interactions of clients and therapists.

Research on Gender Bias in Therapy

One of the earliest studies of therapists' gender bias was Brover-man, Broverman, Clarkson, Rosenkrantz, and Vogel's (1970) exam-ination of the clinical judgements of mental health professionals. In Broverman et al., psychologists were separated into three groups with each group completing the same questionnaire. The first group was told to respond based on their conceptualization of a healthy female, the second group was instructed to conceptualize a healthy male, and the third group was to base their answers on their idea of a healthy adult. The results indicated that the psychologists had significantly different concepts of what constitutes a healthy female as compared to a healthy male, with the definition of the healthy adult more closely resembling the healthy male. Even though some have challenged these findings (Widiger & Settle, 1987), the Broverman et al. paper set the stage for additional research in the area of therapist gender bias.

More recently, a study by Fischer (1989) indicated that therapists' causal explanations for difficulties in therapy were related to cross-gender pairings of therapists and clients. In other words, if the thera-pist was male and the client was female, he was more likely to see the problems in therapy as having to do with the female client. In contrast, if the therapist was female and the client was male, the therapist saw herself as being responsible for the problems in therapy. These results suggest that both the client and the therapist were contextualized by their gender in that the women were viewed as responsible for thera-peutic impasses regardless of whether they were the client or the therapist.

In an analogue study of clients' gender, Hardy and Johnson (1992) found that therapists believed that female clients would require more therapy to become healthy than male clients. To examine the impact of sex on therapists' perceptions of mental health, the participants were given the same case vignette with the exception of the sex of the client, one vignette describing a female client and the other describing a male client. The therapists predicted that the female client would need sig-nificantly more sessions to make progress than the male client would need. These findings indicate that therapists' clinical judgements were affected by assumptions based on information they received regarding each client's sex beyond the content of the case vignette.

In an examination of gender-related attributions, Stabb, Cox, and Harber (1997) found that a male therapist was more likely to attribute responsibility for negative outcomes to female clients than to male clients. To investigate therapist attributions, Stabb et al. trained five coders to score one male therapist's attributions across three married couples. The coders' interrater reliability, as assessed by Cohen's Kappa, ranged from .71 to .95. Even though the study only scored the attributions of one therapist, this therapist, did demographically resemble a typical marriage and family therapist suggesting that his differential treatment of women and men may have relevance for other clinicians as well.

In a recent study by Werner-Wilson, Zimmerman, and Price (1999), the authors found that the interaction of a client's gender with the treatment modality influenced the therapeutic topic. More specifically, females were more successful in introducing topics and goals in marital therapy, while males were more successful at introducing topics in family therapy.

Defining Gender

In the early 1970's the idea that masculinity and femininity were opposite ends of the sex role continuum came under criticism (Ballard-Reisch & Elton, 1992). It was posited that masculinity and femininity could exist simultaneously and that they were not, as previously believed, mutually exclusive. Bem (1974) referred to masculinity as being oriented toward task completion and leadership and femininity as being related to interpersonal affection and relationship building. The redefinition of the constructs of femininity and masculinity meant that one's gender did not necessarily have to be the same as one's biological sex. The conceptual separation of a person's gender from their biological sex eventually led to the use of the terms expressiveness and instrumentality (Ballard-Reisch & Elton, 1992).

THE PRESENT STUDY

This study explored the role of gendered assumptions and client sex in couple's therapy. It was first hypothesized that therapists would (a) interpret the female actor as more expressive than the male actor and

(b) interpret the male actor as more instrumental than the female actor even when both were performing from the same script. These hypotheses were based on the theory that the sex of the actor would influence therapists' construction of each client's gender. For the purposes of this study, an actor's sex was defined by their apparent biological sex and their gender was defined by the role-related behaviors the actors assumed for the purposes of the different vignettes. Second, it was hypothesized that the therapists would perceive gender and power to be more important issues when the gender roles were consistent with traditional norms than when gender roles violated social norms. Given that most conversations about gender are centered on a conceptualization of a traditional couple, we have theorized that therapists are not as sophisticated at assessing the role of power and gender when couples have nontraditional gender roles as compared to when couples have more traditional roles.

METHOD

Participants

Ninety-nine therapists participated in this study from 4 different states with 32 participants from California, 27 from Florida, 24 from Georgia, and 16 from Colorado. The participants' ages ranged from 20 to over 50 years old with 39% between 20-30 years, 22% between 31-40 years, 26% between 41-50 years, and 13% were 51 years of age or older. Of the 99 people that participated, 73 were female and 26 were male. The therapists were mostly students in marriage and family therapy programs (n = 65), with some practitioners (n = 29), and a couple of researchers/scholars (n = 2). Three participants did not indicate the focus of their work. Primary theoretical orientations of these therapists included: Systemic (n = 32), Humanistic (n = 11), Narrative (n = 10), Cognitive (n = 9), Solution Focused Brief (n = 8), Feminist (n = 5), Collaborative Language Systems (n = 4), Behavioral (n = 2), Psychodynamic (n = 2), Adlerian (n = 1), Cognitive Behavioral (n = 1), MRI (n = 1), Rogerian Gestalt (n = 1), and Other (n = 3). Nine participants did not indicate their primary orientation.

Recruitment

Researchers contacted faculty at doctoral and masters degree programs at each of 4 universities: 3 southern and one western. Therapists and therapists in training who agreed to participate were given a videotape and a research packet to complete after viewing the videotape. In addition, practicing clinicians in a southern state were included in this study. Therapists were contacted by telephone and asked to participate. Therapists who agreed to participate were shown the videotape and then completed the research packet.

Participant Procedures

Therapists and therapists in training were asked to participate in a study of therapist's perceptions and attributions of problem formation and problem resolution in couple's therapy in order to better understand the dynamics of couple's therapy. Therapists who consented to participate were separated into two groups. Each group watched a videotape of a therapy session and completed a brief questionnaire. Group 1 viewed a portrayal of a traditional couple, with a male actor performing an instrumental role and a female actor performing an expressive role. Group 2 viewed a portrayal of a nontraditional couple, with the female actor performing the instrumental role and the male actor performing the expressive role. In order to minimize extraneous differences between the traditional and the nontraditional couples, the same actors were used in both versions. After viewing the videotaped performances of the therapy session, each group of participants completed a questionnaire where they assessed the actors' gender and the importance of power in the relationship. Participants were not told that the focus of this study was on gender and power prior to their completion of the questionnaire.

Videotaped Interviews

To examine the influence of sex on therapists' conceptualizations of issues of gender and power in couple's therapy, excerpts from a videotaped interview were condensed into a 25 minute segment. Actors were then contracted to play the parts of the wife, the husband, and the therapist as seen on the videotape. To facilitate the process of reproducing the original couple's verbal and nonverbal communication, the actors worked from a copy of the videotape and a transcription of the dialogue. After the female actor learned the wife's part and the male actor learned the husband's part, they were videotaped performing these roles. When this first phase of the videotaping was completed, the male actor then learned the wife's part and the female actor learned the husband's part. Once the actors were familiar with their new parts, they were videotaped performing these roles. Therefore, there were two videotaped performances of the interview. In one interview, both the sex and gender roles of the actors matched the sex and gender roles of the original couple. In the second interview, the sex and gender roles were not matched so that the female actor performed the male role and the male actor performed the female role.

The two portrayals of the couple's session were titled the traditional format and the nontraditional format. In the traditional format, the dialogue was representative of a couple with conventional gender roles and in the nontraditional format, the actors switched parts to portray a couple with non-conventional gender roles. For example, in the traditional format the husband spoke lines that tended to be instrumental in content and the wife spoke lines that tended to be expressive. By contrast, in the nontraditional format the husband's lines tended to be expressive and the wife's lines were more often instrumental. Participants then viewed a videotape of one of the two formats and completed a questionnaire. The questionnaire responses were used to determine whether there was a difference in how observers rated gender and power in one version versus the other. The participants did not know whether they were viewing the traditional format or the nontraditional format prior to the completion of the questionnaire.

A Brief Case History of the Couple in Videotaped Vignette

Carrie and Frank are a Caucasian, midwestern couple who were being interviewed by a well-known clinician as part of a master therapist series at a national family therapy conference. They had been married eight years and this was the second marriage for each of them. Frank began individual counseling with a therapist (Jack) approximately two years prior to the interview, following a heart attack. Frank and Carrie had been in couple's therapy with Jack for about six months. Both Carrie and Frank work full time, Carrie as a nurse and Frank as an attorney. Frank has grown children from his previous marriage, and he and Carrie have a seven-year-old son together. Carrie had one child from her first marriage, and he died when he was approximately two years old.

Excerpts from the Videotaped Dialogue

To help demonstrate the differences between the expressive and instrumental roles and the traditional and nontraditional formats, three samples of the dialogue are presented. In the first exemplar, the gender was assigned to each character, but the sex of that person was not stated. In other words, the characters are identified as expressive or instrumental, but there is no indication of whether they are male or female. To conceal each characters sex, all the pronouns were replaced with "my partner" or "your partner." For the other two exemplars, the sex of each speaker is evident. To best highlight the differences between the three exemplars, it may help to read the text aloud and visualize each speaker as you read.[1]

All names have been changed in the transcripts.

Exemplar 1:

Expressive
(person)   Tha-that's, that's the key right there, really. I didn't real- ize that my partner was in control, I guess (Therapist: hm) I-I felt I didn't realize the extent to which my partner was controlling me (Therapist: hm) or, or in control of the situation, un-until, ah, we got into therapy. I suppose really you know its kind of like no matter what I said my partner wanted to change that somewhat, or be, you now, it had to be *more*[2] of I didn't, I didn't. . . .

Therapist: Your partner had, your partner had a better idea. (laughing)

Instrumental
(person):   That's right! (chuckling)

Expressive
(person)   A better idea or, or my idea of my idea wasn't exactly, or my idea just wasn't *quite right,* or (Therapist: yeah) or something was wrong (Therapist: yeah) with my idea. And, an I-I-I felt with my partner, that

it, I was afraid to confront my partner because I was afraid that my partner would get angry, that would, then our relationship would start falling apart again, so I was very hesitant and (Therapist: right, right, right) reluctant to confront my partner with this and I let my partner, then, be in control. "OK, fine, so if you want to be in con . . . "

Therapist: So what changed? What changed?

Instrumental
(person): Seeing Jack. Learning that I um, had (Therapist: sigh) this control problem (Therapist: yeah) and that I probably contributed to the heart attack. I mean, I probably, my partner probably suppressed a lot (Therapist: hm) and, and I continued to let that happen. Really opening myself up (Therapist: mmhm) and, and saying I-I have to listen here (Therapist: mmhm) I have to ah, if I want this to work, this counseling is gonna have to be beneficial for us. Something has to work here for us!

Therapist: Wow, wow.

In the second exemplar, the gender and the sex were assigned with the female character portraying an expressive person and the male character portraying an instrumental person. The second exemplar represents what will be referred to as the traditional format.

Exemplar 2: The Traditional Format

Carrie: Tha-that's, that's the key right there, really. I didn't realize that he was in control, I guess (Therapist: hm) I-I felt I didn't realize the extent to which he was controlling me (Therapist: hm) or, or in control of the situation, un-until, ah, we got into therapy. I suppose really you know its kind of like no matter what I said he wanted to change that somewhat, or be, you know, it had to be *more* of I didn't, I didn't . . .

Therapist: He had, he had a better idea. (laughing)

Frank: That's right! (chuckling)

Carrie: A better idea or, or my idea of my idea wasn't exactly, or my idea just wasn't *quite right* or (Therapist: yeah) or something was wrong (Therapist: yeah) with my idea. And, an I-I-I felt with Frank, that it, I was afraid to confront him because I was afraid that he would get angry, that would, then our relationship would start falling apart again, so I was very hesitant and (Therapist: right, right, right) reluctant to confront him with this and I let him, then, be in control. "OK, fine, so if you want to be in con . . . ."

Therapist: So what changed? What changed?

Frank: Seeing Jack. Learning that I um, had (Therapist: sigh) this control problem (Therapist: yeah) and that I probably contributed to the heart attack. I mean, I probably, she probably suppressed a lot (Therapist: hm) and, and I continued to let that happen. Really opening myself up (Therapist: mmhm) and, and saying I-I have to listen here (Therapist: mmhm) I have to ah, if I want this to work, this counseling is gonna have to be beneficial for us. Something has to work here for us!

Therapist: Wow, wow.

In the third exemplar, the gender and the sex were reversed from the second exemplar with the female character portraying an instrumental person and the male character portraying an expressive person. The third exemplar represents what will be referred to as the nontraditional format.

Exemplar 3: The Nontraditional Format

Frank: Tha-that's, that's the key right there, really. I didn't realize that she was in control, I guess (Therapist:

hm) I-I felt I didn't realize the extent to which she was controlling me (Therapist: hm) or, or in control of the situation, un-until, ah, we got into therapy. I suppose really you know its kind of like no matter what I said she wanted to change that somewhat, or be, you know, it had to be more of I didn't, I didn't . . .

Therapist: She had, she had a better idea. (laughing)

Carrie: That's right! (chuckling)

Frank: A better idea or, or my idea of my idea wasn't exactly, or my idea just wasn't *quite right*, or (Therapist: yeah) or something was wrong (Therapist: yeah) with my idea. And, an I-I-I felt with Carrie, that it, I was afraid to confront her because I was afraid that she would get angry, that would, then our relationship would start falling apart again, so I was very hesitant and (Therapist: right, right, right) reluctant to confront her with this and I let her, then, be in control. "OK, fine, so if you want to be in con . . . ."

Therapist: So what changed? What changed?

Carrie: Seeing Jack. Learning that I um, had (Therapist: sigh) this control problem (Therapist: yeah) and that I probably contributed to the heart attack. I mean, I probably, he probably suppressed a lot (Therapist: hm) and, and I continued to let that happen. Really opening myself up (Therapist: mmhm) and, and saying I-I have to listen here (Therapist: mmhm) I have to ah, if I want this to work, this counseling is gonna have to be beneficial for us. Something has to work here for us!

Therapist: Wow, wow.

This third exemplar was the dialogue as presented by the original couple.

Measures

Bem Sex Role Inventory (BSRI). The Bem Sex Role Inventory (BSRI) was introduced in 1974 to measure femininity, masculinity, and androgyny (Bem, 1974). The original BSRI was composed of 20 items to measure femininity, 20 items to measure masculinity, and 20 neutral items to assess social desirability. The instrument had good internal consistency with alpha's of .80 for femininity, .86 for masculinity, and .85 for androgyny. To test Bem's 3 factor structure, Wheeless and Dierks-Stewart (1981) factor analyzed the BSRI and found only 2 strong factors that they termed "sensitivity" and "instrumental." When these 2 factors were tested for internal consistency, the sensitivity factor had an alpha of .87 and the instrumental factor had an alpha of .74. In 1992, Ballard-Reisch and Elton examined a series of studies that factor analyzed the BSRI and suggested that the factors be renamed "expressiveness" (from femininity) and "instrumentality" (from masculinity) to separate the assessment of gender from "maleness" and "femaleness."

In the present investigation, Wheeless and Dierks-Stewart's (1981) version of the BSRI was used, which is a self-report instrument with 10 items for expressiveness and 10 items for instrumentality (see Table 1 for the expressiveness and instrumentality items). The scale was found to be internally consistent for this study's sample with alphas of .91 and .94 for expressiveness, and .95 and .96 for instrumentality. The BSRI was used as an observational measure. Therefore,

TABLE 1. The Expressiveness and Instrumentality Item Foci in the Bem Sex Role Inventory

Expressiveness	Instrumentality
1. Sincere	1. Willing to take a stand
2. Gentle	2. Aggressive
3. Helpful	3. Assertive
4. Friendly	4. Competitive
5. Understanding	5. Independent
6. Warm	6. Strong personality
7. Tender	7. Acts as leader
8. Compassionate	8. Forceful
9. Eager to sooth hurt feelings	9. Dominant
10. Sensitive to needs of others	10. Has leadership abilities

two scores exist for expressiveness and instrumentality since each participant scored both the woman and the man they viewed in each vignette. The BSRI was chosen as an observational measure even though it was designed as a self-report measure because of its reliability in assessing the constructs of expressiveness and instrumentality. Several studies have asked their participants to rate items in BSRI to discover how well these items reflect the constructs of expressiveness and instrumentality (Ballard-Reisch and Elton, 1992; Wheeless and Dierks-Stewart, 1981). The results of these studies have indicated that the BSRI items are consistent with societal views of gender roles.

Gender and power measures. The authors of this paper wrote two one-item measures to assess the degree to which therapists' saw gender and power as an issue in the case vignette. To assess the therapists' perception of the influence of gender they were asked, "To what degree would this be viewed as a gender issue?" The question about power was similarly phrased, "To what degree is this an unequal power issue?" Participants were asked to respond to each measure on a scale from 0% to 100% (see Appendix A for a copy of the questionnaire). The responses to these two 1-item quantitative measures are reported in the following section.

RESULTS

The Effect of Therapist's Sex

To examine possible differences in the therapists' responses based on their own sex, the participant therapists' responses within Group 1 (who viewed a traditional couple) and within Group 2 (who viewed the nontraditional couple) were divided by the sex of the therapists. Since some research has indicated that a clinician's sex may affect the judgements they make about their clients (Bernstein & Lecomte, 1982; Fischer, 1989), an independent samples t-test was conducted to see if the female and male participant therapists' scores were significantly different. The results were non-significant, however, the differences within the group that viewed the nontraditional format did approach significance (see Table 2). It is possible that the sample size was too small to significantly detect the gender difference between the therapists that watched the nontraditional format even though it may exist (Glenburg, 1988). Since the primary purpose of this study was to

TABLE 2. Sex Differences Within Two Therapist Groups: Traditional and Non-Traditional

Group 1: Therapists Who Viewed the Traditional Format					
		Women	Men	*t*-value	*p*
Expressiveness	*M*	42.1	39.5	0.58	.56
	SD	13.7	14.7		
		Women	Men	*t*-value	*p*
Instrumentality	*M*	52.1	50.9	0.28	.77
	SD	13.2	13.4		
Group 2: Therapists Who Viewed the Nontraditional Format					
		Women	Men	*t*-value	*p*
Expressiveness	*M*	51.9	48.5	1.33	.19
	SD	7.9	6.9		
		Women	Men	*t*-value	*p*
Instrumentality	*M*	59.2	55.5	1.79	.08
	SD	6.5	4.3		

examine the differences between the two groups of the therapists, those who viewed the traditional videotape and those who viewed the nontraditional videotape, the female and male therapists' scores within each group were combined. Throughout this paper, the term "therapists' sex" is used to refer to the biological sex of the participant therapists unless otherwise specified.

HYPOTHESIS 1

Assessment of Expressiveness

It was hypothesized that therapists would interpret the expressiveness of the spoken text differently based on the sex of the speaker. An independent samples *t*-test was conducted to assess whether therapists would be more likely to rate a woman higher on expressiveness than a man simply due to the cultural assumption that this is the role that women are more likely to perform. The results supported this hypothesis with the female actor receiving higher scores on expressiveness (M = 50.9, SD = 7.8) than the male actor (M = 41.5, SD = 13.8) when they were speaking from the same expressive text. The t-test was significant, t (94) = 4.03, $p < .001$, suggesting that therapists are referencing gender norms when assessing the expressiveness of their clients. Data from five therapists were excluded due to missing data.

Given that the expressive text was selected because it represented expressiveness, it was hypothesized that the expressiveness scores assigned by the participants to the expressive role would be higher than the expressiveness scores assigned to the instrumental role. In other words, the expressive role should be rated higher in expressiveness than the instrumental role regardless of whether a woman or a man is portraying that role. To test for this difference, the participants ratings of expressiveness on the expressive role were combined from both groups and were then compared to the expressiveness scores for the instrumental role from both groups. A t-test indicated support for this hypothesis with the expressive role (M = 45.9, SD = 12.3) receiving higher scores on expressiveness than the instrumental role (M = 42.6, 10.0), t (96) = 2.01, $p < .05$. Data from three therapists were excluded due to missing data. The results suggest that therapists' assessments of expressiveness were affected by the role the actor played in addition to what they expected to observe based on gender norms. It could be argued that the therapists in the present investigation were constructing expressiveness based on a combination of clients' expressive behavior and culturally defined gender norms.

Assessment of Instrumentality

It was hypothesized that therapists would interpret the instrumentality of the spoken text differently based on the sex of the speaker. As was found with the therapists' ratings of expressiveness, an independent samples t-test indicated the existence of an assumed difference between women and men. For example, even though the actors were performing from the same instrumental text, the male actor received higher scores (M = 58.4, SD = 6.3) than the female actor (M = 52.0, SD = 13.1) and the t-test was significant, t(96) = 3.00, $p < .003$. Data from three therapists were excluded due to missing data. These findings suggest that cultural assumptions based on gender affect therapists' assessment of clients' instrumentality.

Since the instrumental text was selected to represent instrumentality, it was hypothesized that the instrumentality scores assigned by the therapists to the instrumental role would be higher than the instrumentality scores assigned by the therapists to the expressive role. The results of a *t*-test were consistent with this hypothesis with the instrumental role ($M = 54.9$, $SD = 10.9$) receiving higher scores on instrumentality than the expressive role ($M = 35.6$, 12.1), $t(99) = 9.96$, $p < .001$. As was the case with expressiveness, these results indicate that the therapists were constructing instrumentality based on a combination of clients' instrumental behavior and culturally defined gender norms.

HYPOTHESIS 2

The Issue of Gender and Power

It was hypothesized that gender and power would be more frequently identified as a central issue in the traditional format since it depicted the traditional roles that men and women perform in our culture. This supposition was based on the belief that therapists would consider the influence of gender and power in traditional couples more readily because of clinical foci on this type of relationship dynamic. The danger, however, is not considering these macro level variables when a couple violates gender norms. This concern was evident in the vignette where the roles were reversed. The significant results of two *t*-tests indicated that therapists were not considering gender (see Table 3) and power (see Table 4) as readily when the couple was performing nontraditional gender roles. For example, therapists viewing the traditional vignette ($M = 66.2$, $SD = 22.1$) were more attentive to gender

TABLE 3. The Importance of the Issue of Gender in the Traditional vs. the Nontraditional Format

	Format		
	Traditional	Nontraditional	*t*-value
M	66.2	42.9	−4.19***
SD	22.1	30.9	

***$p < .001$, two-tailed.

TABLE 4. The Importance of the Issue of Power in the Traditional vs. the Non-traditional Format

| | Format | | |
	Traditional	Nontraditional	*t*-value
M	72.6	60.8	–2.49*
SD	20.6	25.8	

*p < .02, two-tailed.

than therapists viewing the nontraditional vignettes ($M = 42.9$, $SD = 30.9$), $t (87) = -4.19$, $p < .001$. Similarly, therapists viewing the traditional vignette ($M = 72.6$, $SD = 20.6$) were more attentive to power than therapists viewing the nontraditional vignettes ($M = 60.8$, $SD = 25.8$), $t (89) = -2.49$, $p < .02$. Data from 12 and 10 therapists respectively were excluded due to missing data. These results suggest that power may be obscured when gender norms are atypical.

DISCUSSION

The therapists in the present investigation perceived the male as more instrumental and the female as more expressive when they were performing from a culturally matching gender and sex script. This indicates that the biological sex of the speaker influenced the therapists' assessment of the client's gender beyond what can be accounted for by the content of the interaction. Even though they were saying the same words and using the same gestures, it seems apparent that by switching roles the actors created a different context for the therapists' constructions of gender. The script may have been the same in both the traditional and nontraditional formats, but the meanings that were received were different. For example, when the female actor was being instrumental, different sets of cultural referents seem to have been employed to create an understanding for that behavior than when the male actor was being instrumental. In other words, it may have been the same script in both formats, but it wasn't the same "text." From this perspective, it is believed that we are all embedded in a gendered discourse that co-authors our constructions of expressiveness and instrumentality. Therefore, a client's gender may be best understood as a combination of what we have observed and what we have learned to assume are the essential characteristics of women and men based on culturally manufactured gender norms.

Culture also seems to have affected the therapists' ratings of the importance of the issues of gender and power. The therapists reported that gender and power issues were more influential within the session where the sex of the speaker matched the gendered content of the communication. When the male was speaking from the instrumental text and the female was speaking from the expressive text in the traditional format, both gender and power were perceived as more important issues than when the sex and the gendered content were not matched in the nontraditional format. If therapists were not organized by culturally created gender roles, their ratings of the importance of gender and power would not be different in either format. Since their ratings were affected, this suggests that therapists are less attentive to power and gender when a woman is more instrumental and a man is more expressive than expected in American culture. The danger is that the therapist may downplay a woman's strengths in a relationship because she is seen as too powerful, thereby forgetting that she is embedded in a context that already minimizes her instrumentality. These findings suggest that the therapists' constructions of gender and power were significantly influenced by cultural ideologies.

The present study's findings contradict researchers and therapists who assume that we can assess our clients' behavior without also considering social norms and cultural discourses. The problem with maintaining the assumption that clinicians can separate cultural ideas about gender from clients' behavior is that it decontextualizes their experience by disconnecting them from their socio-historical context (Scott, 1992). Historically, psychologists have been guilty of this sort of disconnection when they described behavior within a research setting without considering its social context (Riger, 1992). Such separation of the participant from the culture leads researchers and scholars to attribute behaviors to personal characteristics rather than examining how a combination of social, cultural, and historical factors may influence the behaviors that are observed. Not considering contextual variables is dangerous because it allows women to be disproportionately blamed for the problems that occur within couples and families, for example, when women are perceived as controlling at times when they are being instrumental.

Even though these results may suggest that gender discrimination may still be found in clinical practice, there is hope that feminist critiques within the field of marriage and family therapy can have an impact. Leslie and Clossick (1996) found that therapists who had completed feminist oriented coursework on gender were less likely to use sexist interventions with their clients than therapists who did not have the coursework. Thus training clearly can have an impact on therapists' practices. This research implies that the varied literature conclusions on this topic should not discourage feminists from continuing to challenge the actions and assumptions of clinicians.

Limitations

Some limitations to this study are that the sample was not randomly selected, it was largely composed of graduate students, and it was disproportionately female, making comparisons based on the impact of the therapists' gender difficult to assess. We, as researchers, also understand that we are caught in the same discursive machinery that created the sexism that we endeavor to critique, meaning that we will have our gaze diverted from sexist assumptions and practices. Research on gender is further complicated by the competing definitions of the constructs of sex and gender. These varying definitions include some researchers' assertions that biological sex is a continuum and that the relationship of sex to gender, though connected, is not easily understood (Reinisch & Sanders, 1984).

It is important to note that feminist researchers have voiced skepticism about the utility of quantitative methods. This critique is understandable given the male-bias that has been found throughout the history of social science research (Riger, 1992). The combination of this male bias and the adherence to a belief in objectivity has allowed value laden scientists to assert neutrality thereby disguising their values and maintaining the existing power structure. Avis (1994) has discussed the problem of privileging scientific knowledge with exclusive value in her writing on the distance between researchers and practitioners or advocates for victims' rights. She argues that assumed objectivity is problematic because it leads to a disconnection between participants and researchers, and thus a decontextualization of the research setting. The separating of a woman from her context enables researchers to more readily conclude that her behaviors are the result of some internal characteristic rather than an artifact of the socio-cultural milieu. Since patriarchy is the prevailing ideology, the presumed objectivity found in the social sciences facilitates the marginalization of women's perspectives and interests. Keeping these concerns in mind is crucial as we proceed with further research into therapists' construction of gender.

Future Research

What this study does indicate, however, is the importance of ongoing critical inquiry. The contradictory findings in the extant literature should signal a call for more work, not the conclusion that it is too early to say what is occurring. Researchers cannot be satisfied that the absence of significant results means that gender bias does not exist. Who is it that is concluding that the evidence for gender bias is inconclusive? What evidence is being used to support this argument? And what are the consequences of the position that gender does not organize the conversations between therapists and clients? To address these questions and many others, we encourage researchers and practitioners to further investigate gender theory and the impact of clients' sex and gender on therapy.

Implications for Training

The idea for this study began in a family therapy class. After watching a couple's session conducted by a well-known family therapist, the question was asked, "What if the husband had said what the wife did, and visa versa?" This led to an invigorated discussion on gender, power, and therapist's roles in addition to a challenging of each of our own assumptions about gender and therapy. Our assumptions and views about gender, power, and communication need to be continually critiqued and appraised in training programs. We are all embedded in cultural and institutional discourses that shape our views and actions on these issues in often "seen but unnoticed ways." It is crucial that we read the literature, engage in exercises, carry out research, self-reflect, and critically challenge our understanding of gender, power, and human interaction.

NOTES

1. All names have been changed in the transcripts.
2. If a word was emphasized by the speaker, it was italicized in the transcript.

REFERENCES

Avis, J. M. (1989). Integrating gender into family therapy curriculum. *Journal of Feminist Family Therapy, 1*(2), 3-26.

Avis, J. M. (1992). Where are all the family therapists? Abuse and violence within families and family therapy's response. *Journal of Marital and Family Therapy, 18,* 225-232.

Avis, J. M. (1994). Advocates versus researchers–A false dichotomy? A feminist, social constructionist, response to Jacobson. *Family Process, 33,* 87-91.

Ballard-Reisch, D., & Elton, M. (1992). Gender orientation and the Bem Sex Role Inventory: A psychological construct revisited. *Sex Roles, 27,* 291-306.

Barak, A., & Fischer, W. A. (1989). Counselor and therapist gender bias? More questions than answers. *Professional Psychology: Research and Practice, 20,* 377-383.

Bateson, G. (1972). *Steps to an ecology of mind.* New York: Ballantine.

Bem, S. L. (1974). The measurement of psychological androgyny. *Journal of Consulting and Clinical Psychology, 42,* 155-162.

Bernstein, B. L., & Lecomte, C. (1982). Therapist expectancies: Client gender, and therapist gender, profession, and level of training. *Journal of Clinical Psychology, 38,* 744-754.

Bograd, M. (1992). Values in conflict: Challenges to family therapists' thinking. *Journal of Marital and Family Therapy, 18,* 245-256.

Broverman, I. K., Broverman, D. M., Clarkson, F. E., Rosenkrantz, P. S., & Vogel, S. R. (1970). Sex-role stereotypes and clinical judgements of mental health. *Journal of Consulting and Clinical Psychology, 34,* 1-7.

Dell, P. F. (1989). Violence and the systemic view: The problem of power. *Family Process, 28,* 1-14.

Fischer, E. H. (1989). Gender bias in therapy? An analysis of patient and therapist causal explanations. *Psychotherapy, 26,* 389-401.

Glenburg, A.M. (1988). *Learning from data: An introduction to statistical reasoning.* New York: Harcourt Brace Jovanovich.

Goodrich, T. J. (Ed.) (1991). *Women and power: Perspectives for family therapy.* New York: W.W. Norton.

Hardy, D. M., & Johnson, M. E. (1992). Influence of therapist gender and client gender, socioeconomic status and alcoholic status on clinical judgements. *Journal of Alcohol and Drug Education, 37*(2), 94-102.

Hare-Mustin, R. T. (1978). A feminist approach to family therapy. *Family Process, 17,* 181-194.

Hare-Mustin, R. T. (1987). The problem of gender in family therapy theory. *Family Process, 26,* 15-27.

Hare-Mustin, R. T. (1988). The meaning of difference: Gender theory, postmodernism, and psychology. *American Psychologist, 43,* 455-464.

Hare-Mustin, R. T. (1991). Sex, lies, and headaches: The problem is power. In T. J. Goodrich (Ed.), *Women and power: Perspectives for family therapy* (pp. 63-85). New York: W. W. Norton.

Hare-Mustin, R. T. (1994). Discourses in the mirrored room: A postmodern analysis of therapy. *Family Process, 33,* 19-35.

Kaufman, G. (1992). The mysterious disappearance of battered women in family therapists' offices: Male privilege colluding with male violence. *Journal of Marital and Family Therapy, 18,* 233-243.

Keeney, B. P. (1983). *Aesthetics of change.* New York: Guilford.

Knudson-Martin, C., & Mahoney, A. R. (1996). Gender dilemmas and myth in the construction of marital bargains: Issues for marital therapy. *Family Process, 35,* 137-153.

Leslie, L. A., & Clossick, M. L. (1996). Sexism in family therapy: Does training in gender make a difference? *Journal of Marital and Family Therapy, 22,* 253-269.

Libow, J. A., Raskin, P. A., & Caust, B. L. (1982). Feminist and family systems therapy: Are they irreconcilable? *The American Journal of Family Therapy, 10*(3), 3-12.

Lichtenberg, J. W., & Heck, E. J. (1981). Much ado about nothing? *Personnel & Guidance Journal, 59*(5), 317-320.

Luepnitz, D. A. (1988). *The family interpreted: Psychoanalysis, feminism, and family therapy.* Basic Books.

McGoldrick, M., Anderson, C. M., & Walsh, F. (Eds.). (1989). *Women in families: A framework for family therapy.* New York: W.W. Norton.

Reinisch, J.M., & Sanders, S.A. (1984). Prenatal gonadal steroidal influences on gender-related behavior. *Process in Brain Research, 61,* 406-416.

Riger, S. (1992). Epistemological debates, feminist voices: Science, social values, and the study of women. *American Psychologist, 47,* 730-740.

Scott, J.W. (1992). Experience. In J. Butler & J. W. Scott (Eds.) *Feminists Theorize the Political* (pp. 22-40). New York: Routledge.

Stabb, S. D., Cox, D. L., & Harber, J. L. (1997). Gender-related therapist attributions in couple's therapy: A preliminary multiple case study investigation. *Journal of Marital and Family Therapy, 23,* 335-346.

Weiner, J. P., & Boss, P. (1985). Exploring gender bias against women: Ethics for marriage and family therapy. *Counseling Values, 30,* 9-23.

Werner-Wilson, R. J., Zimmerman, T. S., & Price, S. (1999). Are goals and topics influenced by gender and modality in the initial marriage and family therapy session? *Journal of Marital and Family Therapy, 25*(2), 253-262.

Wheeless, V. E. & Dierks-Stewart, K. (1981). The psychometric properties of the Bem sex-role inventory: Questions concerning reliability and validity. *Communication Quarterly, 29,* 173-186.

Widiger, T. A., & Settle, S. A. (1987). Broverman et al. revisited: An artificial sex bias. *Journal of Personality and Social Psychology, 53,* 463-469.

APPENDIX A. Therapists' Perception of Couples in Therapy

Instructions: For questions numbered 2-7, please answer according to the following method. You have ten (10) points to distribute among the three or four items per question. Assign values based on the degree of importance you place on the items. Use only whole numbers to rate your responses and be sure that your rating within each question adds up to 10.

SAMPLE QUESTION

In your estimation, who expressed their concerns the most clearly?

        3 *the wife*
        2 *the husband*
        5 *the therapist*
        +_____
        10 points

1. In your own terms describe how would you define the problem?

2. Problem Formulation
    The contribution(s) to the problem follow from:
        _____ Husband's individual characteristics
        _____ Wife's individual characteristics
        _____ Shared aspects of the husband and wife system
        _____ Societal norms and socialization
        +_____
        10 points

3. Who is most affected by the problem?
        _____ Husband
        _____ Wife
        _____ Couple system
        +_____
        10 points

4. Who has most responsibility for change?
        _____ Husband
        _____ Wife
        _____ Couple system
        _____ Society
        +_____
        10 points

5. To what degree does the therapist understand the husband's and wife's concerns from:
        _____ Husband's perspective
        _____ Wife's perspective
        _____ The couple's perspective
        _____ Societal norms and socialization perspective
        +_____
        10 points

APPENDIX A (continued)

6. In your view, interventions should focus on:

        _____ The husband individually
        _____ The wife individually
        _____ The couple/family system
        _____ Societal norms
        +_____
        10 points

7. To what degree do the following impact the couple's problem?

        _____ Non-verbal communication
        _____ Verbal communication (content of what is said)
        _____ Combined aspects of both verbal and non-verbal communication
        +_____
        10 points

8. What is the distribution of interpersonal power in this relationship?

        _____ Husband
        _____ Wife
        +_____
        10 points

9. To what degree would this be viewed as a gender issue?

        _____ Specify an amount between 0 and 100%

10. To what degree is this an unequal power issue?

        _____ Specify an amount between 0 and 100%

In the following question you will be presented with twenty personality characteristics. Please indicate, on a scale from 1 to 7, how true these characteristics are of the individual as viewed in this session. Please do not leave any characteristic unmarked.

12. Describe **Carrie** according to the following scale:

1	2	3	4	5	6	7
never or almost never true	usually not true	sometimes but infrequently true	occasionally true	sometimes true	usually true	always or almost always true

_____ 1. Sincere   _____ 11. Gentle
_____ 2. Willing to take a stand   _____ 12. Aggressive
_____ 3. Assertive   _____ 13. Helpful
_____ 4. Competitive   _____ 14. Friendly
_____ 5. Understanding   _____ 15. Independent
_____ 6. Warm   _____ 16. Strong personality
_____ 7. Dominant   _____ 17. Acts as leader
_____ 8. Compassionate   _____ 18. Forceful
_____ 9. Has leadership abilities   _____ 19. Tender
_____10. Sensitive to needs of others   _____ 20. Eager to sooth hurt feelings

APPENDIX A (continued)

In the following question you will be presented with twenty personality characteristics. Please indicate, on a scale from 1 to 7, how true these characteristics are of the individual as viewed in this session. Please do not leave any characteristic unmarked.

13. Describe **Frank** according to the following scale:

1	2	3	4	5	6	7
never or almost never true	usually not true	sometimes but infrequently true	occasionally true	sometimes true	usually true	always or almost always true

_____ 1. Sincere
_____ 2. Willing to take a stand
_____ 3. Assertive
_____ 4. Competitive
_____ 5. Understanding
_____ 6. Warm
_____ 7. Dominant
_____ 8. Compassionate
_____ 9. Has leadership abilities
_____ 10. Sensitive to needs of others

_____ 11. Gentle
_____ 12. Aggressive
_____ 13. Helpful
_____ 14. Friendly
_____ 15. Independent
_____ 16. Strong personality
_____ 17. Acts as leader
_____ 18. Forceful
_____ 19. Tender
_____ 20. Eager to sooth hurt feelings

Differences Making a Difference: Cross-Cultural Interactions in Supervisory Relationships

Kyle D. Killian

SUMMARY. As the field of family therapy continues to gain exposure both in the U.S. and abroad, family therapists and their supervisors are increasingly likely to come from diverse cultural backgrounds. This study examines how differences in culture of origin influence supervisory relationships. Twelve individual interviews were conducted with six supervisors and six supervisees who had worked with one or more supervisees or supervisors whose culture of origin differed from their own. The descriptive data was analyzed using the method of constant comparison. Results reflect cross-cultural supervisees' acclimation to a Western/U.S. training context, specific challenges associated with cross-cultural supervision, and ways in which supervisors can sensitively and effectively supervise culturally different supervisees. Implications for education and training in family therapy are presented. *[Article copies available for a fee from The Haworth Document Delivery Service: 1-800-342-9678. E-mail address: <getinfo@haworthpressinc.com> Website: <http://www.HaworthPress.com> © 2001 by The Haworth Press, Inc. All rights reserved.]*

Kyle D. Killian, PhD, is Assistant Professor of Family Therapy at the University of Houston-Clear Lake. Address correspondence to: Kyle D. Killian, Box 201, UHCL, 2700 Bay Area Boulevard, Houston, TX 77058-1098.

Portions of this research were presented at the 56th Annual Conference of the American Association for Marriage and Family Therapy, Dallas, TX, October 15, 1998. The author wishes to acknowledge Dr. Anna M. Agathangelou for her insightful comments and critiques that contributed significantly to the quality of this work. He would also like to thank the reviewers for their many helpful suggestions for revising the manuscript.

[Haworth co-indexing entry note]: "Differences Making a Difference: Cross-Cultural Interactions in Supervisory Relationships." Killian, Kyle D. Co-published simultaneously in *Journal of Feminist Family Therapy* (The Haworth Press, Inc.) Vol. 12, No. 2/3, 2001, pp. 61-103; and: *Integrating Gender and Culture in Family Therapy Training* (ed: Toni Schindler Zimmerman) The Haworth Press, Inc., 2001, pp. 61-103. Single or multiple copies of this article are available for a fee from The Haworth Document Delivery Service [1-800-342-9678, 9:00 a.m. - 5:00 p.m. (EST). E-mail address: getinfo@haworthpressinc.com].

KEYWORDS. Cross-cultural, supervision, training, family therapy, culture, ecosystemic, difference

INTRODUCTION

In the twenty-first century, supervisors and trainers of all helping professions will experience a demand to adapt to an increasingly multicultural and multiracial environment. As persons of color become the numerical majority, and whites the minority (Yutrzenka, 1995), supervisors and clinicians will encounter increasing diversity in the supervisees and clientele with whom they work (Lappin & Hardy, 1997). And as the field of couple and family therapy continues to gain exposure both in the U.S. and abroad, family therapists and their supervisors are increasingly likely to come from diverse cultural backgrounds. In regard to delivery of services, there are currently insufficient numbers of minority supervisors and therapists to meet the needs of this expanding and diverse population. Are supervisors adequately prepared for the differences in values, beliefs, and expectations that can be encountered in these working relationships? This study seeks to examine how differences in culture of origin influence supervisory relationships and discover ways in which supervisors can sensitively and effectively supervise culturally different supervisees.

Along with the sweeping social, demographic, and technological changes occurring today, people find themselves reverberating with the impacts of philosophical and epistemological shifts as well. For example, the terms "multicultural" and "postmodern" have become commonplace in personal and professional interactions over the past ten years. With the critique of positivist objectivity and the embracing of reality as a subjective experience (Anderson & Goolishian, 1988; Maturana & Varela, 1980; von Glaserfeld, 1984), family therapists and supervisors are encountering the complexity of multiple realities, multiple identities, and their social locations relative to others within the therapy room, behind the one-way mirror, and in their daily interactions. In light of these developments, to which variables does one attend, under which circumstances, and why? Faced with complex, new ways of understanding social relations, supervisors are being challenged to go beyond what they already know how to do well and to begin to acknowledge and explore the crucial role contextual variables (e.g., culture, gender, race, and class) play in therapy and supervision. Interview data from supervisees and supervisors who have experienced cross-cultural supervisory relationships may provide insight into specific issues associated with such relationships and recommendations for how supervisors can conduct effective supervision in this context.

REVIEW OF THE LITERATURE

Few studies in the literature of the helping professions in general and marriage and family therapy in particular have examined the impact of contextual variables such as race and culture on supervisory and training experiences. A notable exception to the pattern of inattention to context is the feminist critique of systems theory, which, over the past two decades, has highlighted the influence of gender in both therapeutic and supervisory relationships (Allen & Laird, 1991; Ault-Riche, 1986; Avis, 1985; Goldner, 1985; Luepnitz, 1988; Storm, 1991; Turner & Fine, 1997; Walters et al., 1988; Wheeler et al., 1989). This critique of how the issue of power has and has not been addressed in family therapy has been the harbinger of multi-systemic and ecosystemic frameworks that foster an awareness of the social contexts within which couple and family systems are embedded. Nevertheless, there are many differences "which make a difference" (Bateson, 1979), and the influences of race and culture in the context of training and supervision have not been adequately addressed in the family therapy literature (Anderson, 1994; Hare-Mustin, 1994; Lappin & Hardy, 1997; Kliman, 1994; Preli & Bernard, 1993; Storm, 1992; Watson, 1993). Since we all inhabit various social locations on ecosystemic axes of race, gender, class, and culture (Mirkin, 1990), to name but a few, and these locations intersect in unique and sometimes contradictory ways (Kliman, 1994), we are all multicultural, and our interactions with others must necessarily be so as well. As awareness of this ubiquitous diversity continues to increase (Falicov, 1988; Haley, 1996; McGoldrick, Giordano, & Pearce, 1996; Pedersen, 1994), so does the need for studies exploring the relationships between culturally different supervisors and supervisees.

In the fields of clinical psychology and counseling, the impact of race and culture in training contexts has been addressed in a handful of books (Bernard & Goodyear, 1992; Gopaul-McNicol & Brice-Baker, 1998; Peterson, 1991; Pope-Davis & Coleman, 1997) and articles

(Bradshaw, 1982; Casas, 1984; Hilton, Russell, & Salmi, 1995; Remington & DaCosta, 1989; Vasquez & Eldridge, 1994). In their review of the literature, Leong and Wagner (1994) stated that "the scarcity of empirical information on which to base our understanding of cross-cultural supervision is striking" (p. 117). Leong and Wagner found only three empirical studies addressing race in the supervisory context. Cook and Helms (1988) tapped 225 minority supervisees' recollections of their supervisory experiences with their white supervisors. Asian Americans reported higher levels of supervisor approval than Blacks, Hispanics, and Native Americans. This study was retrospective in nature and lacked a white supervisee group that would have enabled a comparison of within-race and between-race supervisory relationship experiences. Cook and Helms (1988) postulated that the limited number of multicultural trainees in graduate counseling programs (Casas, 1984; Killian & Hardy, 1998; McGoldrick, 1998; Preli & Bernard, 1993) may translate to fewer opportunities for supervisors to participate in cross-cultural relationships, resulting in a continued uncertainty as to how they might best proceed with culturally different supervisees. In another study examining the effects of supervision support and supervisor race, Hilton, Russell, and Salmi (1995) found a main effect for supervisor level of support but no significant effects for race. Studying factors related to students' positive or negative anticipation of their supervisory relationships, Vanderkolk (1974) found that Black students expected their supervisors to be less empathic, respectful, and congruent than their white counterparts. Weaknesses of the study included a limited sample size and no data about supervisees' actual experience of their supervisory relationships.

The bulk of the existing research has been clinical and theoretical in nature. Cook (1983) and Guiterrez (1982) found that disregarding the influence of cultural factors on supervisory relationships could contribute to conflictual and nonproductive training experiences. Helms (1982) also found that cross-cultural or racially mixed supervisory relationships tend to be more conflictual than homogenous relationships. Helms also suggested that supervisors may contribute to the level of conflict, a reasonable finding considering supervisors occupy a power position over their trainees and are necessarily a part of the interactions that occur in supervision. In the *Handbook of Multicultural Counseling,* a typology of philosophical assumptions underlying multicultural counseling and training and cross-cultural perspectives on supervision were addressed (Carter & Qureshi, 1995; Brown & Landrum-Brown, 1995). Remington and DaCosta (1989) discussed ethnocultural factors in a process approach to Black and White supervisory relationships, but their recommendations were limited to Black-White interactions. Sue and Zane (1987) and Zane and Sue (1991) concluded that therapists who establish credibility with their culturally different clients are more likely to have positive treatment outcomes. These researchers and others (Hunt, 1987; Lago & Thompson, 1996; Sue et al., 1992; Watson, 1993) suggest that effective training demands that supervisors help therapists establish credibility with clients from different cultural backgrounds. In a parallel fashion, supervisors can model the process of establishing credibility with cross-cultural clients by effectively working with their own culturally different supervisees.

THEORETICAL RATIONALE

An ecosystemic theoretical framework (Auerswald, 1985; Keeney, 1983) guides this study. Ecosystemic theorists emphasize the importance of the historical and cultural contexts in which relationships and presenting problems are embedded. Individuals, couples, families are embedded within larger ecosystems or social structures, and these social contexts influence the values, beliefs, experiences, and daily practices of people and groups of people. Oppressive social institutions such as racism and sexism impose imbalances of power and privilege, locating white persons and men as normative and superior and persons of color and women as inferior in an invidious hierarchy.[1]

In addition, both researchers and family professionals are influenced by the ethnocentrism of the dominant culture that permeates all institutions. A paradigmatic shift toward epistemologies that acknowledge contextual variables of race, gender, class, and culture will facilitate a growing awareness and sensitivity to thinking about people in the context of social and political structures. By helping us place individuals, couples, and families *in context,* ecosystemic epistemology can open our eyes to how social relations are informed by power and how larger systems interact to perpetuate presenting problems.

The emphasis of ecosystemic theory on culture and context is congruent with the Race-Based approach to understanding and teaching about cultural differences (Carter & Qureshi, 1995). The Race-Based approach defines culture interactively as a function of both race and ethnic background. Race is considered the most significant difference because racial characteristics tend to be more enduring, whereas ethnicity and culture are seen as more fluid and flexible (Carter & Qureshi, 1995). Thus, membership in a cultural group is ascribed and dialectically defined, partially through the invidious hierarchical relationship between the most powerful and less powerful social groups. In North American society, the dominant group who has possessed the power to define who is normative, superior, and/or "ingroup," and who is deviant, inferior, and/or "outgroup" has been white persons of European descent. In sum, the ecosystemic framework and the Race-based approach highlight the importance of historical and cultural contexts for understanding social phenomena and emphasize that intergroup power relations must be accounted for in all steps of the research process, from the questions asked by the researcher to the analysis of subjects' interpretations of their situations and experiences.

METHOD

Sample

Twelve interviews were conducted with six supervisors and six supervisees. Five of the supervisors were AAMFT Approved Supervisors, and the sixth had taken coursework in Marriage and Family Therapy and held a supervisor credential in another clinical field. The supervisees were enrolled in masters and doctoral MFT programs at two universities located in central New York and Texas. The supervisors ranged from 36 to 60 years old and the supervisees were from 24 to 38 years old, and all participants had worked with one or more supervisees or supervisors whose culture of origin differed from their own. The supervisors interviewed were a Latina woman from Mexico, a black male of mixed ancestry from South America, a white, Persian woman from the Middle East, and three supervisors from the U.S., a white male of Dutch and English descent, a white female of English and German descent, and a white, Jewish female of German descent. The three white supervisors from the U.S. identified themselves as feminists. The six supervisees were four women and two men from six different countries: three Asian women, one from Japan, one from Korea, and one from Vietnam, a Latina woman from Mexico, a white man from Russia, and a man from Spain who identified himself racially as white and ethnically as Arab. The Latina female supervisee identified herself as a feminist.

Procedure

Blumer (1969), a founder of the inductive tradition in the social sciences, suggested that qualitative researchers enter the field with "sensitizing questions" to help guide their thinking. Sensitizing questions serve as points of reference for researchers as they approach data collection and can help them avoid predetermining what it is that they hope to find. A reading of the relevant literature led to the formation of several sensitizing questions about how cultural differences influence clinical supervision, and these questions were utilized in the interviews. Phenomenology, the analysis of consciousness, is an important part of feminist research (Humm, 1995). Feminist analyses include the consciousness of both the observer and the observed, and phenomenological researchers try to use first-hand and immediate contact with their subjects, reflecting on their own experiences and observations of what women (and men) say and do (Humm, 1995; Patton, 1990). The semi-structured interviews were conducted individually and featured open-ended questions (see Appendix) regarding the participants' customs, values, and traditions in their cultures of origin and their experiences of cross-cultural supervision. Ten interviews were conducted face-to-face, and two were conducted over the telephone. The interviews were audiotaped with the participants' permission and were approximately an hour and a half in duration.

A major tenet of qualitative research is that the researcher is part of the process (Moon, Dillon & Sprenkle, 1990). Situating myself ecosystemically in this study, I am a white, middle class, bilingual, well-educated U.S. citizen. My social locations as a family therapist, educator, supervisor, and the spouse of a non-citizen played a role in how I interacted with the research participants and conducted the interviews. For example, two interviewees inquired as to why I was interested in the topic of cross-cultural supervision, and my locations as a fellow clinician and/or trainer and a person who has worked with persons from many different countries and experienced immersion in several cultural contexts helped to increase the comfort level of these participants. I conducted and transcribed all the interviews.

I transcribed the interviews verbatim, and the data were subjected to a coding process facilitated by the software program HyperRE-

SEARCH (ResearchWare, 1995). Coding involves the categorization and sorting of data into labels or codes which serve to separate, compile, and organize descriptive data (Charmaz, 1983). HyperRE-SEARCH permits one to import data from a variety of sources, allows one to assign multiple codes to the same data, and then store and retrieve coded data. For example, as the user views a segment of an interview, HyperRESEARCH presents an index of code names or categories. The researcher chooses an existing code or creates a new one as it emerges from the data, and the program records the exact location of the text along with the code name. Coding categories can be retrieved over a set of interviews through data reports, which are organized through the use of descriptors or the selection of multiple codes. Subsequent stages of focused coding involve the renaming and condensing of codes and the use of larger "family" codes or categories that bring together the underlying codes they represent. Via a method of constant comparison, recurring topics, key words, and phrases in the data were used as coding categories and relationships among the data sources and the coding categories were mapped out through repeated sifting of the data (Strauss & Corbin, 1998). The codes and themes that emerged from the participants' narratives were analyzed by examining the participants' social locations on the contextual variables of culture, gender, race, and class and how these locations informed their supervisory experiences.

RESULTS

Responses by the participants were coded under many codes, including the following major categories: supervisor/supervisee cultural identity, issues and challenges in supervision, finding common ground, recommendations for cross-cultural supervision, and supervisor sensitivity.

Supervisor/Supervisee Cultural Identity

Each of the six supervisees described a culture of origin comprised of particular customs, values, and assumptions, many of which were non-Western. For instance, the three Asian supervisees described groups and communities as the basic social unit as opposed to a

Western focus on the individual. They also suggested that helping professionals, professors, and supervisors were viewed as high-ranking authority figures in their respective cultures. Three of the six supervisees planned to return to their culture of origin, and so assimilation to Western/U.S. cultural norms was less of a priority for them. The three supervisors from other countries also demonstrated some salient differences in cultural assumptions, but had been in the U.S. from 16 to 34 years and had more or less adjusted to life in the U.S. The three supervisors from the U.S. possessed a more diffuse sense of cultural heritage, sometimes identifying one or two European cultures from which they were descended, but not making concrete and explicit how these ethnicities informed their current identities, perceptions, and relations. It is possible that while they held a strong interest in the influence of culture in therapy and supervision, the three white supervisors were not immune to the effects of the dominant US culture in which they were born and raised. Their responses to questions about their cultural identity appeared to be influenced by the paradigm of assimilation (see Schlesinger, 1998), which views the retaining of a specific cultural identity (other than the homogenized "North American" white identity) as a "divisive threat" to unity in the United States.

Developing a concept of "culture." Supervisees and supervisors were asked about how their culture of origin had affected their expectations for life in the U.S. and clinical supervision in particular (the three supervisors from the U.S. were also asked to talk about cultural difference and how the concept had impacted their ideas about training). A middle class, Russian male supervisee shared the following:

> When I came here, I considered myself very international, very good with different races, not homophobic, and very open. While I was thinking that, I found that my emotional reactions showed some cultural stereotypes about sexuality and gender. There were homosexuals in a few classes, and sometimes I had a hard time with this issue; to some extent it is more difficult for me because in Russia it was still prohibited legally. . . . Regarding gender relationships, in my first year here, all of my female colleagues would call me a sexist pig because I would make this statement that women who aren't happy just need sex. Culturally, in Russia, people say the first thing that women want is sex, and if they have it, they are happy, and if they don't, they are not. Doing a

sexual analysis like that here, people, especially female colleagues, reacted vigorously. They cured me in a year (laugh).

This supervisee's immersion in a new culture challenged his perspective of himself as "international" and "open." He had also come
here "with a sense that this was a country where they pay a lot of
attention to freedom, individual freedom," but quickly discovered that
there were some limits to this liberalist[2] ideal. Hence, for some supervisees, immersion into mainstream U.S. culture represents a shock and
requires a period of adjustment (Leong & Chou, 1996). This supervisee
experienced intense admonitions from his peers for sexist and homophobic stereotypes that purportedly were never challenged in the Russian context.

An upper middle class supervisee from Mexico discussed an intersection of variables that contributed to her cultural identity and how
people ascribed an identity to her without seeking information:

I never really thought about my heritage until I lived in the
States. I began to question my background because of the way
people reacted towards me. I do know that I'm not so white
looking, it is evident to me, but that is not such a big deal in
Mexico. . . . I think that it's a combination of race, class, ethnicity, and gender in some cases. My first recollection is that in my
late teens we used to go up to Texas to go shopping. One time we
were waiting in line to pay the bill and the people behind the
counter were talking. One said, "You know, I feel sorry for these
Mexican people who have to wait until so-and-so gets here so
someone can speak to them in their language." I said, "Excuse
me, are you talking about us?" And she was shocked. But I was
really annoyed that she could make such an assumption, and that
was the first time I became aware of this idea of "these Mexican
people" and I did not even understand what I now know as the
construction of "the other." We learned that to get attention and
service we had to be short and sharp, which is considered very
rude in our culture.

Interviewer: Were you ever the designated "the Spanish-
speaking, Mexican person" or "expert" in any of your training
contexts?

That came about when I was in Texas and in New York. I found people asking me about working with Spanish people, and I didn't know!

This supervisee speaks about an intersection of various contextual variables all informing her evolving sense of her cultural self and how her first experiences with prejudice and faulty generalization in the U.S. affected her understanding of how others perceived her. She critiques the others' presumption that she did not know English based on her appearance or the fact that she does speak Spanish. In addition, despite having access to a Latina and Mexican identity, this supervisee highlights that identity does not "expertise" make, that is, that her culture of origin does not translate into her being a spokesperson for all "Spanish" clients.

The 58-year-old, middle class, white female supervisor from the U.S. shared a critical incident abroad that deepened her understanding of the concepts of culture and worldview:

The summer after my freshman year I stayed in Vienna with a family in a German language program. I was furious all the time, because my friends would show up late. Six weeks into the summer, standing at a bus stop, waiting for people who were running forty-five minutes late, it hit me like a lightning bolt: "*This* is culture. It's not that they're bad people. They always show up an hour late because that's their culture, and everybody knows it, and I've been told it, but I want them to play by my rules instead of me playing by their rules." Then when I began the MFT program here, I seriously could not imagine trying to train people who had not lived in another culture to be a family therapist. It seemed to me that for anybody who wanted to do this kind of work, it was crucial that they have the experience of knowing what a mind set or paradigm was, and having to break out of one mind set and experience another.

This participant experienced anger when her Viennese acquaintances challenged her implicit worldview that emphasized the importance of punctuality. The angry and indignant response of this participant to this cross-cultural encounter (i.e., "these bad people should play according to my rules") may have been connected to her status and privilege as a white, well-educated citizen of the United States.

Becoming "Westernized." Three participants discussed the importance of adjusting to the cultural context of the United States and doing things the "Western" way. The Middle Eastern, middle class, 50-year-old female supervisor talked about the adjustment process she and her compatriots experienced when they first came to the U.S. to start their graduate education. She said that her family had been exposed to much information about the U.S. through movies and books, but still had experienced culture shock in some areas: "For instance, people freely express themselves in public as boyfriend and girlfriend, men and women, and sometimes same-sex. I knew that they do that here, but it's different when it happens right next to you." In commenting on the initial strangeness of experiencing public displays of affection firsthand, this participant pointed out that her basic knowledge of many aspects of Western culture was quite detailed, while the depth of her fellow supervisees' and supervisors' knowledge of her culture was likely to be limited. This participant also talked about the importance of cross-cultural supervisees having time to acclimate to and develop a voice in the U.S. training context:

> Especially in cultures where they respect their professors, students do not talk back and would not think to comment or disagree. Especially in male to female types of interactions, supervisors and their supervisees may end up missing a lot of opportunities to discuss issues. Supervisees may need a little more time, a period of adjustment to get used to American cultural ways, so that they can say whatever they think and feel, really benefit from discussion, get feedback, and learn more.

In talking about her cultural self, a 24-year-old Japanese supervisee noted how "Westernized" she had become:

> All my college education was received in the U.S., so my salient culture at the time of supervision was going towards U.S. culture, and that was where I was coming from. And because in the academic field I was trained to analyze, I was thinking in a more Western scheme. I think because we travel and interact with people from other cultures, I think individuals have some range in terms of culture; sometimes I'm so Japanese, and sometimes I'm so Westernized (laugh).

This supervisee did not speak exclusively as an "Eastern" or "Westernized" subject, but as both, stressing a *range* of cultural identity rather than a single, monolithic subjectivity. Her reference to the dialectic, "both/and" nature of cultural identity highlights the inadequacy of reductionistic, monolithic, or stereotypical constructions of culture if one hopes to capture the uniqueness and complexity of each supervisee's cultural self. This supervisee went on to describe how her culture of origin influenced her experience of supervision:

> I think that my culture of origin came into play in my expectations about roles. I was expecting a very explicit, structured form of supervision–more like telling me what to do, step by step, very clearly–a very structured supervision, versus "let's explore what will happen, what this means." In my culture, in high school, I was used to lecturing, and we had so many rules that we had to obey and there were many consequences.

While she had been in the U.S. five years and she had begun to be socialized into Western values and ways of thinking, this supervisee was nevertheless more familiar with a hierarchical, didactic, and very structured style of education and training. Thus, the styles and cultural expectations of different supervisors can vary greatly in terms of their initial "goodness of fit" with a given supervisee's expectations.

Issues and Challenges in Cross-Cultural Supervision

> To enter a family system, unless it's one's own, is to enter another culture.

> *Jay Lappin, 1983, p. 123*

While their experiences had been positive in many ways, all 12 subjects in this study reported experiences of tension or discomfort in some of their cross-cultural supervisory relationships. All six supervisees reported instances in which at least one trainer had made faulty generalizations, or times when they had felt that they did not "fit in" with their peers in training programs. The interviewer asked the Latina female supervisor to describe her experience when she first came to the U.S.:

> Interviewer: Anything about these training programs or job contexts that was a challenge or struggle for you?

> Always. But I don't know what to ascribe it to. It could have been my race, it could have been ethnicity, my language, it could have been my trying to adapt to a new country. At my first job, the director introduced me at a staff meeting–"this is [subject's name], our new therapist"–and everyone is thinking that she is a Jew from Brooklyn, I was fitting whatever image they had as I sat there smiling. But little by little, they began to discover that I was not a Jew from Brooklyn. So my feeling was that these people were a circle and I couldn't come into this circle, and my ticket to getting into this circle was how much I knew and how much I could prove myself. And that was my second taste of having to be some way other than polite like I had been in Mexico.

This participant describes the accumulation of knowledge and skills as a means of garnering approval. In stark contrast to the "politeness" that characterized her social relations in her culture of origin, this supervisor negotiated a new social relations in the U.S. context, explicitly proving herself, as it gained her access to membership in a social and professional "circle."

A few participants discussed feelings of frustration and alienation that they experienced when supervisors and fellow supervisees failed to "connect" with them or did not negotiate divergent expectations. The supervisees from Vietnam and Korea stated that they felt awkward or uncomfortable approaching their trainers and professors to voice specific needs or concerns. Here the Japanese supervisee expressed the feelings she had had about a supervision style that was less structured than she had expected:

> I didn't feel uncomfortable because I was already used to it in my classes. It was maybe a little bit frustrating . . . and it was true of all my supervisors, that I couldn't get a clear answer. Coming from my background, studying counseling in general was very frustrating, because here I didn't get specific answers most of the time and that made me feel like I wasn't learning anything. But now I do feel that I learned something, after I got a job. . . . In talking about culture, I tend to think that it's coming from how I grew up and was trained in Japan. Even now I tend to really listen

to my boss, and follow her first and then find out whether it's true or not later. I don't even question her from the beginning. Later on I might find out she was wrong.

This supervisee said that she was uncomfortable questioning the authority of her supervisors or volunteering feedback to them regarding what she liked or didn't like about supervision. Her previous experiences with a top-down, lecturing style meant that experiential and process-oriented approaches to supervision were unfamiliar and initially less comfortable to her.

When supervisors and/or supervisees did not co-construct a space for respectful discussion of differences, culture of origin differences were perceived as having a negative impact on supervision. Here a 36-year-old, white, middle class male supervisor relates how unexamined assumptions impeded the supervisory process:

> Looking back at supervising a Japanese female student, I don't think I was able to speak in her "language." I did broach the subject of culture, and we did discuss some cultural concepts explicitly, and we were comfortable. But I did not take into account her own background in terms of the education system and how that might influence her expectations of the training she would receive from me as a teacher or supervisor. And so, I was approaching supervision with a self-of-therapist model, and I was trying to be collaborative and non-hierarchical and just "getting together to talk about some clinical scenarios." And now, I think that's not at all what she was expecting. These differences had an impact on our relationship, but, unfortunately, they were not always processed or made explicit during supervision. For example, I think that now we would be much more likely to talk about our respective values around indirect communication, saving face, training style, and power.

A 50-year-old supervisor from the Middle East shared the following experiences:

> When you come from other countries, the political situation in the world can be a big factor, and it was for me. When I came to the U.S., it was '78, less than a year before the hostage situation started [at the American embassy in Iran]. It was nerve-wracking–

it was really, really, bad. They were counting the days on television, every day and every night, and you couldn't get away from it. I was taking a class, and this teacher was so indifferent towards me, and I was still struggling at that time with my English. I remember asking something about when an assignment was due, and he said he didn't know why I was there in his class. I didn't know what to say! In my culture, you don't raise your voice or talk back to a professor; you always show respect in your words and tone of voice. I was shocked! . . . One way that my culture affects my work that is very obvious is my accent. Sometimes clients would ask where I was from, and I immediately wondered about how to answer that question. I learned from my supervisor to talk about that; to ask, "How do you feel about talking with someone with an accent? Do you feel like it is affecting the therapy session?" And people in general don't have that much information about other countries, but when people ask where you are from and the answer is "Iran" or "Iraq" in the middle of a major political situation, then a few times, I think, clients felt like, "Oh, she's not from here, she doesn't know a thing about American culture, how can *she* help *us?*"

The international political situation can inform the degree of comfort and security international students feel in and out of the classroom and can influence their clients', supervisors', and professors' perceptions of them. A strong cultural tradition for showing deference to the authority of a teacher or professor is common in many countries, especially in the Middle East and Southeast Asia. A cultural proscription against "talking back," combined with learning a second language, and other contextual factors such as gender, may make it very difficult for culturally different supervisees to effectively respond to the direct or indirect hostility of a professor or trainer or doubts about the supervisees' efficacy or competence expressed by clients.

The Russian male supervisee communicated his perception that some trainers seemed burdened by having an "international" member in their group of supervisees:

I felt like sometimes they didn't know what to do with me, like they didn't know how to approach me. They were very cautious. It felt like they had to go an extra mile and I felt like a burden. I could see that they were having to make an extra effort. I couldn't help thinking that they would prefer to have an American student as a supervisee because it makes their life easier.

Some supervisors, from their own perspectives and those of their trainees, appear to grapple with unique concerns and issues when working with an international supervisee. The male supervisor from South America expressed the following concern about training international supervisees in U.S./Western therapy techniques:

> I think it is a little arrogant and a bit unsettling to think that you can take someone from Kuwait, teach them how to do therapy in the United States, and that that is going to be applicable to Kuwait. They simply do not perceive things the same way and families are not structured the same way there. In fact, psychotherapy is seen as something that's not done. . . . If I have students from Japan, and a young adult child is talking about problems with parents, you can ask them if they would encourage him or her to do things their own way and not get their parents' permission to do certain things, and they would probably say "No, that's not done; that's not part of the Japanese culture," and then you try to get a solution that is within the boundaries of their particular culture. Now if they are not going back home and they are going to stay in the U.S., that's a different thing. Then you have to train them to be effective in this culture.

This supervisor expressed a wish that trainers clarify which cultural context trainees would be practicing in and be certain to explicitly discuss cultural differences as part of the supervision.

A 58-year-old, white middle class female supervisor with 22 years experience conducting supervision with trainees of various races and cultures was quite familiar with intergroup power dynamics:

> I had three young, white women who had taken feminist therapy and had found their voice, and three non-white women, one African-American, one Vietnamese, and one Japanese. I paired them up originally across cultures so that they could support each other and learn from each other. The first thing that happened was one of the white women said, "I don't want to work with *her*; I want to work with my friend here," who was also a young, white woman, "be-

cause we have a lot to learn from each other." I said, "Well, maybe next time, but we are going to start out like this." . . . I made the Anglo group be quiet while we sat for thirty seconds, and I would ask the Vietnamese student, "What do you think about this?," and I would use my hands to be sure no one else took the floor, while we waited the minute it took for her to start to respond. She would say wonderful things, and after I'd modeled it five or six times, I said, "You see? There's a cultural difference here. These guys aren't going to participate at all in the supervision group unless we make a space for them. We have a lot to learn from them. Why don't we work on this?" And the answer was: "No. We just got our voice. We're going to use it. If they want their turn, they can take the floor." So, from the Anglo side, the willingness to consider [culture] wasn't there. . . . They refused to accommodate people from other cultures because their culture was right. And they'd just taken feminist family therapy and that proved it (laugh).

This incident demonstrates that a sensitivity to one ecosystemic axis of power, such as gender, can sometimes override consideration of other axes of power, such as race, class, and/or culture. Supervisors and supervisees who are accustomed to holding power and privilege, such as white persons from the U.S., have a persistent tendency to define what is "right" or proper, and may succeed in supplanting one hierarchical, hegemonic set of social relations (i.e., a patriarchal system with men positioned over women) with another (i.e., a racist system which privileges white persons over all "others," and U.S. citizens over internationals). On this theme, the 45-year-old Jewish female supervisor from the U.S. shared the following: "As trainers, we want to be sensitive to gender, ethnicity, race, culture, class, but we tend to see one of these more clearly than the others, possibly because it's been experienced as crucial to our own sense of being, possibly because we tend to look at only one thing at a time." This supervisor speaks to difficulties of sustaining the complexity of identity, social location, and social relations because as people, therapists, and supervisors, we tend to privilege or resonate with a particular ecosystemic axis of power more than others. Nevertheless, it is the *intersections* of our locations on various axes of power that inform our social relations in and out of training contexts and organize who does and does not speak, what is and is not spoken about, and whose beliefs, values, and expectations are deemed normative and granted a privileged, implicitly superior, status in the room.

Finding Common Ground

The six supervisees shared that while some differences in expectations and personal style related to culture of origin are inevitable, a rapport could be established by focusing on commonalties between supervisor and supervisee. Here the Japanese female supervisee addresses how supervisors and supervisees can create a space where culture can be acknowledged in the supervision process:

> It was comfortable that we [she and her supervisor] were both coming from the counseling field, so that we were open to discuss feelings. So in that sense, we were coming from the same culture, if I can say that that was the culture. . . . and we were aware of cultural differences, and had so much interaction with other people from different cultures, it made it possible to make a balance and not be so much into stereotypes. So it created a space for us to deal with it and not to go to either extreme, stereotyping or looking at everyone as just individuals.

Supervisors who hold an active interest in other cultures and value ecosystemic differences are likely to foster an atmosphere where difference can be discussed in supervision. The Russian supervisee reported having a similar experience with a minority supervisor:

> I felt lucky because I had a really good connection with him and I trust him a lot because it seems like he understands what I'm going through in terms of the cultural adjustment. Some of the processes that he went through I also had to go through.

> Interviewer: Which processes?

> The cultural adjustment to the white American world that he had to go through–I'm doing this too–even though he's black and I'm white, and I'm a foreigner, so there is a little twist in that–but still, he does seem sensitive to me. I feel he treated me equally, *and* he also saw me as different. But I never felt like something extra.

In this case, supervisee and supervisor connected around their mutual adjustment to a culture where white male and female U.S. citizens occupy a normative, non-prefixed position. The supervisee perceived the supervisor's being black as a contributing factor in his empathy and sensitivity to the supervisee's status as an international student. Note that the supervisee felt he was treated as an equal and also as different, indicating that these two experiences are not mutually exclusive. He also shared that he had felt understood by another supervisor who had been to his home country: "He knew a little bit about where a person like me is coming from. I think experience with different people, traveling, knowing that there can be different views and different meanings is all helpful."

The supervisor from South America shared the following on the theme of common ground:

> Traveling a lot before I came to this country, I saw that people had different roles and ways, and that made an indelible impression on me that people can be different. I always tell my students that people are unique, *in predictable ways.* You are a unique person, but you behave in ways that are predictable for humans. You may be different, but if your parents died, you would experience some kind of bereavement. . . . But you could never know all the cultures. The best thing you can do is to ask people who you are working with to teach you about their culture. It has many benefits: (1) you establish a good rapport with them, (2) they know that you are not infallible, that you have weaknesses just like them, and (3) it gives them a refresher about their own culture.

This supervisor comments that a "both/and" perspective is useful in thinking about cross-cultural interactions because there are basic human emotional processes at work across contexts and also significant differences in how these processes are conceived and expressed from place to place. He also states that therapists (and supervisors) cannot be cultural anthropologists with expertise on every culture, so their interest in clients' (and supervisees') worldviews can create opportunities to connect with them and help them to review the cultural beliefs, values, and assumptions that are persisting as organizing principles in their family lives.

Recommendations for Cross-Cultural Supervision

Supervisees were asked to talk about how they would approach supervision and training of their own supervisees in light of their experiences. The first quotation is from the Japanese female supervisee, the second from the Russian male supervisee:

> I think the first thing I might do is to constantly remind myself where I'm coming from and what my style is and how it's created, and where my supervisees are coming from, so that would clarify expectations, and when we know what we expect it will be less complicated, less miscommunications, and less disappointments.

> Being very open, and providing a personal support system, making a human connection, and sharing my own personal and professional struggles.

> Interviewer: Just being human and personable. Personable, and curious about the difference in culture. So if I encounter something, say, a student who is doing poorly in my class, I will try to get a sense about what is happening rather than assuming it's his individual responsibility.

The supervisees suggested that supervisors be aware of differences in perspectives and meaning, have an interest in supervisee's challenges and struggles to adjust to a new cultural context, and be vulnerable and willing to share their own struggles. The Russian supervisee pointed out the importance of maintaining curiosity and avoiding individualistic, Western assumptions such as that individuals can achieve success (professionally or academically) if they only work hard enough. Cross-cultural supervisees who do not share these assumptions may experience interactions organized around these principles as confusing, frustrating, and isolating.

Another theme that emerged from the interviews was trainers' adopting a proactive stance and taking the leadership in discussing differences in expectations, goals, and personal style. The male supervisor from South America said, "When international students are in my classes, I ask them, 'Are you going back home?', and if they say 'Yes', I make it clear that I am going to call on them a lot to translate whatever I say here into their own culture. We need to remember that every therapeutic thing can be explained in a different way through a cultural lens. I would suggest that supervisors ask their supervisees to place what they are learning in supervision into the context of their culture, because that enriches everybody." This supervisor also recommended that trainers avoid overgeneralizing about different supervisees' needs:

> Supervision has to be tailored to each person. Making a blanket statement about anything about people can get you into trouble. . . . If you get two Americans together, you don't necessarily expect to get a consensus. If you get two culturally different people together, you wouldn't expect a consensus there either. So what I do is let the person present, talk to them about their culture, talk to them about what psychotherapy is, talk to them about family therapy, and if they are going to stay here versus go home, and give them some ideas about whether they may have problems applying interventions done here back at home.

The Middle Eastern female supervisor noted the importance of knowing in which cultural context a supervisee plans to practice:

> If the supervisee is from a different ethnic background, then that has to be part of the supervision. They have to discuss how their culture informs their perception of interventions and their comfort level with how things are done here. The supervisor should make a point of finding out if the supervisee will be taking back this experience to their home culture. If so, the supervisor should be asking "How would you do this back home? How would you change it so it would work there?"

In addition to the issue of the cultural context that cross-cultural supervisees expect to apply their family therapy training, this quotation highlights the importance of white supervisors and therapists also learning to discuss how their culture informs their perception of what are "appropriate" therapeutic interventions and their comfort level with diverse clientele (e.g., persons of color).

The 58-year-old, white female supervisor from the U.S. had the following suggestions for increasing comfort for and opening space for feedback from culturally different supervisees:

Listening, personal sharing, learning about the family of origin, and getting the students to talk about their experience in this culture. Practically speaking, it would be better to have more than one of the minority people in the room so that they can support each other. I think a group might be better, or at least once a month getting together with more than one culturally different supervisee and asking them to talk with each other about their experiences working in this culture, and then listen carefully to their discussion. A supervisor could ask everybody in the group to write down one thing the supervisor could do better if you were going to start working with a culturally different supervisee.

Supervisor Sensitivity to Culture

In light of supervisors' power positions in relation to their trainees (e.g., professionally, educationally, and, frequently, along the variables of race, nationality, gender, class, and others), I asked about ways that supervisors from the U.S. could attain and maintain cultural awareness and sensitivity in their work with culturally different supervisees. Distinguishing cognitive knowledge and emotional sensitivity, a Mexican female supervisor talked about how important it is to avoid placing the culturally different supervisee in the supervision "hot seat":

> In understanding culture intellectually, it takes a while to take in all that information; that's cognitive. Then there's the affective part, and when you have the two, then you are really getting somewhere. But to put it into practice, what you actually do as a therapist or supervisor, that takes even longer. In the past, I think I put myself in the center as an authority person without even knowing it. I think that while theoretically and intellectually I agree with this equality thing–you are the supervisee, I am the supervisor, and we're equal here because we're both learning, blah, blah–it's a great thing to say, but when it translates into practice, I think more often than not I've put myself at center as the authority. Let's say you are my supervisee–instead of me talking with you about how I feel with you being white and me not being white, what I have done in the past is to ask the supervisee how he feels about being supervised by someone who is not white. I have an issue with that approach because if I ask you

how you feel about me, I'm putting myself in the center and I'm making you wiggle and explain to me how you feel. Forget that! I now think that the way to do it would be something like sharing with you how uncomfortable or comfortable what I am experiencing is in that process, and *then* gingerly invite you to do the same.

This participant articulated a collaborative supervisory process where the supervisor never unilaterally demands that the culturally different supervisee ecosystemically locate himself or herself and disclose his or her feelings in the relationship before the supervisor has done so.

Finally, the 58-year-old, white female supervisor stated that she is now "more willing to listen and to try to find out what the internal experience and culture of a family is because I do know that I *don't know*":

I am willing to risk that I'll be made a fool of because there's something obvious I missed or didn't know, and having someone get mad at me, because I'm capable of backing off, apologizing, and being open to learning, which I think most white people are not. They're too afraid of coming across as an idiot or racist. In my classes, I say things like, "All of us are a little bit racist, we just have to discover our racism and learn how to deal with it." And the supervisor has to know that it's okay to be imperfect, to make mistakes. You're never going to learn if you have to pretend that you already know it all. . . . I could see it being helpful having an African-American person watching me supervise a Chinese person–I would get something totally different if I had a Chinese person watching me supervise a Chinese person–but either way, I would get information, especially if they could watch the supervision, and then discuss it with me and the supervisee together. They could say "Now, did you feel that [supervisor's name] was doing such and such," and "How did you feel when she said this?" or "I would have done this" in some kind of three-way discussion. *That* would be training. And everybody who *trains* ought to have that kind of training.

DISCUSSION

If we are always arriving and departing, it is also true that we are eternally anchored. One's destination is never a place but rather a new way of looking at things.

Henry Miller, 1957, from "The Oranges of the Millennium"

Ecosystemic theory facilitates the examination of power relations along ecosystemic axes of power: culture, gender, race, class, and nationality, among others. Just as "gender" does not mean women, but refers to the social institutions and history that support particular sets of relations between men and women, culture also cannot be reduced to only "others," people who are different from the normative, white, U.S. citizen. Culture instead refers to institutions, practices, and histories which locate persons "from here" and from other countries differentially in terms of the privilege and power they possess in relationship to one another. As the opening quotation to this section suggests, it is important for us to anchor or locate supervisors in terms of their own privilege and power ecosystemically so that they can more fully understand how that social location informs what happens in supervision with a culturally different supervisee. This section begins with a critical engagement of power issues as they are linked with race and culture, and proceeds with an analysis of the ideas and experiences shared by the participants in the results section.

Locating Self in Relation to "Other": Enhancing Sensitivity to Whiteness

The vast majority of Approved Supervisors are white men and women from the U.S., and most of their families have been in the U.S. for several generations. It is all too easy in a country that places considerable stock in the "melting pot" paradigm of mass assimilation to learn to occupy a normative, non-prefixed social location as the culturally generic white person. The more implicit one's sense of normativity and accompanying privilege, the easier it is to reap the benefits of white privilege unconsciously, in the sociopolitical sense. However, whiteness as a racial and ethnic category has become the subject of academic study, and key components to the constitution of white privilege and identity have been examined (Frankenberg, 1993;

hooks, 1990; Hurtado, 1999). Interestingly, there is considerable overlap between core aspects of whiteness and the culture of psychotherapy and counseling (see Sue & Sue, 1990). Part and parcel of these two cultures are rugged individualism, an internalized locus of control and responsibility, dichotomous thinking, and a belief in competitive economic system where status is measured in the accumulation of material. Because white people, therapists, and supervisors from the U.S. have been socialized into and informed by these basic tenets of white culture and psychotherapy all their lives, the identification of and sensitization to these beliefs and values can be quite difficult. Therapists and trainers who operate from this framework are most likely person- or individual-centered (Sue & Sue, 1990), and while this may not be "wrong" or "bad," it may be inappropriately imposed on clients and trainees who do not share these assumptions. An imposition of views without a regard for the legitimacy of other views (e.g., collectivism, dialectics, cooperative economics) is a form of cultural oppression (Sue & Sue, 1990). But while the effects of oppression on its victims have been explored and documented (Fine, Weis, Powell & Wong, 1997; Hardy, 1996), "we have yet to chronicle how those who oppress make sense of their power *in relationship* to those they have injured" (Hurtado, 1999, p. 226, emphasis in the original).

In the interviews, several white persons provided examples of how unexamined assumptions had led to misunderstandings, frustration, and insensitivity in cross-cultural interactions. The white male supervisor spoke about having entered into his working relationship with a Japanese supervisee without engaging in a dialogue about what education, training, and supervision was like in her culture of origin. His spontaneous, collaborative, self-of-therapist, and self-of-supervisor, approach to supervision was experienced as awkward, discomfiting, and, as the supervisee disclosed, "a little bit frustrating." She had been accustomed to both getting "the" answer to her questions and to relations with her professors and supervisors in Japan characterized by a top-down hierarchy and a more aloof, less disclosing stance from these authority figures. However, these expectations were not communicated because the supervisor had not broached the subject and the supervisee did not initiate such a discussion out of deference to his authority. The supervisor's expectations that his supervisee would enjoy the relaxed atmosphere and open format to supervision were also not made explicit until near the end of the supervision process, and even then were not questioned or critiqued by a supervisee interested in "saving face." An impasse developed but remained largely invisible because of a complex interlocking of cultural values and assumptions blocked their explicit discussion in the supervisory conversation.

The 58-year-old, white, female supervisor's first awareness of her cultural paradigm around punctuality occurred in an interaction with her acquaintances in Vienna. Her furious response to others' consistent "lateness" reveals her sense that her worldview was "correct" and theirs totally unacceptable. Decades later, to this supervisor's chagrin, a similar Anglo U.S. citizen worldview organized the social relations in her own supervision group. The three young white women in the group felt they had "a lot to learn from each other" but were unable or unwilling to deepen their understanding of and sensitivity to culture even as opportunities abounded. Having "found their voice," and resonating with a newly discovered sense of empowerment, they refused to relinquish the floor to their fellow supervisees of color in the group. However, this display of white privilege demonstrates unspoken rules of power, and Hurtado (1999) articulates some of these rules in the following quotation:

> If I am not the central actor in the drama, I will not listen to you, I will not acknowledge your presence. . . . my ability not to see you is my power. . . . I claim my right to be central to all action by claiming my special needs as a . . . (white) woman with special demands that supersede the needs of anybody else involved in the situation. If you claim your own needs, I will proceed as if I did not hear you and reassert my initial claim. . . . Unless I want you to exist, you do not. (pp. 228-229)

In the critical incident in the supervision group, the three white women ignored the needs of their culturally different peers even after the white female supervisor explicitly advocated for them. As the supervisor related, "from the Anglo side, the willingness to consider [culture] wasn't there." A liberalist discourse of individual responsibility and their inalienable right to their own voice seemed to inform their marginalization of their racially and culturally diverse fellow supervisees. Clearly, a supervisor's or supervisee's awareness and sensitivity to gender as an ecosystemic axis of power is crucial to sustaining a contextually informed perspective in supervision and therapy. However, the privileging of one axis of power over all others does not sustain the complexity of various ecosystems' intersections with one another, and a narrow punctuation around one ecosystemic axis can marginalize other crucial and ongoing processes, rendering them invisible.

Related to this issue of white privilege and "otherness," the female supervisor from the Middle East and the male supervisee from Russia discussed the experience of being ignored, unappreciated, or viewed as burdensome during some of their training experiences. Because of a lack of experience with cultural diversity, personal prejudices, or historical and recent international crises (Agathangelou, 2000), some supervisors and educators are uncomfortable or even overtly hostile toward particular students due to their culture, race, nationality, or permutations of these and other contextual variables such as gender or class. For example, U.S. foreign policies with Russia, Iran, and Iraq have involved, respectively, a Cold War, economic sanctions, and consecutive bombing campaigns. A student from Russia may have to contend with a cool reception in his or her classes due to decades of antagonism between the two super powers, an Iranian student may encounter resistance connected to the U.S. embassy hostage crisis from decades before, and an Iraqi student may detect residual resentment surrounding the Persian Gulf War. Aversion or reluctance on the part of supervisors or peers need not be overt and intentional to adversely affect the atmosphere in the training context.

According to Breunlin, Schwartz, and Kune-Karrer (1992), multiculturally skilled therapists are aware of and sensitive to their own racial/cultural heritage and understand how it affects psychological processes and definitions of health and normality. I posit that cultural awareness and sensitivity is important for the "person of the therapist" as well as the "person of the supervisor" who hopes to facilitate the development of these skills and knowledges in his or her trainees (Watson, 1993). With these multicultural competencies in mind, I offer seven sets of sensitizing questions for supervisors and supervisors-in-training to reflect upon to help them assess their cultural competence and potential effectiveness in working with culturally diverse supervisees:

- To what extent do you possess cultural knowledge of groups other than your own in terms of race, nationality, ethnicity, and sexual orientation? What groups would you feel most and least competent to supervise, and why?

- To what extent are you familiar with current literature (journals, books, and conference proceedings in the past 5 years) on multicultural therapy and contextual issues in supervision?
- How do you respond when you find yourself having difficulty understanding the words or ideas of a cross-cultural supervisee or client?
- Would you expect a favorable supervisory relationship with a supervisee from: Russia, Japan, Kenya, Germany, India, Mexico, China? Why or why not?
- What feelings do you have toward other races, ethnicities, and classes? What do you think other races, ethnicities, and classes feel towards your race, ethnicity, and class? Reflect on an interaction with an upper class person. What were your feelings during it? How did the interaction affect how you felt about yourself? If such feelings were elicited by a higher class supervisee during supervision, how might your work be affected?
- Reflect on an interaction with a person from a working class background. What were your feelings during it? How did that interaction affect how you felt about yourself? If such feelings were elicited by a working class supervisee, how might your work be affected?

Working with Cross-Cultural Supervisees

While differential locations on ecosystemic axes of power should be mapped, discussed, and negotiated in culturally sensitive supervision, supervisor awareness of and sensitivity to social location also opens entry points to connection with culturally different supervisees. Regardless of their personal experiences and therapeutic or research interests, supervisors and supervisees from nearly any background can focus on common experiences that can foster rapport and a sense of partnership in supervision, even if the supervisor is a U.S. citizen who has never been a "world traveler." In several of the interviews, it was apparent that supervisors and supervisees who shared an interest in cultural diversity already possessed one means of connecting with one another. One supervisee said he had felt understood by two supervisors, one who shared his own personal struggles with "otherness" and another who had visited his country. Trainers who view difference with interest and empathy rather than discomfort or distrust will be more at ease with supervisees whose first language, pigmentation, ethnicity, nationality, gender, social class, or some combination of these variables differs from their own. An obvious shared interest through which joining could occur is their choice to become a marriage and family therapist and the process of professional identity development. Trainers and trainees can share their respective journeys that culminated in their decision to enter this field, and describe what aspects of therapeutic theory, practice, and/or research interest them most. In addition, since we carry multiple selves within us, and numerous experiences and contextual variables determine our totality of "self," each of us carries a social location or experience through which we can resonate, connect, and empathize with persons who appear very different from ourselves. For example, supervisor and supervisee might be from different countries and different ethnic, racial, and religious groups, yet share in common gender, age, marital status, or the role of parent. Supervisor and supervisee can connect along lines of similarity and then proceed to explore and/or engage how their differences in social location also inform who they are and how they see and experience what is happening in the therapy room and in supervision.

It is helpful if supervisors and trainers possess a sincere interest in how their culturally different supervisees are adapting to education and life in general in the U.S. Asked how he would approach his students if he was in the role of trainer, the Russian supervisee said:

> I would invite the student in and ask, "In your culture, did you get C's, and what happens in your culture when something like that happens?" You see, I didn't know when I first came here that one's GPA was so important. I wondered, "What's most important here: grades, conferences, personality?"

Checking in with one's supervisees and adopting a stance of perpetual curiosity in regard to the particular meanings and values of their culture of origin can be invaluable in helping cross-cultural students critically examine the different, sometimes implicit expectations of their new environment (see Lappin, 1983, and Leong & Chou, 1996). As discussed by the Middle Eastern supervisor, world events, such as geopolitical crises and catastrophes, can have profound impact on a supervisee's acclimation process in the U.S. For example, current or historical tension or armed conflict between the U.S. and another country (e.g., Russia and Iran) can impact interchanges among participants in the therapy room and in supervision. During political crises, supervisors may wish to "check in" with supervisees to see how they are coping with relevant developments on the international front.

Since some culturally different supervisees report feeling awkward about approaching their supervisors and professors, training programs might wish to assign them mentors and/or more advanced peers to insure they do not "fall between the cracks." A genuine desire to learn more about how culturally different supervisees perceive family relationships and psychotherapy through their cultural lens can go a long way to establishing a training context that validates these trainees' perceptions. And as two supervisors in this study noted, the topics of cultural difference and the cultural context in which a given supervisee plans to apply his or her training are part and parcel of the supervision process. Supervisors can invite meaningful exchanges of different cultural perspectives on relationships, family, and community and lead discussions on the belief systems that inform these perspectives. Such exchanges can broaden participants' conceptions of what constitutes a "legitimate" or "valid" worldview beyond their own particular perspective.

Finally, supervisors and trainers can more effectively establish rapport by not presuming they know their supervisee's cultural identity or worldview simply because they have visited that supervisee's country or have worked with another student from that cultural background. As one supervisee articulated, each student possesses a range of culture based on their particular family of origin, individual differences, and degree of acculturation to Western beliefs and values. Clearly, supervisors should challenge the "myth of sameness" by avoiding the assumption that all persons from the same country possess the same monolithic cultural identity (Hardy, 1990).

Supervisor Accountability and Availability

> When Monica first wrote the book *Ethnicity and Family Therapy,* it was a shock and wasn't necessarily accepted. There was no awareness of culture. We were "value-free" (laugh), and there was no focus on gender. The women's movement was just getting started, it wasn't in family therapy yet at all, and there was no focus on class. We were all saving the world because we had

discovered *systems*. In the 70s, the fight was against all those idiots who thought you had to treat individuals. (58-year-old, white female supervisor from the U.S.)

Our professional practices as therapists and supervisors are embedded in intergroup power relations. With dramatic shifts in social demographics in the US, and a rise in the number of trainees from other countries, active consideration of race, ethnicity, nationality, class, gender and other contextual variables in the social relations of both therapy and supervision has become obligatory (Ridley, Mendoza, & Kanitz, 1994). For instance, the social locations of being white, male, heterosexual, or of Northwest European descent or a combination of these contextual variables serve to augment the power differential already present in the hierarchical relationships of therapist to client, and supervisor to supervisee. It is crucial that supervisors gain the capacity to be aware of and sensitive to issues of power and privilege if they are going to (a) be culturally competent, and (b) assist their trainees in becoming so.

But the task of addressing culture in supervision carries risks, and many supervisors may wish to "play it safe." One way supervisors have remained safe is by embracing a color- or culturally-blind perspective and questioning the motivations of anyone who suggests race, culture, or ethnicity might be salient in a therapeutic or supervisory situation. Another way is to assert that basic therapy skills and theories, as the core of training programs, must be addressed first and foremost, and multicultural therapy and training is auxiliary to this primary goal (Baird, 1999; Dobbins & Skillings, 1991). Another option, alluded to by a participant in this study, is for supervisors to invite supervisees to unilaterally "come clean" regarding their identity, experiences, cultural biases, and struggles in the supervisory context, while never locating themselves, their own culture, and their experiences in a dialogic space. Such a position concedes the existence of culture and difference, but features the supervisor's retreat into a normative or non-prefixed position, leaving the culturally different supervisee as a spectacle in the supervision group. Since we are all located on the ecosystemic axes of power of race, ethnicity, culture, and gender, these contextual variables are relevant to everyone, not just culturally different supervisees. A qualitatively different position is for the supervisor to initiate mutual discussions about culture which "enrich everybody" in supervision. Thus, supervisor accountability begins with a personal awareness of how he or she thinks and feels about culture, power, and difference in both therapy and supervision (Kaiser, 1992).

The person of the supervisor is interrelated with the person of the therapist, and both contribute to what occurs in therapy and supervision (Aponte, 1992; 1994). The quality of the supervisory relationship is influenced by the degree to which it is "safe" for the supervisee to disclose person of the therapist issues. A foundation of safety and trust can be created by supervisors' willingness to disclose their own feelings and reactions along cultural lines before expecting supervisees to "bare their souls." Making oneself available through self-disclosure demonstrates empathy and can reduce feelings of isolation and hopelessness in cross-cultural supervisees facing new and difficult challenges. When the supervisor is willing to participate in the supervisory process in a deep or personally meaningful way, supervisors and supervisees are "in training" together in a bilateral supervisory commitment (Garfield, 1987). This process runs parallel to that proposed by Hoffman (1981), who stated that growth, or second order change, demands interdependent involvement and shifts by all participants in the system to a qualitatively different kind of functioning. Availability is also demonstrated in supervisors' capacity to "be there" and be interested in how their supervisees are doing professionally and personally.

Strengths and Challenges of Cross-Cultural Supervision

The advantage of having a supervision group with culturally different persons is the diversity of perspectives available, if those different perspectives are valued and affirmed by the supervisor. Culturally different supervisees can work together with the supervisor to triangulate on a clinical phenomenon and provide meaningful alternative explanations and interventions during live supervision and case presentations. In a qualitative study on clients' perspectives on reflecting teams, Smith, Yoshioka, and Winton (1993) found a recurrent theme of clients valuing multiple perspectives, especially when they contained "dialectic tensions": "This suggests that teams with a diverse membership in gender, class, and/or ethnicity will provide clients with the richest set of meaningful options" (p. 40). As one supervisor stated in an interview, cross-cultural exchange "enriches everybody," possibly even the people paying for services.

Whether this dialectic tension becomes a boon or bane depends on many variables: supervisor experience and comfort with trainees with very different points of view, supervisor sensitivity to overt and covert expressions of conflict among supervisees, and the ability to constructively respond to critical incidents in the cross-cultural supervision group. As discussed by the 58-year-old, white female supervisor from the U.S., statements by majority group supervisees can clearly demonstrate ethnocentrism and presumptions of cultural superiority which often inform intergroup power dynamics. The supervisor must be able to process such incidents as constructively and non-reactively as possible, helping to render visible stereotypic and prejudiced thoughts, feelings, and behaviors at the level of personal experience and values (Lappin & Hardy, 1997; Preli & Bernard, 1993). One way of setting the stage for an exploration of supervisees' values is to begin supervision by saying that contextual variables are important and that they are going to be focused upon repeatedly in supervision. As one participant recommended, "First, say from the beginning, 'We're going to be talking about race, gender and culture, and you might get tired of me pointing out these kinds of things, but that's one of the things we have to do.' Second, always make an effort to engage the people in some kind of conversation about differences." Asserting the importance of culture and other contextual variables in the supervision group and making discussions of difference a mainstay of the process increases the chances that supervisees can learn from each other in a meaningful way. Another way of exploring the terrain of personal experiences and values is to ask supervisees in one's group some of the following questions from time to time:

- How is therapy/a therapist viewed in your culture?
- What cultural groups do you believe you will have the most difficult time working with, and which will be the easiest?
- How does your cultural self (your race, class, ethnicity, gender, etc.) play out in the therapy room? In supervision?
- What are your experiences of how a professor or teacher conducts class?
- How do you think your educational experiences affect your expectations of supervision here in this training group?
- In which cultural context do you think you will be practicing your skills as a therapist?

- In what ways does your cultural context differ from that in the U.S.? How useful or effective would therapy in general, or this particular intervention, be with clients in your culture of origin? How do these differences in cultural context inform how you would design therapy and therapeutic interventions to enhance their efficacy?

Education and Training of Culturally Competent Supervisors

Population statistics (Hall, 1997; Yutrzenka, 1995), the well-known inadequacy of mental health service delivery to minorities (Rosado & Elias, 1993), and the poor frequency and quality of cross-cultural therapy courses (Bernal & Castro, 1994; Mintz, Bartels, & Rideout, 1995) highlight the need for multicultural training for therapists and supervisors alike. If an important task of supervisors is preparing therapists to work with culturally different clients, and supervisors are increasingly likely to encounter culturally different trainees, it seems that the training of supervisors should also include an acknowledgement of the significance of contextual variables in therapeutic and supervisory contexts. I also challenge the view of academic institutions and some MFT programs that multicultural therapy does not constitute a "basic" component of clinical training. As the supervisor from the Middle East stated:

> Cultural issues should be addressed in supervisor training. The willingness to develop cultural sensitivity comes from the supervisor's personality and letting themselves be exposed to different cultures, being willing to talk, exchange, and get to know culturally different individuals as people really helps to develop the sensitivity. When the experience goes beyond the facts in a book and becomes a personal connection, then that cultural sensitivity starts to develop and begins to translate to other cultural groups as well. Once you have it, it doesn't go away.

For cultural sensitivity to be encouraged, Program Directors and Approved Supervisors must work hard to create opportunities for supervisors in training to develop the concept of culture and to experience cultural difference in ways that permit them to become both cognitively aware and emotionally sensitive to the ways in which culture, gender, race, and class interweave and interact in therapy and supervision. Courses in multicultural therapy and counseling, cultural diversity, and the didactic components of the education and training for the supervisor designation provide opportunities to enhance therapists' and supervisors' awareness of their own assumptions, values, and biases and to acquire basic knowledges and skills. Cultural genograms and supervision-of-supervision by culturally diverse consultants are specific experiences which can facilitate the achievement of these goals. Culturally competent supervisors-in-training should be able to demonstrate the following: (a) knowledge about the ecosystems of culture, ethnicity, race, class, and gender, how they relate to their own cultural self, and how they affect their perceptions of the world; (b) an understanding of past and present relations between their own culture and others; (c) an understanding of how racism, prejudice, classism, and xenophobia operate to marginalize and oppress persons of color and/or international origin; (d) the ability to see themselves and their trainees as cultural and racial beings (Sue et al., 1992, pp. 480-481). In addition, Breunlin, Schwartz, and Kune-Karrer (1992) suggested the following questions to help family therapists examine their own cultural beliefs: "Do we explore commonalities in sociocultural background with families? . . . Do we believe that our views also need expanding? . . . Are our interventions detrimental to the members of the family? . . . Do we believe that all sociocultural contexts offer opportunities for change as well as constraints?" (p. 235).

The standards for AAMFT Approved Supervisor status must include specific attention to contextual variables in all written materials submitted for the designation. Also, basic standards for the philosophy statement and supervision case study submitted by supervisors-in-training (i.e., requisite content areas to be addressed and quality of submitted materials) should be re-established and upheld by the Standards Committee. A lack of consensus on basic standards at the local level of supervisor training relationships is isomorphic to the lack of accountability and consensus at the level of the national organization. While a "rubber stamp" approach to bestowing the Approved Supervisor credential is expedient, the Standards Committee should enforce the requirement that candidates submit evidence of their active reflection on the impact of contextual variables in supervisory and therapeutic processes as part of their written materials.

CONCLUSION

Just as supervisors and trainers have a professional responsibility to prepare therapists to be effective with clients from different cultural groups, they also have a responsibility to be effective with their culturally different trainees. Since the culture of origin influences the isomorphic relationships of supervisor/supervisee and therapist/client in parallel processes, culturally competent supervisors can use cross-cultural supervisory experiences to model an effective helping relationship with their supervisees. Vulnerable, available, and culturally competent supervisors can create a space for meaningful exchange through an acknowledgement of difference and a willingness to consciously negotiate a "goodness of fit" with their culturally different supervisees. Since many trainers are embedded in a particular cultural perspective their entire lives, they may be culturally encapsulated and lack an awareness or sensitivity to how their customs, values, and traditions organize their interactions with persons from other cultures. Supervisors may perceive an open discussion of differences in ethnicity, nationality, gender, race, and class as risky and may avoid addressing culture for fear that they will stereotype, or be seen as stereotyping, the culturally different supervisee. Other supervisors may choose to place their supervisees in the "hot seat" by asking them to initiate a soliloquy on their degree of comfort in the supervisory relationship. But by proactively opening a bilateral dialogue about culture in supervision, supervisors can start with themselves by sharing their own assumptions, beliefs, curiosities, and even ignorance in as respectful manner as possible. In this way, supervisors and supervisees can work together to explore alternative understandings of family, community, and culture and ways of making meaning of interpersonal and professional relationships. Since our social locations on multiple ecosystemic axes of power inform and organize power dynamics with or without our awareness, concerted efforts to make explicit our privilege and power on the ecosystems of race, ethnicity, gender, class, and others are crucial part of culturally sensitive supervision practices. When cultural difference is viewed as an opportunity for meaningful discussion, rather than a problem or burden, supervisors and supervisees together can more readily acknowledge and process a host of social locations, cultural selves, and differentials in privilege on both sides of the one-way mirror.

NOTES

1. See McIntosh, P. (1988). White privilege: Unpacking the invisible knapsack. In M. McGoldrick et al. (Eds.) *Re-envisioning family therapy: Race, culture, and gender in clinical practice* (pp. 147-152). New York: Guilford.

2. Rather than the dualistic sense of liberal versus conservative, liberalist here refers to the philosophy of liberalism, which holds that individuals are created equal and are free to pursue happiness and success. These individualistic premises guide the politics of both "liberals" and "conservatives" in the U.S.

3. Non-prefixed refers to the implicit notion that whiteness is the standard to which all "others" are compared. Therefore, whiteness is seen by the dominant group as normative, never the difference (see Minich, 1990).

REFERENCES

Agathangelou, A. M. (2000). Nationalist narratives and (dis)appearing women: State sanctioned sexual violence. *Canadian Woman Studies, 19,* 12-21.

Allen, J., & Laird, J. (1991). Men and story: Constructing new narratives in therapy. In M. Bograd (Ed.), *Feminist Approaches for Men in Family Therapy* (pp. 75-100). New York: Haworth.

Anderson, H., & Goolishian, H. (1988). Human systems as linguistic systems: Preliminary and evolving ideas about the implications for clinical theory. *Family Process, 27,* 371-393.

Aponte, H. J. (1992). Training the person of the therapist in structural family therapy. *Journal of Marital and Family Therapy,* 18, 269-281.

Aponte, H. J. (1994). How personal can training get? *Journal of Marital and Family Therapy, 20,* 1-15.

Auerswald, E. H. (1985). Thinking about thinking in family therapy. *Family Process, 24,* 1-12.

Ault-Riche, M. (Ed.). (1986). *Women and Family Therapy.* Rockville, MD: Aspen.

Avis, J. (1985). The politics of functional family therapy: A feminist critique. *Journal of Marital and Family Therapy, 11,* 127-138.

Baird, B. N. (1999). *The Internship, Practicum, and Field Placement Handbook: A Guide for the Helping Professions.* Upper Saddle River, NJ: Prentice Hall.

Bateson, G. (1979). *Mind and nature.* New York: Dutten.

Bernard, J. M., & Goodyear, R. K. (1992). *Fundamentals of Clinical Supervision.* Boston, MA. Allyn & Bacon.

Blumer, H. (1969). *Symbolic Interactionism: Perspectives and Method.* Englewood Cliffs, NJ: Prentice-Hall.

Bradshaw, W. (1982). Supervision in black and white: Race as a factor in supervision. In M. Blumfield, *Applied Supervision in Psychotherapy.* New York: Grune & Stratton.

Breunlin, D. C., Schwartz, R. C., & Kune-Karrer, B. M. (1992*). Metaframeworks: Transcending the Models of Family Therapy.* San Francisco: Jossey-Bass.

Brown, M. T., & Landrum-Brown, J. (1995). Counselor supervision: Cross-cultural perspectives. In P. Ponterotto, J. M. Casas, L. A. Suzuki, and C. M. Alexander (Eds.) *Handbook of Multicultural Counseling* (pp. 263-286). Thousand Oaks, CA: Sage.

Carter, R. T., & Qureshi, A. (1995). A typology of philosophical assumptions in multicultural counseling and training. In P. Ponterotto, J. M. Casas, L. A. Suzuki, and C. M. Alexander (Eds.), *Handbook of Multicultural Counseling* (pp. 239-262). Thousand Oaks, CA: Sage.

Casas, J. M. (1984). Policy, training, and research in counseling psychology: The racial/ethnic minority perspective. In S. D. Brown & R. W. Lent (Eds.), *Handbook of Counseling Psychology* (pp. 785-831). New York: Wiley.

Charmaz, K. (1983). The grounded theory method: An explication and interpretation. In R. M. Emerson (Ed.) *Contemporary Field Research* (pp. 109-126). Prospect Heights, IL: Waveland.

Cook, D. A. (1983). *A Survey of Ethnic Minority Clinical and Counseling Graduate Students' Perceptions of Their Cross-cultural Supervision Experiences.* Unpublished doctoral dissertation, Southern Illinois University, Carbondale.

Cook, D. A., & Helms, J. E. (1988). Visible racial/ethnic group supervisees' satisfaction with cross-cultural supervision as predicted by relationship characteristics. *Journal of Counseling Psychology, 35,* 268-274.

Dobbins, J. E., & Skillings, J. H. (1991). The utility of race labeling in understanding cultural identity: A conceptual tool for the social science practitioner. *Journal of Counseling and Development, 70,* 37-44.

Falicov, C. J. (1988). Learning to think culturally. In H. A. Liddle, D. C. Breunlin, & R. C. Schwartz (Eds.), *Handbook of Family Therapy Training and Supervision* (pp. 335-357). New York: Guilford.

Fine, M., Weis, L. Powell, L. C., & Wong, M. (Eds.). (1997). *Off White: Readings on Race, Power, and Society.* New York: Routledge.

Frankenberg, R. (1993). *White Women, Race Matters: The Social Construction of Whiteness.* Minneapolis: University of Minnesota Press.

Garfield, R. (1987). On self-disclosure: The vulnerable therapist. *Contemporary Family Therapy, 9,* 58-78.

Goldner, V. (1985). Warning: Family therapy may be dangerous to your health. *Family Therapy Networker, 9,* 19-23.

Gopaul-McNicol, S., & Brice-Baker, J. (1998). *Cross-cultural practice: Assessment, treatment, and training.* New York: Wiley and Sons, Inc.

Guiterrez, F. (1982). Working with minority counselor education students. *Counselor Education and Supervision, 21,* 218-226.

Haley, J. (1996). *Learning and Teaching Therapy.* New York: Guilford.

Hall, C. C. I. (1997). Cultural malpractice: The growing obsolescence of psychology with the changing U.S. population. *American Psychologist, 52,* 642-651.

Hardy, K. V. (1990). The theoretical myth of sameness: A critical issue in family therapy training and treatment. In G. W. Saba, B. M. Karrer, & K. V. Hardy (Eds.), *Minorities and Family Therapy* (pp. 17-33). New York: Haworth Press.

Hardy, K. (1996). *The Psychological Residuals of Slavery.* New York: Guilford.

Hare-Mustin, R. T. (1994). Discourses in the mirrored room: A postmodern analysis of therapy. *Family Process, 33,* 19-35.

Helms, J. E. (1982). *Differential Evaluations of Minority and Majority Counseling Trainees' Practicum Performance.* Unpublished manuscript, University of Maryland, College Park.

Hilton, D. B., Russell, R. K., & Salmi, S. W. (1995). The effects of supervisor's race and level of support on perceptions of supervision. *Journal of Counseling and Development, 73,* 559-563.

Hoffman, L. (1981). *Foundations of Family Therapy.* New York: Basic Books.

hooks, b. (1990). *Yearning: Race, Gender, and Cultural Politics.* Boston: South End.

Humm, M. (1995). *The Dictionary of Feminist Theory. 2nd ed.* Columbus, OH: The Ohio State University Press.

Hunt, P. (1987). Black clients: Implications for supervision of trainees. *Psychotherapy, 24,* 114-119.

Hurtado, A. (1999). The trickster's play: Whiteness in the subordination and liberation process. In R. D. Torres, L. F. Miron, & J. X. Inda (Eds.), *Race, Identity, and Citizenship: A Reader* (pp. 225-243). Malden, MA: Blackwell Publishers.

Keeney, B. (1982). *Aesthetics of change.* New York: Guilford.

Killian, K. D., & Hardy, K. V. (1998). Commitment to minority inclusion: A study of AAMFT conference program content and members' perceptions. *Journal of Marital and Family Therapy, 24 ,* 207-223.

Kliman, J. (1994). The interweaving of gender, class, and race in family therapy. In M. P. Mirkin (Ed.), *Women in Context: Toward a Feminist Reconstruction of Psychotherapy* (pp. 25-47). New York: Guilford.

Lago, C., & Thompson, J. (1996). *Race, Culture and Counseling.* Philadelphia: Open University Press.

Lappin, J. (1983). On becoming a culturally conscious family therapist. In C. Falicov (Ed.), *Cultural Perspectives in Family Therapy* (pp. 122-136). Rockville, MD: Aspen.

Lappin, J., & Hardy, K. V. (1997). Keeping context in view: The heart of supervision. In T. C. Todd & C. L. Storm, *The Complete Systemic Supervisor: Context, Philosophy, and Pragmatics* (pp. 41-58). Needham Heights, MA: Allyn & Bacon.

Leong, F. T. L., & Chou, E. L. (1996). Counseling foreign students. In P. B. Pedersen, J. G. Draguns, W. J. Lonner & J. E. Trimble (Eds.), *Counseling Across Cultures. 4th ed.* (pp. 210-242). Honolulu, HI: University of Hawaii Press.

Leong, F., & Wagner, N. S. (1994). Cross-cultural counseling supervision: What do we know? What do we need to know? *Counselor Education and Supervision, 34,* 117-131.

Luepnitz, D. (1988). *The Family Interpreted: Feminist Theory in Clinical Practice.* New York: Basic Books.

Maturana, H. R., & Varela, F. (1980). *Autopoiesis and Cognition: The Realization of the Living.* Dordrecht, Netherlands: D. Reidl.

McGoldrick, M. (1998). *Culture, Class, Race and Gender: Clinical Implications of Our Clients' Context.* Conference in Houston, TX, March 28.

McGoldrick, M., Giordano, J., & Pearce, J. K. (1996). *Ethnicity and Family Therapy. 2nd ed.* New York: Guilford.

Miller, H. (1957). "The Oranges of the Millennium." From *Big Sur and the Oranges of Hieronymous Bosch.* Microsoft Bookshelf 98.

Minnich, E. K. (1990). *Transforming Knowledge*. Philadelphia: Temple University Press.

Mintz, L. B., Bartels, K. M., & Rideout, C. A. (1995). Training in counseling ethnic minorities and race-based availability of graduate school resources. *Professional Psychology: Research and Practice, 26*, 3.

Mirkin, M. P. (Ed.). (1990). *The Social and Political Contexts of Family Therapy*. Needham Heights, MA: Allyn & Bacon.

Moon, S. M., Dillon, D., & Sprenkle, D. H. (1990). Family therapy and qualitative research. *Journal of Marital and Family Therapy, 16*, 357-376.

Patton, M. Q. (1990). *Qualitative Education and Research Methods. 2nd ed.* Thousand Oaks, CA: Sage.

Pedersen, P. B. (1994). *A Handbook for Developing Multicultural Awareness, 2nd ed.* Alexandria, VA: American Counseling Association.

Pedersen, P. B., Draguns, J. G., Lonner, W. J., & Trimble, J. E. (Eds.). (1996). *Counseling Across Cultures, 4th ed.* Thousand Oaks, CA: Sage.

Petersen, F. K. (1991). *Race and Ethnicity*. New York: Haworth.

Ponterotto, J., & Casas, J. (1991). *Handbook of racial/ethnic minority counseling research*. Springfield, IL: Charles C. Thomas.

Pope-Davis, D. B., & Coleman, H. L. (Eds.). (1997). *Multicultural Counseling Competencies: Assessment, Education and Training, and Supervision*. Thousand Oaks, CA: Sage.

Preli, R., & Bernard, J. (1993). Making multiculturalism relevant for majority culture graduate students. *Journal of Marital and Family Therapy, 19*, 5-16.

Remington, G., & DaCosta, G. (1989). Ethnocultural factors in resident supervision: Black supervisor and white supervisees. *American Journal of Psychotherapy, 43*, 398-404.

ResearchWare, Inc. (1999). *HyperRESEARCH: A content analysis tool for the qualitative researcher*. PO Box 1258, Randolph, MA 02368-1258.

Ridley, C. R., Mendoza, D. W., & Kanitz, B. E. (1994). Multicultural training: Reexamination, operationalization, and integration. *Counseling Psychologist, 22*, 227-289.

Rosado, J. W., & Elias, M. J. (1993). Ecological and psychocultural mediators in the delivery of services for urban, culturally diverse Hispanic clients. *Professional Psychology: Research and Practice, 24*, 450-459.

Schlesinger, A. M. (1998). *The disuniting of America: Reflections on a multicultural society. 2nd ed.* New York: W. W. Norton.

Smith, T. E., Yoshioka, M., & Winton, M. (1993). A qualitative understanding of reflecting teams I: Client perspectives. *Journal of Systemic Therapies, 12*, 28-43.

Storm, C. (1991). Placing gender in the heart of MFT masters programs. *Journal of Marital and Family Therapy, 17*, 45-52.

Strauss, A., & Corbin, J. (1998). *Basics of Qualitative Research, 2nd edition.* Newbury Park, CA: Sage.

Sue, D. W., Arrendondo, P., & McDavis, R. J. (1992). Multicultural counseling competencies and standards: A call to the profession. *Journal of Counseling and Development, 70*, 477-486.

Sue, D. W., & Sue, D. (1990). *Counseling the Culturally Different: Theory and Practice. 2nd ed.* New York: Wiley.

Sue, S., & Zane, N. (1987). The role of culture and cultural techniques in psychotherapy: A critique and reformulation. *American Psychologist, 42,* 37-45.

Turner, J., & Fine, M. (1997). Gender and supervision: Evolving debates. In T. C. Todd & C. L. Storm (Eds.), *The Complete Systemic Supervisor* (pp. 72-82). New York: Allyn & Bacon.

Vanderkolk, C. J. (1974). The relationship of personality, values and race to anticipation of the supervisory relationship. *Rehabilitation Counseling Bulletin, 18,* 41-46.

Vasquez, M. J. T., & Eldridge, N. S. (1994). Bringing ethics alive: Training practitioners about gender, ethnicity, and sexual orientation issues. *Women & Therapy, 15,* 1-16.

Von Glaserfeld, E. (1984). An introduction to radical constructivism. In P. Watzlawick (Ed.), *The invented reality: How Do We Know What We Believe We Know?: Contributions to Constructivism.* New York: W. W. Norton.

Walters, M., Carter, B., Papp, P., & Silverstein, O. (1988). *The Invisible Web: Gender Patterns in Family Relationships.* New York: Guilford Press.

Watson, M. F. (1993). Supervising the person of the therapist: Issues, challenges and dilemmas. *Contemporary Family Therapy, 15,* 21-31.

Wheeler, D., Myers-Avis, J., Miller, L., & Chaney, S. (1989). Rethinking family therapy training and supervision: A feminist model. In M. McGoldrick, C. Anderson, & F. Walsh (Eds.), *Women in Families* (pp. 135-152). New York: W. W. Norton.

Yutrzenka, B. (1995). Making the case for training in ethnic and cultural diversity in increasing treatment efficacy. *Journal of Consulting and Clinical Psychology, 63,* 197-206.

Zane, N., & Sue, S. (1991). Culturally responsive mental health services for Asian Americans: Treatment and training issues. In H. F. Myers, P. Wohlford, L. P. Guzman, & R. J. Echemendia (Eds.), *Ethnic Minority Perspectives on Clinical Training and Services in Psychology* (pp. 49-58). Washington, DC: American Psychological Association.

APPENDIX

Culture of Origin Interview Questions for Supervisees and Supervisors

I would be interested in your telling me about your cultural background; where are you from? Please identify your background in terms of race, ethnicity, and class.

Could you say what expectations you had when you first came to the United States about what life would be like, what the culture would be like?

Why family therapy, why this program?

When you first came to _____ and started the program, can you recall any incidents or events that stand out in your memory as something that was a challenge or struggle? What about incidents in the context of clinical training?

What was your experience in your first year (or years) here?

Did you have any experiences of alienation or feeling separate from your classmates or colleagues? What about sources of social support?

In what ways, if any, have you changed or adjusted to acclimate to U.S. culture and society? How is [interviewee's name] different now?

You identified a number of different ethnicities in your cultural self; how do you think being raised in _____ and your current cultural self play into your role as therapist? How is your cultural self communicated in the therapy room?

Coming from your culture of origin and in light of your expectations, could you draw me a picture of what an optimal training situation would be? If you were to receive the best possible supervision, please identify some of the crucial characteristics of the supervisor and major processes that would be part of the optimal supervisory experience.

What are some ways that supervisors, regardless of their particular backgrounds, could try to maintain an awareness and sensitivity to issues of cultural difference in supervision? How might a white male or white female supervisor from the United States achieve a sense of accountability in their work with culturally different supervisees?

For supervisees: Say you are a clinical trainer or supervisor somewhere; how would you approach working with someone from a cultural background that differs from your own?

For supervisors: How have you approached supervision with supervisees of a different cultural background? What experiences have you had with culturally different therapists in training? What might you do differently in the future in light of these experiences?

Neither Mask nor Mirror:
One Therapist's Journey to Ethically
Integrate Feminist Family Therapy
and Multiculturalism

Laura A. Bryan

SUMMARY. Feminist family therapy focuses on the gendered context of clients' lives, but has been criticized for mirroring the needs of White, middle-class women only. The multicultural approach to therapy emphasizes respect for diverse cultural values, but is vulnerable to using tradition to mask abuses. Integration of these two perspectives can address these criticisms, but also raises ethical concerns. Therapists need to be aware of these dilemmas as well as suggestions for managing them. *[Article copies available for a fee from The Haworth Document Delivery Service: 1-800-342-9678. E-mail address: <getinfo@haworthpressinc.com> Website: <http://www.HaworthPress.com> © 2001 by The Haworth Press, Inc. All rights reserved.]*

KEYWORDS. Gender, therapy, multicultural ethics

Feminist family therapy (FFT) uses feminist philosophy to expose the gender biases in family therapy. FFT has long been concerned with the client's context, especially the patriarchal structure of most societies. However, critics point out that this approach is based on the perceived needs and wants of White, middle-class American women, as though

---

Laura A. Bryan is affiliated with Texas Tech University.

[Haworth co-indexing entry note]: "Neither Mask nor Mirror: One Therapist's Journey to Ethically Integrate Feminist Family Therapy and Multiculturalism." Bryan, Laura A. Co-published simultaneously in *Journal of Feminist Family Therapy* (The Haworth Press, Inc.) Vol. 12, No. 2/3, 2001, pp. 105-121; and: *Integrating Gender and Culture in Family Therapy Training* (ed: Toni Schindler Zimmerman) The Haworth Press, Inc., 2001, pp. 105-121. Single or multiple copies of this article are available for a fee from The Haworth Document Delivery Service [1-800-342-9678, 9:00 a.m. - 5:00 p.m. (EST). E-mail address: getinfo@haworthpressinc.com].

105

they mirrored the needs and wants of all women (Brown & Brodsky, 1992; Hare-Mustin & Marecek, 1994). In response, multiculturalism tries to avoid this ethnocentric approach by advocating for the consideration of diverse cultural mores and values. Many cultural traditions, however, are patriarchal and sexist, and giving them too much regard can mask their detrimental effects (May, 1998a). The attempt to respect both feminism and culture can lead to ethical dilemmas for therapists, and creativity and training are needed to manage the struggle.

Before continuing, I would like to be transparent about my biases. I am a White, middle-class female doctoral student in a marriage and family therapy program located in a conservative mid-sized town in the Southwest. In my training I have been exposed to feminist family therapy and am interested in applying the premises as I understand them. Currently I am working as an in-home therapist as part of a university-sponsored project. The majority of clients are low-income ethnic minority (most are Hispanic) mothers with children. In my desire to be sensitive to cultural differences, I have found myself questioning whether and how I should introduce feminist ideas to clients who will remain in a traditionally patriarchal culture with little support after I am gone. For example, one young Hispanic mother with four children, separated from her abusive husband, has a new boyfriend who wants him to move in with her. How much do I discuss her value as a woman alone when her culture–including son and brother-in-law–tell her differently? She sees constrained futures for her young daughters; how do I introduce other options without ignoring important cultural values about women and men? When she parentifies her young son because he is the only male, should I talk with her about not depending on him too much although the community sanctions this behavior? In this paper, I will describe my struggle to find a therapy that honors both cultural and feminist values and some of the quandaries I face. I will begin by providing a brief overview of the tenets and critiques of FFT and multiculturalism, followed by an analysis of their ethical integration, and will conclude with suggestions and further questions.

FEMINIST FAMILY THERAPY

FFT is a therapeutic philosophy rather than a specific theory of therapy (Brown & Brodsky, 1992), and focuses on the application of feminist theory to family therapy (Coe, 1993). The FFT approach is diverse, and different members promote varying beliefs and techniques. Noting this heterogeneity, Coe (1993) examined FFT literature and found three common principles of theory and practice. The first principle highlights gender as a variable that structures interactions, historically resulting in unequal relationships between men and women. In practice, this means that therapists explicitly explore power imbalances and stereotypical gender beliefs. Techniques for introducing and discussing power imbalances during therapy sessions include: (a) directly or indirectly naming the issues as power differences, (b) using separate sessions to raise power issues, (c) putting issues in the larger context of family history or society, (d) identifying consequences for each partner and the relationship, and (e) challenging the woman to insist on justice (Parker, 1997a; 1997b). This principle regarding the primacy of gender as an organizing construct provides the foundation for the other two tenets of FFT.

The second principle relates to the therapeutic relationship. Feminist family therapists use the relationship with their clients to model an egalitarian relationship. In this relationship, therapists do not even pretend neutrality, but rather perceive the personal as political. Therapists are straightforward about their bias and agenda, and recognize how they influence the definition and treatment of problems in therapy. Feminist family therapists are active social change agents (Coe, 1993; Rodis & Strehorn, 1997), but this intensity is tempered by a respect for the clients' beliefs and value systems. Often this results in a tension between advocating change and demonstrating acceptance. For example, if the client's goal is to come to terms with his/her oppression, a feminist family therapist faces the difficult high-wire act of respecting beliefs while pushing those beliefs to change.

The third principle describes the therapeutic process. In FFT, therapists validate women's experiences, skills, and strengths, and collaborate to generate goals for the client. In addition, feminist family therapists avoid manipulative or deceitful therapeutic strategies. By confirming women's experience and demystifying therapeutic interventions, therapists further model egalitarian relationships and value the clients' expert knowledge about themselves. By questioning previous understandings, the therapist acts as a catalyst for clients' insight and understanding of their situation, thus empowering clients to change their own relational environment (Brown & Brodsky, 1992).

For all its support and advances, FFT is not without critics. Although feminism has resulted in advances for some, minority and poor women have been neglected in most feminist theory and research (Brown, 1990). Assuming that the findings from studies of White, middle-class women apply to all women is analogous to assuming that the findings from studies of men apply to women. Related to this criticism is the charge of "cultural colonialism," that feminist family therapists want other cultures to mirror their own culture (that is, the feminism of Western, White, middle-class women). To do FFT, then, is to risk imposing the values of a group that is in some respects dominant. Therapists may find themselves in the role of social *control* (rather than *change*) agent unless they are particularly careful and aware of their own cultural bias. Otherwise FFT is another mode of acculturation to the dominant discourse, which means for the United States blending diverse cultures into a great melting pot. This may also lead to internal colonization, where individuals internalize the values of the dominant society and denigrate the worth of their minority culture (Brown, 1990).

It seems that FFT needs a way to think about and consider the influence of culture. This addition seems to be a natural extension of the feminist ideal of privileging oppressed voices (Brown & Brodsky, 1992). Hare-Mustin (1994) specifically placed the responsibility on therapists to reflect something other than the dominant view. Paterson and Trathen (1994) argued that recent epistemologies such as post-structuralism provide guidelines for feminists to put aside the mirror that reflects all women as though they were like White, Western, heterosexual, middle-class women; and instead to see women in all their racial, class, age, and sexual diversity.

THE MULTICULTURAL COMPONENT

One way to address this criticism of FFT is to include a multicultural component. Hardy and Laszloffy (1995) noted that "culture" is related to, yet distinct from, "ethnicity." Specifically, ethnicity is defined as race, religion, and history combined to provide a sense of identity beyond any of these elements alone (McGoldrick, Garcia-Preto, Hines, & Lee, 1991). Culture includes not only ethnicity but also other factors such as social class and religion united to form the whole of an individual's cultural identity (Hardy & Laszloffy, 1995).

Culture shapes everything from eating habits and mating rituals to family structure and problem definition (McGoldrick et al., 1991), and is constantly evolving and changing meaning (Laird, 1998). Culture influences not only the value placed on particular elements of life, but also helps determine who has the power in the system–whose opinions are important, whose decisions are followed. In this paper I will use the term multiculturalism to refer to the influence of many different cultures. For the sake of simplicity and clarity, I will refer to ethnic groups as though there was no variation within the group itself. Although I run the risk of perpetuating stereotypes, my purpose is to describe the dilemmas of considering both multicultural and feminist approaches (McGoldrick et al., 1991).

Like FFT, multiculturalism is a perspective rather than a coherent theory, and is more concerned with diversity than achieving agreement (Rodis & Strehorn, 1997). In general, multicultural therapy considers a client's culture to be a source of strength and guidance, ties that many do not recognize or have severed. This ideal may conflict with that of FFT, whose goal is to break free of the bonds of traditional forms of authority perceived as damaging to women. Such multicultural approaches will become more important as the population becomes increasingly diverse (Brown & Brodsky, 1992). The four largest racial and ethnic minorities–African Americans, Hispanics, Asians/Pacific Islanders, and American Indians–accounted for 25% of the U.S. population in 1992; by 2050, these minorities may account for 47% of the U.S. population (O'Hare, 1992).

Recognizing the influence of culture takes different forms. McGoldrick and her colleagues (McGoldrick, Garcia-Preto, Hines, & Lee, 1989; 1991) provide valuable information to consider when working with families of various ethnic backgrounds. For example, Garcia-Preto (1996) pointed out that Hispanics often share the following characteristics: emphasizing spiritual values, valuing personalism (i.e., unique inner qualities), placing importance on family unity, and conceptualizing gender roles according to machismo and marianismo. Kurilla (1998) also noted that racial/ethnic minority individuals respond better to directive, active, structured, and explicit approaches rather than nondirective, passive, unstructured, and ambiguous approaches. These studies highlight the importance of considering the influence of culture in clients' struggles.

Although healing may come through using cultural tradition as a resource, many of the problems that bring people into therapy have a specific cultural root (Rodis & Strehorn, 1997). McGoldrick, Giordano, and Pearce (1996) highlighted some traditional cultural values that have therapeutic treatment implications: African Americans view therapy as a process for "crazy people"; it is acceptable for upper-class Jamaican men to have mistresses; covert communication is used in Mexican families in the interest of family harmony; Asian Americans are likely to express emotional problems through physical symptoms; and Iranian parents value boys more than girls. The challenge for therapists is to decide, and help clients decide, what parts of their culture are helpful.

Some authors suggest respecting the values of a client's culture but challenging them when they are not functional (e.g., Nichols & Schwartz, 1995). This attitude raises the question of defining what is "functional." Just because a belief or behavior pattern is normative in another culture, does that mean it is healthy and should not be challenged in that culture? For example, when speaking with women in Afghanistan, does the therapist help a client come to terms with the restrictive fundamentalist Muslim attitude toward women because it is the norm? McGoldrick et al. (1991) encouraged therapists not to push their clients beyond culturally determined limits even if the therapist thinks it would be helpful. Therapists, then, have to decide where helpful pushing ends.

A mirrored reflection of this dilemma applies to minority clients in a different majority culture (e.g., Hispanics in the United States). Should the values of the traditional culture be abandoned for the values of the dominant culture? For example, McGoldrick et al. (1991) described machismo in Hispanic cultures and suggested that when the dominant society does not reinforce traditional cultural values, rigid adherence to the value ceases to be functional. This could be interpreted to mean that clients should adopt the beliefs and values of the dominant society in order to "fit in," the ultimate definition of functional. Recognizing this potential, Doherty and Boss (1991) warned that "unless family therapy engages in a careful examination of its own assumptions and metaphors about normal family functioning, it will inevitably engage primarily in a resocializing of families to the dominant culture or to another ethnic culture favored by therapists" (p. 611). Again, therapists need to be aware of their own cultural biases and decide (with clients) how to be functional without losing their cultural identity to the dominant view.

Although the multicultural perspective has emphasized an important contextual variable in working with families, it is not without its critics. For instance, May (1998a) cautions against hiding behind the "cultural mask," referring to family dynamics perceived as part of the culture and therefore not challenged to change and grow. Similarly, cultural relativism refers to the practice of defending customs as tradition even when they violate human rights. Therapists and clients must decide when a family practice based on cultural values is unacceptable, but there are no clear answers to this question. Nichols and Schwartz (1995) point out that ethnicity and culture are often not considered by recent theory paradigms (e.g., constructivist), although these factors are seen as powerful meaning generators. Unfortunately, failing to consider culture does not diminish its influence any more than failing to consider the importance of gender. It seems the multicultural perspective needs a way to evaluate the helpfulness of cultural values, and using FFT may provide the necessary critical skills.

ETHICAL CONSIDERATIONS

FFT and multiculturalism are similar in some respects. First, FFT examines power differences between men and women, and multiculturalism examines differences in power of minority and majority cultural groups. Second, FFT encourages respect for women's experiences and skills, and the multicultural perspective values diverse cultural beliefs. Finally, both approaches focus on the strengths of their respective populations: FFT examines the strengths of being a woman, and multiculturalism explores the strengths of various cultures.

In spite of these similarities, however, there are times when a situation appears to call for the therapist to make a choice between FFT and multiculturalism. The differences between these approaches guarantee that a true integration will not be simple, and indeed will create ethical dilemmas for therapists. Five ethical principles guide the integration (Huber, 1994): autonomy, beneficence, nonmaleficence, justice, and fidelity. Autonomy is the recognition that all people have the right to make decisions and choose to act on them. The principle of beneficence calls for therapists to actively benefit the client. Nonmaleficence means "do no harm"; one must avoid causing harm to another. The principle of justice toward clients insists that all individuals be treated fairly; equals must be treated as equals and unequals must be treated in a way that recognizes their uneven status. Fidelity refers to the principle of honesty and loyalty.

Often these principles are in tension with one another. Both FFT and multiculturalism describe themselves as beneficent, and argue that neglecting their respective variables (gender, culture) is unethical. Unfortunately, "doing good" for the client may take different forms, including modifying the principle of fidelity. Lageman (1993) pointed out that fidelity is not simply a matter of divulging every thought, but rather "it is in how carefully we tell the truth to our clients that we give clear indication of our respect for them" (p. 49). Fidelity, then, is not an absolute, but rather should be modified according to what will be beneficial for the client.

Two principles often in conflict are autonomy and nonmaleficence. Feminist family therapists sensitive to cultural differences have addressed autonomy by making culturally sanctioned gender differences and inequities overt, then leaving it up to the client how s/he will change. Even this more "hands-off" approach has its problems however, as previous authors (e.g., McGoldrick et al., 1989) have noted that women who become aware of such inequalities often reject their entire culture and history in an attempt to break those bonds. Unfortunately, this escape also separates a woman from her heritage, including her legacy of strong female role models, a violation of the principle of nonmaleficence. McGoldrick et al. (1989) suggested that therapists find creative ways to help clients reinterpret their traditional culture such that they can "take along into the future what they will need from the past" (p. 197).

Therapists may attempt to promote autonomy by following Lageman's (1993) advice: "I maintain that it is essential for family therapists to respect (not agree with) the belief systems of clients" (p. 32). Although many therapists would agree with this sentiment, in choosing between FFT and multiculturalism it is often unclear what "respect" looks like. May (1998a) described a case of an Asian American woman having difficulty with her husband's family that she was not able to correct herself because of cultural proscriptions. Her therapist worked within the cultural system of values to help her find a respected male family member to plead her case. Although this solution showed respect for cultural values, FFT would call for more social action, questioning, and change. May (1998a) pointed out that to address issues of gender inequality (which she defined as cultural values as well) would cause greater harm to the family dynamics, a violation of the principle of nonmaleficence.

I struggle with justice, nonmaleficence, and autonomy when I consider whether to address feminist ideals with clients who will remain in patriarchal cultures after I am no longer present to give support. I wonder if I am doing them harm by providing the information, giving them the autonomy to choose to change, then abandoning them. For example, Comas-Diaz (1988) pointed out that Puerto Rican women often use indirect manipulation. They use this style of communication not because there is something inherently peculiar about Puerto Rican women, but because these strategies are characteristic of all oppressed people regardless of gender and/or ethnicity. By pointing out their oppression and helping to develop a more direct communication style, there is a risk that these Puerto Rican women will actually be in more jeopardy than if they had continued using such methods. I feel a sense of responsibility to the client who lives in a world that may not accept her newfound ideas of equality and power. Is it a violation of the principle of justice to provide information to a socially oppressed woman and then leave her to fight her own battles? Is the alternative–I stay and "help" her–too dominating, a form of cultural colonialism? Who am I to step in for her? Yet, I am the one with a certain amount of power; if I use that for her good, am I being disrespectful of her autonomy or cognizant of her situation (justice)?

Family therapists must often deal with the tension between what is best for the family unit and what is best for the individual. Lageman (1993) described individual problems as primarily dealing with issues of well-being while system problems deal with issues of justice, and said therapists have a duty to work for justice and to eliminate prejudice. The FFT technique of pointing out power differences, even those that are culturally approved, follows the principle of justice, but it may conflict with nonmaleficence for the couple, especially those in a culture hostile to more egalitarian relationships. Although feminism focuses on the self in relation to others, it does advocate for equality. If that equality is not possible within a given system, then alternatives –including leaving the system–are considered without regard (or with less regard) for the outcome of the system. While some may see FFT as inherently individual, I agree with Rodis and Strehorn (1997) who argued that by focusing on issues of social justice, feminism is a movement for the fulfillment of moral life for all people.

INTEGRATION OF FFT AND MULTICULTURALISM

In the integration of FFT and multiculturalism, researchers note that rather than being forced to choose one culture over another, it is possible to have a cultural identification with more than one culture simultaneously (Kurilla, 1998). This fits well with the feminist ideals of not needing absolute and universal truths, and valuing a means of evaluating alternative knowledges in order to make moral and ethical decisions while still accommodating differences (Paterson & Trathen, 1994). In this vein, some researchers have used feminist theory with minority clients. For example, using FFT with Hispanic women can result in a greater awareness and understanding of the oppressive effects of traditional sex roles while functioning within the mainstream society (Comas-Diaz, 1988). A feminist family therapist could also challenge cultural assumptions using culture itself, through conversations that make cultural values explicit, normalizing the fact that a client has trouble following incongruent cultural messages, challenging cultural messages by externalizing them, advertising nondominant (e.g., minority culture) discourses, or introducing beliefs from yet another culture (Coale, 1994).

These studies show that it is possible for FFT and multiculturalism to be integrated in spite of, or maybe because of, their differences. The struggle to integrate FFT and multiculturalism reflects a common problem of social activism: should one work for change from within the system, or must change come from outside the system? Multicultural approaches work within the system, while FFT often functions outside the system. There may be a way to combine them so they complement rather than conflict with each other. Clearly we want neither a cultural mask that protects biased traditions nor a mirror that reflects the values of a dominant culture. By integrating FFT and multiculturalism, we get the best of both worlds. Therapists and clients can work together to co-create unique adaptations that are not considered by either approach alone. This requires creativity and flexibility, especially from therapists who may strongly hold principles particular to either FFT or multiculturalism.

Such blending will require adjustment of the principles of FFT described earlier. The first principle emphasized the importance of gender as a variable that structures interactions. This principle can be modified to reflect the understanding that although gender as an organizing factor is central to a feminist analysis and understanding, it may not be central to all women in all cases (Brown, 1990). Pinderhughes (1986) pointed out that both racism and sexism affect the minority woman, and her circumstances are unique because of this intersection. Therapists should be open to hearing from people experiencing these interacting factors (Falicov, 1995). Unfortunately FFT has alienated some minority therapists who are ideologically feminist but refuse to identify with FFT because of its overly White bias. Feminist family therapists need to be humble and listen to the voices of feminists from other cultures. Although it is not the responsibility of the oppressed to educate the privileged (Akamatsu, 1998; Brown, 1990), these women are our best teachers.

The second principle described the egalitarian therapeutic relationship and defined the therapists' responsibility as social change agent, providing information and support to improve clients' gender-biased life circumstances. This activism goes beyond simply naming the problem of gender inequity; it exerts itself to advocate for a more just distribution, a more moral way of life. Feminist family therapists must realize, however, that this activism takes place in the client's cultural context, a context that must be respected and validated even as it is questioned and challenged. Therefore, although striving for an egalitarian relationship and being a social change agent will continue to be in conflict at times, multiculturalism provides another variable to consider in the respect of clients' values.

The third principle focused on the therapy process in which therapists validate women's experiences, challenge traditional understandings, and empower clients to change their own environment. Therapists have a responsibility to be aware of and respect the cultural context, yet remain challenging within ethical guidelines. Therapists must ask themselves whether such challenges will be beneficial for the client, whether they may be doing harm, and whether the choice is up to the client. According to Rodis and Strehorn (1997), feminist approaches have had a fortifying influence on real people because this active stance "conveys to such a client that what was violated was not only her own person, but the moral law" (p. 22). By appropriately challenging traditions, clients gain insight into their situations and are able to make more informed decisions.

Integrating the principles of both FFT and multiculturalism necessitates some creative adjustments. For example, Falicov (1995) suggested one way to consider the multiple influences–culture, gender, social class, etc.–clients face using a multidimensional comparative framework. In this approach, therapists use concepts such as cultural borderlands, those overlapping zones of similarities and differences within and between cultures, and ecological niches, the unique combination of a family's multiple contexts. Through these lens, therapists examine key parameters–ecological context, migration and acculturation, family organization, and family life cycle–situated in the web of simultaneous group membership. In another example, Almeida, Woods, Messineo, and Font (1998) created the Cultural Context Model to respectfully examine outside influences. This model contains several unique elements, including sponsorship, in which clients who have been through the program are used to keep current clients accountable for their issues; socioeducational orientation, in which film clips and readings are used to raise consciousness regarding gender, race, class, and culture; and cultural circles, gender specific open-ended groups that provide an opportunity to tell and hear stories. These approaches are consistent with both FFT and multicultural principles.

SUGGESTIONS FOR THE FUTURE

Integration of FFT and multiculturalism is the goal, but it will be a process with continuing ethical dilemmas. There are several ways to address those dilemmas. One suggestion is to obtain informed consent from clients. According to Huber (1994), it is the ethical responsibility of therapists to give adequate information regarding entering and continuing a therapeutic relationship with a particular therapist so the client can make informed choices. Feminist family therapists sensitive to cultural differences must inform clients of our feminist ideology–that we will be challenging traditions and talking with them about how to choose among cultural values. This would lay the foundation for a conversation about what this ideology means to the client and what concerns they may have about future changes. These are steps many therapists already take. One possible dilemma in this situation is the client who decides to go to another therapist who does not challenge his/her cultural beliefs. Do we let them choose (autonomy) even though it is not what we believe is best for them and may even be harmful (nonmaleficence)?

Another strategy to minimize the ethical dilemmas of integration is to focus on other issues. An overemphasis on ethnicity (Nichols & Schwartz, 1995) or gender (Hare-Mustin, 1994) can obscure the influence of factors such as economic class and education. For example, Rabin (1989) examined gender issues using the feminist approach with couples on welfare. She pointed out that using middle-class subjects in studies of gender assumes that sexist values similarly influence all families. McGoldrick et al. (1991) acknowledged that ethnicity intersects with other factors such as class and gender, and indeed separating their respective influence may be impossible. Laird (1998) noted that all elements of culture are constantly acting on each person, although one part may be more salient in one context and time than in another. As noted earlier, both Falicov (1995) and Almeida et al. (1998) have developed unique approaches to address these multiple issues.

Another suggestion for therapy that integrates FFT and multiculturalism is to be more proactive in seeking out network resources. Rather than working with a client, then leaving him/her in a culture potentially hostile to feminist ideas, therapists should find out about network resources. These may be people in the community who feel the same way, or may be just someone safe to talk to about the challenges proposed by the therapist (e.g., Almeida et al., 1998). This network support can make the difference for a client's autonomous choices.

IMPLICATIONS FOR TRAINING

This tension between FFT values and cultural values also has ramifications for family therapy training. Unfortunately, awareness of gender and cultural inequalities is not consciously available to all people. Therefore family therapists need training to become aware of their own values and the extent to which they use stereotypes in their ideas about differences among people. Cultural sensitivity requires that therapists not only develop an awareness and appreciation of difference, but also give up power and the assumption of superiority (May, 1998a). A number of authors have made specific suggestions for improving multicultural competence in training programs. One method of becoming aware of cultural influences is for trainees to complete an in-depth cultural genogram of their own families (Hardy & Laszloffy, 1995). In addition, May (1998b) suggested that culturally sensitive therapists be able to (a) determine whether clients' "problems" result from external factors such as racism, (b) conduct training/educational interventions to combat oppression, (c) use institutional interventions on behalf of clients, and (d) educate clients to their personal and legal rights. Green (1998) suggested establishing multicultural competencies as goals, having multicultural faculty leadership, employing faculty members who represent a proportional balance of diverse cultures, and inclusion of multicultural content in clinical supervision. When training the multidimensional comparative approach, Falicov (1995) recommended that trainees have a curious attitude about client's cultural views, make comparisons across at least three cultures in order to lessen the tendency toward right-wrong dichotomies, and first interview non-clinical families in order to focus on the multiple cultural influences. Supervisors should help trainees differentiate between cultural patterns that are to be respected and inequities that are human rights issues (McGoldrick et al., 1999).

Many of the suggestions for training culturally sensitive therapists could also be applied to training gender sensitive therapists. For example, Whipple (1996) stated that training programs should (a) encourage trainees to examine ideas and awareness of gender issues, (b) require reading feminist theory, and (c) promote discussion of gender issues with colleagues and supervisors. Both gender and culture material should be integrated into all aspects of the training program and a regular topic of discussion, rather than relegated to one course (e.g., Falicov, 1995). The multidimensional comparative framework (Falicov, 1995) and the Cultural Context Model (Almeida et al., 1998) hold promise for the ethical integration of FFT and multicultural principles, and could be considered as patterns for training programs to follow. Designing and maintaining such a training program is not easy, yet engaging in this effort could provide the necessary ethical environment for dealing with many of these dilemmas.

CONCLUSION

In conclusion, I believe that integrating FFT and multiculturalism offers the opportunity for much soul-searching in family therapy. The tensions between ethical principles will continue to challenge those of us who strive to honor both of these approaches. We have a responsibility to clients, but there are the limits to what we can and should do.

I will continue working with minority clients, trying to be sensitive to their cultural context by neither hiding behind the cultural mask nor forcing them to mirror my own biases. For example, in the case I described earlier of the Hispanic mother with four children, I could clearly state my feminist agenda and biases, and explore with the client what this approach means to her. We, the client and I, could reach out to relatives or others in the community, possibly women who have been in a similar situation, in order to broaden the possible alternatives. I could also learn more about her culture and my own, openly discuss and challenge the biases of both, and find out what a third culture might have to offer. This is not to say that my dilemmas will be easily resolved, but rather there will be an on-going struggle to recognize and honor them.

Lageman (1993) warned "attachment to our own idealism can prevent us from examining the realities of our work as well as looking at the shadow side of professional life" (p. 33). It is time now for feminist and multicultural family therapists to look at the shadow of our work and at the realities of clients' situations once they leave the therapy room. I believe that by offering families a viewpoint emphasizing an egalitarian and empowering relationship, we benefit our clients. Our reasons for employing this approach and our actions within the relationship, however, are matters worthy of further discussion.

REFERENCES

Akamatsu, N. N. (1998). The talking oppression blues: Including the experience of power/powerlessness in the teaching of "cultural sensitivity." In M. McGoldrick (Ed.), *Re-Visioning Family Therapy* (pp. 129-143). New York: Guilford.

Almeida, R., Woods, R., Messineo, T., & Font, R. (1998). The cultural context model: An overview. In M. McGoldrick (Ed.), *Re-Visioning Family Therapy* (pp. 414-431). New York: Guilford.

Brown, L. S. (1990). The meaning of a multicultural perspective for theory-building in feminist therapy. *Women & Therapy, 9*(1-2), 1-21.

Brown, L. S., & Brodsky, A. M. (1992). The future of feminist therapy. *Psychotherapy, 29*(1), 51-57.

Coale, H. W. (1994). Using cultural and contextual frames to expand possibilities. *Journal of Systemic Therapies, 13*(2), 5-23.

Coe, M. J. (1993). *The Practice of Feminist Family Therapy: A Qualitative Analysis of the Literature of Theory and Practice.* Unpublished doctoral dissertation, Florida State University.

Comas-Diaz, L. (1988). Feminist therapy with Hispanic/Latina women: Myth or reality? *Women & Therapy, 6*(4), 39-61.

Doherty, W. J., & Boss, P. G. (1991). Values and ethics in family therapy. In A. S. Gurman & D. P. Kniskern (Eds.), *Handbook of Family Therapy: Vol. 2* (pp. 606-637). New York: Brunner/Mazel.

Falicov, C. J. (1995). Training to think culturally: A multidimensional comparative framework. *Family Process, 34*(4), 373-388.

Garcia-Preto, N. (1996). Latino families: An overview. In M. McGoldrick, J. Giordano, & J. K. Pearce (Eds.), *Ethnicity and Family Therapy* (2nd ed., pp. 141-154). New York: Guilford.

Green, R.-J. (1998). Training programs: Guildelines for multicultural transformation. In M. McGoldrick (Ed.), *Re-Visioning Family Therapy* (pp. 111-117). New York: Guilford.

Hardy, K., & Laszloffy, T. (1995). The cultural genogram: Key to training culturally competent family therapists. *Journal of Marital and Family Therapy, 21*(3), 227-237.

Hare-Mustin, R. T. (1994). Discourses in the mirrored room: A postmodern analysis of therapy. *Family Process, 33*, 19-35.

Hare-Mustin, R. T., & Marecek, J. (1994). Asking the right questions: Feminist psychology and sex differences. *Feminism & Psychology, 4*(4), 531-537.

Huber, C. H. (1994). *Ethical, Legal, and Professional Issues in the Practice of Marriage and Family Therapy* (2nd ed.). Upper Saddle River, NJ: Prentice-Hall.

Kurilla, V. (1998). Multicultural counseling perspectives: Culture specificity and implications in family therapy. *The Family Journal: Counseling and Therapy for Couples and Families, 6*(3), 207-211.

Lageman, A. G. (1993). *The Moral Dimensions of Marriage and Family Therapy*. Lanham, MA: University Press of America.

Laird, J. (1998). Theorizing culture: Narrative ideas and practice principles. In M. McGoldrick (Ed.), *Re-Visioning Family Therapy* (pp. 20-36). New York: Guilford.

May, K. M. (1998a). Family counseling: Cultural sensitivity, relativism, and the cultural defense. *The Family Journal: Counseling and Therapy for Couples and Families, 6*(4), 296-299.

May, K. M. (1998b). A feminist and multicultural perspective in family therapy. *The Family Journal: Counseling and Therapy for Couples and Families, 6*(2), 123-124.

McGoldrick, M., Almeida, R., Garcia Preto, N., Bibb, A., Sutton, C., Hudak, J., & Hines, P. M. (1999). Efforts to incorporate social justice perspectives into a family training program. *Journal of Marital and Family Therapy, 25*(2), 177-189.

McGoldrick, M., Garcia Preto, N., Hines, P. M., & Lee, E. (1989). Ethnicity and women. In M. McGoldrick, C. M. Anderson, & F. Walsh (Eds.), *Women in Families: A Framework for Family Therapy* (pp. 169-199). New York: W. W. Norton.

McGoldrick, M., Garcia Preto, N., Hines, P. M., & Lee, E. (1991). Ethnicity and Family Therapy. In A. S. Gurman & D. P. Kniskern (Eds.), *Handbook of Family Therapy: Vol. 2* (pp. 546-582). New York: Brunner/Mazel.

McGoldrick, M., Giordano, J., & Pearce, J. K. (Eds.). (1996). *Ethnicity and Family Therapy* (2nd ed.). New York: Guilford.

Nichols, M. P., & Schwartz, R. C. (1995). *Family Therapy: Concepts and Methods* (3rd ed.). Boston, MA: Allyn and Bacon.

O'Hare, W. P. (1992). America's minorities: The demographics of diversity. *Population Bulletin of the Population Reference Bureau* [On-line], *47*(4). Abstract from: Internet: www.cicred.ined.fr/rdr/rdr_a/revues/revue67-68/13-67-67_a.html.

Parker, L. (1997a). Keeping power issues on the table in couples work. *Journal of Feminist Family Therapy, 9*(3), 1-24.

Parker, L. (1997b). Unraveling power issues in couples therapy. *Journal of Feminist Family Therapy, 9*(2), 3-20.

Paterson, R., & Trathen, S. (1994). Feminist in(ter)ventions in family therapy. *Australian & New Zealand Journal of Family Therapy, 15*(2), 91-98.

Pinderhughes, E. B. (1986). Minority women: A nodal position in the functioning of the social system. In M. Ault-Riche (Ed.), *Women and Family Therapy* (pp. 51-63). Rockville, MA: Aspen Systems.

Rabin, C. (1989). Gender issues in the treatment of welfare couples: A feminist approach to marital therapy of the poor. *Contemporary Family Therapy, 11*(3), 169-188.

Rodis, P. T., & Strehorn, K. C. (1997). Ethical issues for psychology in the postmodernist era: Feminist psychology and multicultural therapy (MCT). *Journal of Theoretical and Philosophical Psychology, 17*(1), 13-31.

Whipple, V. (1996). Developing an identity as a feminist family therapist: Implications for training. *Journal of Marital and Family Therapy, 22*(3), 381-396.

Conversations with the Founders
of the Women's Project on the Integration
of Gender and Culture in Family
Therapy Training

Shelley A. Haddock

Marianne Walters

Shelley: As you look back over the past twenty years as the field began to grapple with integrating the organizing principles of gender, culture, and power in its training programs, what are your reflections on this process?

Marianne: I think that there has been a sensitization–in the field and in the larger culture–to the issues of gender, culture, ethnicity, race, sexual orientation, and power. But, it is a mistake to think that we have integrated these concepts in our practice or training programs. In general, the field has treated these issues quite separately. There have been special classes, workshops, and conferences, particularly intended to sensitize people to the issues of gender, sexual

Shelley A. Haddock, MS, is a Lecturer and Clincal Supervisor in the Marriage and Family Therapy Program, and Interim Director of the Marriage and Family Therapy Clinic at Colorado State University.

Address correspondence to: Shelley A. Haddock, MS, 119 Gifford Building, Colorado State University, Fort Collins, CO 80523.

[Haworth co-indexing entry note]: "Conversations with the Founders of the Women's Project on the Integration of Gender and Culture in Family Therapy Training." Haddock, Shelley A. Co-published simultaneously in *Journal of Feminist Family Therapy* (The Haworth Press, Inc.) Vol. 12, No. 2/3, 2001, pp. 123-149; and: *Integrating Gender and Culture in Family Therapy Training* (ed: Toni Schindler Zimmerman) The Haworth Press, Inc., 2001, pp. 123-149. Single or multiple copies of this article are available for a fee from The Haworth Document Delivery Service [1-800-342-9678, 9:00 a.m. - 5:00 p.m. (EST). E-mail address: getinfo@haworthpressinc.com].

orientation, race, and class. There also have been parts of curriculum specific to these issues in training programs. The topics have been raised, but not yet really integrated into everything that we do. But, we have come a long way in terms of recognizing that there are issues of gender, race, ethnicity, class, and sexual orientation; earlier, we only looked at the intra-dynamics of a family.

Shelley: Do you have other reflections or comments on the field's development with regard to training?

Marianne: As far as I can see, we are training people primarily in techniques. Depending upon the particular banner under which you received your training–whether it is called solution-focused, cognitive-behavioral, structural, integrative, or narrative–you learn some specific and concrete techniques. There has been more and more of an effort to add more techniques. There seems to me to be "the flavor of the week"–one new technique after another, EMDR, Imago. We learn this and then we learn that. I find that the techniques are devoid of ideology. What ideology underlies them? For instance, do the techniques have anything to do with how we understand the impact of homophobia or racism on families, on people? I worry about this proliferation of a technological way of thinking in our field. I understand that it certainly reflects our culture–where life is increasingly more technologically dependent–but I think it reduces the power of relationships and the artistry of therapy to a series of techniques. This is my general concern at this point.

Shelley: What would you like to see instead?

Marianne: I would like to see more critical thinking. I have been amazed to find that I will speak to an audience that seems to be very much "in tune" with and like what I am saying and the tapes that I show. Then, they listen to the next person who is diametrically different from me–who thinks differently, who has a different ideology, who has a different way of working, or who in fact can be quite sexist–and they love that, too. I have seen huge audiences look at work either of mine or someone else's and not be critical of what is being presented in terms of gender, culture, homophobia–power relationships. They focus on the technique, but there is not much critical thinking.

Shelley: Are you saying that the focus is on the presumed out-come–on what supposedly worked–rather than the pro-cess? Or, that the focus is on solving the presenting prob-lem rather than on the messages that are given to the clients?

Marianne: Yes. Very well put. We need to consider at whose ex-pense was the problem supposedly solved. As therapists, we need to develop an ideology that guides our work–one that integrates gender and culture. One of few places that integrates gender and culture is my Center–the Family Therapy Practice Center. We do not raise these issues as special or hold a special class on them. Rather, these issues are part of everything we say and do–integrated into every case, every situation, every presentation, and every conference. All of our supervision and training incorporates this ideology–an ideology that the field as a whole has not yet developed.

Shelley: I would like to hear more about specifically how you train at your Institute–is that what you called it?

Marianne: The Family Therapy Practice Center. We call it The Cen-ter–as in "the Center of the Universe" (chuckle).

Shelley: Are you the "center" of the Center?

Marianne: The sun.

Shelley: Could you describe how you train at your Center?

Marianne: My training is all case based. My faculty and I do only one full-day didactic presentation to orient new trainees to our way of working and thinking. We move quickly to seeing families using live supervision and reviewing videotapes. We work from "inside out"-from the case to the thinking. Even when we train in welfare departments, or foster care and child protective service agencies, we do some orientation, but mostly we develop the thinking out of the work. By this I mean that we talk with our trainees to elicit their attitudes and assumptions-their belief systems-about what constructs behavior and what constructs change. For instance, if we are going to see a single, twice-divorced mom with a sexually acting out daughter-a daughter that she conceived when she was sixteen-we ask what the therapists are thinking. What are their assumptions? Do they think that the child is repeating family patterns by sexually acting out like her mother did when she was sixteen? Is that what they think? And, if so, why? Then, we begin to challenge this thinking. Our thinking is not about repeated patterns of family behavior. We think in terms of culture and a society that pushes young women-particularly those who are in a financially deprived situation or who are members of an at-risk family lacking social supports and so on-to engage in sexual behavior. We also are looking at the fact that this child could not be sexually active if boys were not encouraging that kind of behavior. Ninety percent of our trainees would initially say that this daughter is repeating her mother's pattern. It is this kind of thinking that we would begin to challenge.

Shelley: Where does this thinking about repeating family patterns come from-our training programs?

Marianne: Not necessarily; these kind of assumptions are not just in our training programs or our field. If you read the current or past issues of *Harper's, Good Housekeeping*, or any popular magazine, you can see that the current common wisdom is that children repeat the patterns of their parents. For instance, we believe that children who are abused frequently abuse their own children. It is far more complex.

Shelley: What you do in your training, then, is to help trainees articulate these cultural assumptions or beliefs as they pertain to a particular case, and then challenge these beliefs. Is that correct?

Marianne: Yes. This is what I mean by ideology–what are your priorities? What are your concerns? How do you understand socialized roles and rules? Where do you help a family to look at the possibilities and the options for change–within or without, or both? It is not that we cannot work with what is going on in the family–obviously we must and we do–but we have to enter that kind of work in a non-linear way; in other words, rather than the family as the locus of problems, let us look at the gendered, ethnic, or economic construction of relationships and how these operate within a family.

The whole notion of dysfunction has been so trivialized that dysfunctional can be anything from benign neglect of children to a beating. We do not know what dysfunctional means anymore. For instance, I am finding out that an awful lot of young women–unmarried women who are in their late thirties who are high-powered professionals, attractive, wonderful, lots of friends–who are miserable because they are not married and their biological clock is running out. When you ask them why don't they have a kid if they want a family, the idea has not even occurred to them. It seems so impossible because in our culture, you do not have children without marriage. Well, why don't you? If you want a child and you are financially able, healthy, and a loving person, then have a child. If we are not critical thinkers and have not developed an ideology, we start working with this kind of woman in terms of what kind of family did she come from, why is she having trouble with relationships, what are her boundary issues, or God knows what. Let us, at least, consider cultural inhibitors; the social messages that construct behavior.

Shelley: So, you are saying that as therapists, we should not accept these cultural "myths" about how we should lead our lives. We should become critical thinkers–even about issues that many would argue are accepted traditions of our culture, such as "marriage comes before babies."

Marianne: Yes. And it is important to remember that these traditions are very much a part of professional lives. Many of the people who read this journal belong to an organization called the American Association of Marriage and Family Therapy. The title indicates that "marriage" and "family" are attached, and does not recognize that marriage is not allowed to 10% of our population. So, it is a discriminatory institution. We would never belong to an organization that was called "marital and family therapy" if only those who could marry were white. This is what I mean by critical thinking.

Shelley: How do you teach this kind of critical thinking at the Center?

Marianne: We are always talking and thinking about these issues. As we talk about marriage, we ask: Why marriage? What about divorce, and is it a problem? Why is it a problem? When is it a success? When does it show intelligence, thoughtfulness, and a taking care of one another in life? Do children need two parents? Why? What do we expect of our children? Do we have different expectations of boys and girls? Why? We challenge all the assumptions that our culture and therapists have about the families that we see.

Shelley: How do you teach trainees to take what they have learned from these conversations into the room with clients?

Marianne: We talk a lot about the use of self–about using your wisdom and experiences as a grown-up person. We use a lot of coaching or scripting. We might say, "Here is something you might say," or "Here is one way you could approach this guy." We offer a lot of scripts; we do not ask trainees what they think they should do with the client, unless we think they have a real answer. We never ask them the question that we do not want them to ask their clients, which is, "What do you think you should do?" Clients come to therapy not knowing how to do something or what to do next. So, for therapists to ask them, "How could you control your daughter?" seems to be a foolish question. If they knew, they would not be here. That is how we begin to apply notions of competence.

We also do not teach trainees to discuss these issues-society, or culture, or homophobia-with their clients. Instead, we teach them to enact them, and we offer specific ideas about how to enact them. We teach them to talk with people about how they are reacting to or dealing with various issues that come up within their lives. You are working with the family; you are not working on society.

Shelley: How might you teach a trainee to enact these issues with the previous case you were describing-the one with the mother and the daughter who was sexually active?

Marianne: The first thing that we would do is to talk about how alike these two are in wonderful ways. For instance, we would look at the way they interact with each other and find the first time when the mother and daughter laugh at the same things or share an idea about a film that they saw recently. We would begin to point out where this mother and daughter have really good connections and good values. Then, we would begin talking with the mother about how she can help her daughter to negotiate the minefield that is out there for any young, beautiful, attractive girl. The mother has survived this minefield; we ask her to help her daughter to cope with a minefield that says that to be attractive, you have to have a boyfriend and have sex with him.

We first talk about their connectedness. We would not focus on being sexually dysfunctional, but about the wonderful things that they have in common–maybe they share a dimple, beautiful black hair, or a smile. You first establish the connectedness on something other than the sexuality, and then you go for the mother's capacity as a survivor, and her strengths.

Shelley: Do you ever experience resistance to this ideology in training? And, if so, how do you handle it?

Marianne: Yes, I love resistance. I worry if there isn't any resistance because it means that the ideology isn't being integrated or taken in. But, when there is resistance, we discuss it. As people often do when you have any ideology, they bring up the exceptions–well, that isn't true in this situation or the people that I have met are not like that. We talk about it; I might agree that there are exceptions, but I am adamant about how I think. We have differences that we discuss, and we end the discussion by saying, "I am right, and you are wrong" (chuckle). And, we do a lot of laughing and eating, and people get very connected with one another.

Shelley: Previously, you mentioned that you focus on the use of self in your training. How do you work with trainees in this regard?

Marianne: I always ask my trainees these questions: "What about you turns other people on? How do you turn people on? When you enter a crowded room at a party, how do you attract people? How do you get people to trust you, think you're smart, think you are funny, attractive, or interesting? What do you do?" I have them talk about their answers because it is a stunner. No one wants to say, "Well, I do this and that . . . . " But, all of that has to go into the room with you–that is your technique. Most people do not want to think that they do something to attract other people or make themselves attractive or engaging to other people. That is one of the first things I say to people when we talk about use of self–how do you get noticed, how do you convince someone that you know something, how do you present your ideas.

Shelley: What a thought-provoking question! Unfortunately, it is time to close. What closing message or comments would you like to say to trainers or trainees who are committed to continuing this work in their training programs?

Marianne: Do not make race, class, gender, sexual orientation separate issues. Find ways to make these a part of your every day living, your every day work, your every day thinking. Then, think of new kinds of ways of working that fit within this ideology. Do not do it the opposite way; that is, think of new techniques and then think of how they fit. Always have a context from which you figure your interventions rather than just thinking up techniques.

Shelley: Thank you, Marianne, for your many significant contributions to our field over the years. It is my hope that we can follow in your footsteps, finding ways to truly integrate gender and culture in every case, conversation, and interaction.

Betty Carter

Shelley: As you look back over the past couple of decades as the field began to recognize and grapple with incorporating the organizing principles of gender, culture, and power, what are your reflections on the field's development?

Betty: We all know that in the beginning, we just ignored the issue. All the founders in the field were white men, and they just assumed that everyone else was like them. In the 1980's, the feminist critique put gender on the table, and since that time, there has been a lot of movement. However, there have been differences in how the issues of gender, race, class, and sexual orientation have been responded to. Gender was addressed first, and there was a good response because there are many women in the field–most of those in power positions were and are white. And although there was a lot of resistance and turmoil to feminist proposals, the topic of gender was generally more well accepted than the other issues or race, class, and sexual orientation. However, eventually all the issues began to be put on the table–many by feminists who learned from examining gender to look at other inequalities. It seems to me that sexual orientation has been addressed a little better than race or class because there are many gay and lesbian people in important positions in our field to write books and conduct workshops.

However, I would say that, although there has been so much written and discussed on all of these topics, we are still in a situation where there is more lip service than practice. Although national conferences have many workshops and speeches on these topics, I think there is very uneven inclusion in the training programs across the country. For instance, one favorite way that programs deal with these issues–without having to get too upset–is to hold a special course on them. They may have a course down the hall or give a few lectures, and then say, "Good, we have included these topics, and no one can say that we haven't." And, then these topics are generally forgotten about unless a client happens to be a member of a minority group; then, they wonder how they are going to work with this, like somehow it is a new issue.

So, I would say that we are still very much at the beginning of the struggle, in a sense. We have put it all on the table, but there is a lot more lip service than there is actual practice in training programs.

Shelley: Why do you think that is? What might be getting in the way?

Betty: I do not know, but my guess would be because so many of the leading training institutes and leading training programs are populated primarily by white, upper middle-class men and women both as trainers and trainees. They may be "out," maybe not. But the majority continue to be white upper middle-class, and they continue to do what they know.

Shelley: Privilege blinds us.

Betty: Yes, I think so. And, it takes a lot of effort to change it. At the Family Institute of Westchester, we did a couple of pilot programs. One of them was related to working with gay and lesbian clients. One of our staff members who was lesbian worked on this project, and I believe she really helped us develop a more successful program. We also developed a pilot project for working with minority families and people of color. We had no one on the staff to really devote energy to that project, and it just fizzled. My point is that you have to begin by changing yourself. And, that is where the problem is; it is very hard and people are so busy doing things the usual way. It is much easier to stay with the status quo than to change yourself. But, you have to change yourself if you are going to change the situation.

Shelley: And much of our culture is inconsistent with the kind of work, thinking, and questioning that you need to do to change your paradigm. Not only is there little to encourage us to question, but there is often much to discourage us.

Betty: Yes, that is right. For instance, in terms of class, look at the tuition of any institute or training program. We only let upper class people in. The tuition is a barrier for many people. The organization can not necessarily afford to give unlimited scholarships, even if they wished other people would come in. It is just what you said; there is a lot out there to discourage. You have to be very committed to the process in order to truly integrate gender, race, ethnicity, class, and sexual orientation into your training and therapy.

Shelley: Betty, when you look back over the past couple of decades, do you have other reflections or comments?

Betty: I would say that, after having been in the field for almost 30 years, of all of the many different things that I did, my most gratifying work was related to gender and culture–especially when we first started recognizing and working with gender issues. It was mind-blowing to me that we hadn't noticed the most basic of things–the organizing principle of gender. And when I did notice it, nothing was the same. Trying to communicate the importance of gender was the most important and gratifying work that I did of all that I was involved in over those years.

Shelley: In addition to being gratifying, would you say that these insights and changes in your work also made you more effective?

Betty: That was definitely true for me. Before you recognize the importance of gender, race, ethnicity, class, sexual orientation, it is like you are missing one of the main events. Then, all of a sudden, you start tapping into it. When you see the effect that it has on the people that you are working with, you realize even more the importance. And, you get this feedback with every couple or family that you work with.

Shelley: You have said that many training programs need to move from just paying lip service to a full integration of the topics. What are your recommendations for accomplishing this integration?

Betty: First, the person doing the training has to be committed to it, because it will often be the more inconvenient way. If you are not in charge of the institution, the first struggle is to try to get the support of the institution in which you are teaching. You also have to keep in the upper most part of your mind that you are liable to get some flack, resistance, and bewilderment by trainees and by others. You have to be prepared to deal with. To fully integrate means that you never let a single supervision or teaching session go by without referring to the larger context–gender, race, ethnicity, class, sexual orientation. That becomes the priority.

Shelley: So, you're actively putting it on the table in all your discussions?

Betty: Yes. A large part of the way I train is to encourage trainees to look at their own families as part of their training. These family-of-origin issues are often woven into my work with trainees. To the degree that trainees care to share, I encourage them to talk about how these issues play out in their own lives and relationships, with parents and families. I try to make it more personal so that no one can pretend that these topics are something that they never before dealt with.

Shelley: How do you go about doing that? Do you ask questions that facilitate personal exploration separate from case discussion, or do you discuss family-of-origin issues as they seem relevant in case consultation?

Betty: I use an evaluation form that trainees complete as part of presenting the family or couple in supervision. The form asks a series of questions about the family–some of which are: What is stirred up in your own experience by this families situation? Or, is there anyone in this family who reminds you of someone in your own life? Is that memory positive or negative? I would pay particular attention to the answers to these questions. In this way, I am paying attention to the therapist's personal experience, but always as it is connected to their clinical work.

Shelley: How would you work with this material that supervisees would bring regarding connections between their own personal experiences and their cases?

Betty: I always supervise in groups of about four therapists. The presenting therapist often would discuss the connections. Other times, other group members may ask questions about these connections. The therapists actually kind of put each other on alert about these connections so that they could help each other and learn from one another. So, when a trainee got stuck, another member of the group might say, "Hey, maybe she is reminding you of the time when your mother . . . . " If you make help trainees personalize the power issues of class, gender, or race, it makes the material much more live; it is much more likely to get integrated.

Shelley: How do you help trainees translate their understandings of gender, race, class, sexual orientation into their work with clients?

Betty: Monica McGoldrick and I have spent a lot of time talking about how to teach trainees to really talk to clients. Some of our thoughts are in the first chapter of our textbook, *The Expanded Family Life Cycle (Vol. 3)*(in press). The first point we wanted to make is that issues of race, gender, class, and sexual orientation are not just about differences between people. Rather, there are power hierarchies in which whites have more power than blacks, males more than females, heterosexuals more than gays and lesbians, and rich more than poor. We tried to teach trainees to address these issues with the power group because they are the ones with the problem. Gays and lesbians can tell you everything about homophobia because they are oppressed by it. But, they are not the ones with the problem. It is the same with racism. Why talk about racism with black clients? If you are white, for instance, they know more about racism than you do.

We tried to find ways to bring up these topics with clients of the power group *whether the issues are part of the presenting problem or not.* In other words, we believe that these issues exist for most people, and that they should be part of any thorough evaluation of a couple or a family. Therefore, we teach trainees how to talk about racism with whites, sexism with men, classism with rich people, and homophobia with heterosexuals.

Shelley: How do you teach the trainees to do this?

Marianne: We developed several specific questions that can be
              asked in evaluating a couple or family: What community
              groups do you belong to? Is there diversity of member-
              ship in these groups? If not, is that because of exclusion-
              ary policies or attitudes, and what are you doing about
              that? Do you belong to a church, temple, or other
              religious organization? If so, do you agree with their
              attitudes toward people of other religions? If not, why
              not? Do your children have friends of other racial and
              religious backgrounds? How are you teaching your chil-
              dren what they need to know about the rapidly increasing
              multi-culturalism in our society? I notice that your broth-
              er John has never married; do you think that he is gay? If
              he were gay, what would make it hard for him to tell the
              family? Or, to a man: How did you and your wife decide
              on the allocation of household chores? How did you and
              your wife decide who should cut back at work to do
              childcare? To another client: Are you ashamed of your
              son-in-law because he and his parents have less educa-
              tion and money than your family? To a privileged person:
              You have much more education, money, and social status
              than the average person; are you aware of the power that
              that gives you? How do you use it? Do you exercise this
              power to make a difference on the social and political
              issues that concern you? What would it take for you to
              make time to do something along these lines?

Shelley: These are very powerful questions that are rarely asked.

Betty: Very powerful. Monica and I talk about how to integrate
              gender, race, class sexual orientation with every case–not
              just when working with an inter-racial couple.

Shelley: How do your trainees respond to these ideas?

Betty: Trainees are typically intrigued. The most frequent ques-
              tion they ask is, "Aren't we dropping our agenda on
              these people?"

Shelley: What do you say to that?

Betty: I say that our agenda as therapists is the client's life. As therapists, we can raise any question we want to help them with their life. Of course, our theory allows us to include these kinds of questions because our goal is to help people have a better life. We do not have a theory that says, What is the problem; let's get to the solution. Some theories would not permit these kinds of questions because they are not as clearly focused on the presenting problem.

Shelley: When you can critically analyze these issues, you learn to manage your own privilege and your own power more effectively, which improves our life and other's lives?

Betty: Yes. Trainees will often respond by looking at their own life. In fact, there's always a lot of discussion about how they had not really thought about it like that before. They may recognize that their children go to a school where this is only white affluent children, and that they do not want that. They may recognize that they want their children to be friends with children of other races and circumstances. There may be discussion about how to go about changing that. So, the trainees are changing themselves as they try to work on these questions in therapy.

             I don't think many people use this kind of approach. I know Monica McGoldrick does it endlessly. But, I really haven't heard of others paying much attention to this. This is what I consider a complete integration. By the way, I heard that Ken Hardy's presentation at the recent *Networker* conference was inspirational for anyone looking for motivation to really get to work on these issues.

Shelley: Betty, what would you say are some of the current or future challenges for trainers and therapists in our field?

Betty: One of the most serious contemporary challenges of our time is related to managed care. The national ethos is about managing patients, not treating them, about money, not the necessary time for treatments, and about drugs and quick fixes, not the therapy process. For instance, I recently heard that at least several medical schools do not teach any form of psychological treatment anymore. They only focus on drug therapy. This national ethos provides a terrible context for family therapists to do our work, if we define our work as helping people to lead a better life. There is no motivation for helping people lead a better life in the national context. Rather, the motivation is to drug them. Did you ever see that cartoon on one-session of managed care therapy where the therapist is slapping the patient across the face, saying, "Snap out of it!" I used to have it on the wall at the Institute because it's funny, but also because it accurately reflects what the context is telling us. It tells us to just get them to snap out of it, shape up, get in line.

Shelley: And the quicker you get them to snap out of it, the better.

Betty: I think that our only hope is for family therapists to become more aware of how important it is–now more than ever–to commit ourselves to a continuation of our values and beliefs. Our only hope is for therapists to become aware of how much is going against them and what is going to happen if we don't commit ourselves.

The best way to pass these values along is in our training programs. We can't be afraid to do something that might be considered controversial or may cause a little bit of a stir. We have to do something besides business as usual.

Shelley: How would you help trainees prepare to deal with this national ethos?

Betty: I don't think that the national ethos can be totally ignored. We have to help trainees deal with it. For instance, at the Family Institute of Westchester where we worked from a long-term, Bowenian model, we did try to help trainees work in the managed care system. You can do anything you want in private practice, but we had a separate way of teaching how do our long-term therapy within the context of managed care. It may mean that you don't see clients every week; you may see them five or six times, but over a longer period of time. After that, you may see them two or three times a year. The Bowen type model of coaching people and send them out with homework fits well with meeting them once a month or so. In fact, it can be counter-productive to meet weekly. So, if you are working under managed care, you may get six sessions, but see your clients every two months–a year's worth of therapy.

Shelley: So, you help trainees bridge their model and managed care?

Betty: Yes. One thing we said over and over at the Institute was that managed care may change the format of what we are doing, but we cannot let managed care change our belief in what should be done to help people. We may have to figure out a way to bridge and maybe change the format, but we do not have to change our beliefs.

Shelley: Or lose our spirit.

Betty: That is the hard part–not to lose our spirit.

Shelley: Do you have any closing comments?

Betty: Only that training is a very important task. It is like having children and sending them forth. Training is a way that we impart what we have learned over the years and questions that have been raised to the next generation. It's generative. . . so that the next generation is better equipped to go forth and continue whatever work that the previous generation has been doing. I think that training should be taken very seriously. What are you teaching your children? Well, what are you teaching your trainees? Have you stopped to think about it recently?

Shelley: Betty, thank you for your thoughts on this topic. But

mostly, thank you for your incredibly significant contributions to the field over the years. You taught your
children well.

Peggy Papp

Shelley: As you reflect on the past twenty years as the field began
to recognize and grapple with the incorporation of gender,
culture, and power, what are your thoughts about the
field's development–particularly with regard to training?

Peggy: The field as a whole has come a long way–to say the
least. In the beginning of family therapy, there was no
attention paid to gender, class and ethnicity. The field was
focused on the interactional patterns within the family.
Attention was paid only to cycles of interaction, repetitious patterns, reciprocity, feedback–and how to stop
these cycles. These ideas had nothing to do with the
social or cultural context in which the family existed.
Recognition of the social or cultural context is new, occurring over the past 40 years. Feminists were greatly
responsible for first calling attention to the problems with
the concept of reciprocity. We also were the first to call
attention to the discrepancies in power, authority, and
status outside of the system.

Shelley: What is your assessment of where the field is now in
terms of these issues?

Peggy: I think that the field has changed substantially, but not
enough. There is much more to be done. The changes can
be evidenced in the fact that issues of gender, ethnicity,
and race are taken into account much more; they are now
becoming a part of every approach to therapy now raised
continually and are a part of every approach to therapy. I
also think that our world is shrinking; immigration from
country to country has increased enormously, which results in the falling away of many cultural taboos.

Shelley: What is an example of some of these taboos that are
being challenged?

Peggy: For instance, more and more people are daring to cross the boundaries of race, ethnicity, and class to enter into mixed marriages. As therapists, it is absolutely essential that we understand the potential conflicting beliefs of couples in mixed marriages. Often, therapists get stuck trying to resolve the couple's interactional patterns while ignoring the cultural differences in which the patterns are embedded. It is essential to distinguish between the content of the cultural material and the emotional dynamics. In general, this increased immigration leads us to confront differences of every kind on every level.

Shelley: Peggy, would you describe some of the practical ways in which you prepare therapists to recognize and attend to the cultural context in their work with families?

Peggy: First, I think that the way each therapist deals in training with these issues depends very much on the theoretical orientation from which they are working. In other words, if you are working structurally, experientially, Bowenian, from a brief therapy model, or with cognitive ideas, you will train very differently. Although you may be looking at the same issues, your approach in working with these issues will be very different. So, I can only talk about my approach.

Shelley: I think that people are very interested in learning about how others approach training. You have years and years of experience in training students, from which many of us could benefit. It would be wonderful to hear some of your ideas and strategies.

Peggy: Evan Imber-Black and I have been working together on developing ways to teach for about seven years. One exercise that we developed is the "Family of Origin Belief and Theme Exercise," which is published in *Family Process* (1996).[1] This exercise provides a starting point for helping raise the awareness of trainees by facilitating their thinking about their own cultural and gender beliefs and themes. This allows them to recognize their own beliefs, and then those of the families with whom they work. Here are some of the questions:

1. What dominate themes and beliefs about culture, religion, class, ethnicity from your family of origin still influence your life and relationships?
2. How do these beliefs and themes show themselves in your behavior and interactions with others today?
3. How have these beliefs and themes handicapped or enhanced your life?
4. How have you struggled to change or alter them?
5. How would your life be different if you responded differently to them?
6. How have other family members reacted to these?
7. Are these belief and themes that you would pass on to your children?

At the Ackerman Institute, I am the director of the Depression Project. As part of this project, we treat couples in which one spouse is depressed. Because we place special emphasis on gender differences in this work, we developed a gender awareness questionnaire for couples. We give this questionnaire to couples. Because I think that these questions are so important, I also give them to the trainees. Some of these questions are:

1. What were the messages you received from each of your parents about what kind of man or woman you should be?
2. What were the messages you received from each of your parents about marriage?
3. What kind of man or woman were you supposed to marry?
4. How have these ideas affected your relationship both positively and negatively?
5. What do you think the advantages or disadvantages would be if you would have been born the opposite sex?

Shelley: These are very thought provoking questions. How do you introduce and structure this exercise?

Peggy: First, I introduce trainees to my theoretical framework, which in based on looking at themes and beliefs in families and couples. After this introduction, I provide trainees with this exercise as something that they can do on their own.

Shelley: Afterward, do you discuss the exercise as a group?

Peggy: Yes, but only if people want to; it is totally voluntary. I ask the group if they have anything they would like to say about the effect of the questionnaire. I ask what their thoughts and feelings are about the questionnaire. I ask if it was helpful in trying to become aware of your own beliefs? I also ask if there are questions they would add to the questionnaire. We discuss how people become aware of personal beliefs that they were previously unaware, which is the purpose of the questionnaire.

Shelley: Is part of the goal to help therapists facilitate this process with their clients?

Peggy: Each therapist trains within her or his own model of therapy. In my sessions, I do not speak directly about these issues. I very seldom use the word gender. It is my awareness of these issues that influences the direction of therapy. When students observe me work, they often ask, "When are you going to deal with gender?" I respond that I *have* been dealing with gender. I learned long ago that it was not effective to say to clients, "Well, this seems to be a gender issue," and then relate the problem to the larger culture. The feedback that I got from clients was that they didn't want to talk about the larger culture–that they didn't want to be compared to other couples–that they are unique. So, I do not do that anymore. My intention in asking trainees to answer the questionnaire is to help them become aware of how their own beliefs have affected their lives and relationships. They then transfer this understanding into looking at couples within their context and learn to consider some of the clients' myths and beliefs in their therapy.

Shelley: You said that you do explicitly speak about gender or culture in your sessions. How do you address these issues?

Peggy: Let me give an example. In one family that I worked with, a woman was jealous of her brother because she felt he had been the preferred child in the family. She felt that her father favored her brother and that she was not nearly as important as her brother to him. This family was from an East European culture where males held a privileged position in families. The daughter and father had a very conflictual relationship; when I saw them for therapy, the relationship had been cut off and they were not speaking to one another. I got the daughter and father together. First, I helped her to express what was so hurtful and painful to her. I got the father to listen and to acknowledge the fact that he had treated her differently. I then helped her to be able to ask for what she wanted, which was to be treated like her brother. I worked with the father to treat her in a different way.

Shelley: Is there ever a point where you are asking the father if his cultural beliefs influenced the way in which he treated his children?

Peggy: Yes. I would ask questions, such as: What was it like for you when you were growing up? What country did you grow up in? What were the expectations for men and male and female children where you came from?

Shelley: And, these questions allow him to recognize his own cultural beliefs about gender.

Peggy: In one tape of my work that is often shown, I am seeing a couple in which the wife is from a working class New England family and her husband is from the Philippines.

They were both poets. The issues between them are class, gender, ethnicity, and religion. As a therapist, I believe I am mandated to help with the presenting problem, so everything I discuss is relevant to these problems. With this couple, the presenting problem was that in their four years of marriage, the husband had only worked for three months. She was furious about having supported him and taking all the responsibility in the relationship. He came from a very aristocratic, wealthy family in the Philippines, and as he put it, he had been pampered and had all of his needs taken care of. He did not have beliefs about work as Americans do. In her particular working-class New England family, there was an ethic where you worked hard for everything. His work ethic was that making a living was not what life is about; it was more important to write poetry. Another of his cultural beliefs was that you do not show your feelings or allow yourself to be vulnerable. His belief was that you remain inscrutable because otherwise people will take advantage of you. After clients identify beliefs like these, I never just leave it there. I ask how the beliefs are affecting the presenting problem, returning always to the presenting problem and work to resolve the problem. One of the rituals that I gave this couple was for them to create masks. Whenever she felt that he had a mask on, she was to go get the masks, put them on, and play with them. In this way, we took one of the symbolic beliefs and created a kind of playful ritual that debunks the belief.

Shelley: These examples provide good illustrations of how you address gender and cultural beliefs in therapy, and how you teach trainees to address these issues. Earlier, you said that how students train is dependent on their theoretical orientation. How do you teach students to integrate the organizing principles of gender, culture, and power into therapy models that may have been informed by problematic concepts, such as reciprocity? Do you see this as an issue?

Peggy: Gender and cultural biases of all kinds can be present or not present in any model, depending on how you use it. In other words, you can work from any model without having to use the part that is biased. The basic idea of systems, which informs the therapy models–is that no phenomena in the universe can be understood outside of its context. This premise is very consistent with feminist practices. It is the way that systems theory was applied to family therapy–specifically, the use of cybernetics language–where we went awry. Cybernetics is different from systems, and you can talk about systems without using cybernetic language. To me, systems theory means that you look at the total context of a person's life.

Shelley: Peggy, you recently edited a book, *Couples on the Faultline: New Directions for Therapists*, that addresses some of the challenges or issues that current and future trainers and therapists will be grappling with. Would you talk some about some of these challenges or issues?

Peggy: The book deals with the new issues of technology and time pressures that are confronting the field. It deals with the technological, biological, psychological revolutions that are occurring. The kind of problems that our field will be called upon to solve in the next few years will be absolutely mind-boggling; they simply stagger the imagination. With all the new discoveries in biology, we will be called upon to deal with questions about birth and death, issues related to fertility, cloning, and genetic testing. I think our field will be drastically changed in dealing with these issues. It will be an enormous challenge, but who is better prepared to deal with these issues than are family therapists? We are the most well prepared to deal these kind of problems because we think in terms of context, and there is no way we can deal with these problems without thinking in terms of the total context.

Shelley: What do you think we need to begin doing as trainers and therapists to prepare to deal with these problems?

Peggy: We should begin to become knowledgeable about other fields of thought, such as the advances that are being made in fertility or the understanding of how the brain functions. I think that it is our responsibility to become knowledgeable about these different fields of thought.

Shelley: And then there are new problems related to computers and the Internet.

Peggy: Yes, we do not even have language to talk about Internet affairs and computer addictions–two new symptoms. We are going to have to begin to deal with these new symptoms that are being brought into our offices as a result of the technological age.

Shelley: And time pressures.

Peggy: I think that until recently people ignored time pressure as being one of the major factors that interferes with intimacy. I think we are just beginning to deal with that.

Shelley: And, you believe that family therapists have a lot to offer in beginning to address these new areas.

Peggy: Yes, we are the ones that deal with context. You have to deal with context when you talk about these new developments; you can not just focus on trust, intimacy and closeness.

Shelley: In the early days of family therapy, we perceived our lens as relatively broad because we focused on the family rather than on just the individual. Then, with the contributions of feminist and multicultural scholars, we broadened our lens to include the cultural context. Now, are you talking about the need to broaden our lens again?

Peggy: Yes, I am. Over the years, the field of family therapy has been greatly influenced by the historical era–all of the cultural and social beliefs of the era to which it belonged. And now we are entering a new era to which we have to be responsive.

Shelley: As we close, are there any final comments that you have for trainers or therapists?

Peggy: If your work does not incorporate the total context of people's lives–if you deal just with micro interactions without addressing macro beliefs and expectations, you are missing the crux of the problem as well as tremendous resources that you can use to help your clients.

Shelley: Peggy, thank you for your thoughts during this interview. But, mainly, thank you for the many significant and on-going contributions that you have made to the field.

Olga Silverstein

Note: Olga Silverstein did not feel comfortable commenting on the topic of training because she has not actively participated in the training of family therapists for approximately six years and believes that the field has changed significantly during this time. Olga Silverstein has made incredibly significant and long-lasting contributions to our field and to the training of generations of therapists. Thank you, Olga.

NOTES

1. Papp, P. & Imber-Black, E. (1996). Family themes: Transmission and transformation. *Family Process*, 35(1), 5-20.

2. Papp, P. (2000). *Couples on the Faultline: New Directions for Therapists*. New York: Guilford Press.

Feminism, Moral Consultation, and Training

William J. Doherty

If feminism were just another competing clinical model, its impact could have been absorbed and tamed by the field of psychotherapy. If its claims were limited to the treatment of women in therapy, it could have been relegated more easily to a way to treat a portion of the population. The story of how feminist therapists introduced radical notions of social and political justice into the world of therapy has been often told. Less appreciated are the broader implications of feminism for the once-standard notion that therapists must separate moral sensibilities from their work.

As an offshoot of medicine, psychotherapy's traditional goal is to promote psychological and relational health. Health, in the standard way of thinking, is a value-free and morally-neutral idea, quite distinct from moral categories such as good and bad, or right and wrong, fairness and unfairness. Some feminist writings stayed within this health paradigm by stressing how traditional social structures and role patterns were harmful to women's psychological and economic well-being. But the feminist critique also embraced principles of justice or fairness in human relations–the idea that, as full human beings, women are entitled to all rights and opportunities given to men in the domestic and public spheres. Feminism's stance was not just a clinical

William J. Doherty, PhD, is affiliated with the Family Social Science Department, University of Minnesota, 290 McNeal Hall, St. Paul, MN 55108 (E-mail: Bdoherty @che1.che.umn.edu).

[Haworth co-indexing entry note]: "Feminism, Moral Consultation, and Training." Doherty, William J. Co-published simultaneously in *Journal of Feminist Family Therapy* (The Haworth Press, Inc.) Vol. 12, No. 2/3, 2001, pp. 151-156; and: *Integrating Gender and Culture in Family Therapy Training* (ed: Toni Schindler Zimmerman) The Haworth Press, Inc., 2001, pp. 151-156. Single or multiple copies of this article are available for a fee from The Haworth Document Delivery Service [1-800-342-9678, 9:00 a.m. - 5:00 p.m. (EST). E-mail address: getinfo@haworthpressinc.com].

appeal to more effective ways to help women be healthier, but also a profoundly moral appeal for therapists to redress inequities that women experience in private and public spheres.

Here is my main point: Although feminism is many things–a social movement, an epistemology, a political stance, an approach to therapy– at its heart is also a moral enterprise, a naming of what is unjust and a call to redress inequity. A feminist-informed therapy, therefore, must reject moral neutrality as a cornerstone in therapy. Once the Trojan Horse of women's moral claims is allowed inside the gates, the consequences extend beyond gender into the whole realm of human moral experience.

It is time to define my terms. In my book, *Soul Searching: Why Psychotherapy Must Promote Moral Responsibility* (Doherty, 1995), I defined the moral domain as "behavior that has consequences for the well-being of others." In these terms, morality is inherently interpersonal. Being gay or straight is not a moral matter, but how one treats one's sexual partners is a moral matter. Because so much therapy involves behavior that seriously affects the welfare of others, therapists cannot help but deal with morality.

But most therapists have been trained to steer away from moral language, even when clients raise it themselves. By moral language, I mean terms such as good and bad, right and wrong, fair and unfair, truthful and lying, should, owe, ought, and responsibility to others and to community. This language is the way that human beings deal with the moral realm of human life, the realm of what we owe others and how we treat them well or poorly. But most therapists have been trained to concentrate on the language of individual self-interest–what do you need to do for yourself?–and get nervous when the conversation turns to notions of obligations and responsibility to others. Relationships are seen as important, of course, as venues for personal fulfillment, but not necessarily as arenas for enacting responsibilities and obligations. The isolated self that many feminists have critiqued in mainstream psychotherapy is also the self-interested self. The relational world, especially in family life, brings obligations that transcend narrowly-defined self interest. When clients use the moral language of "I should," many therapists reframe it back into the more comfortable language of "I want" or "I need."

You cannot do feminist-informed therapy without an explicit way to work with the moral issues of justice and injustice. Feminism has shone an intense spotlight on how individual men and broader social structures have treated women unfairly–not just inappropriately, ineffectively, and insensitively, but wrongly. Sexual inequality is a moral evil, not just a political fact, because it robs women of their human rights and denigrates their human worth. Since no therapist can avoid dealing with these human realities, every therapist is a moral consultant who must confront what feminism has revealed about families and society.

What about the claim that therapists are not ethicists or clergy, and therefore should stay out of the morality business? In *Soul Searching,* I borrowed from the early feminist response to therapists who said that they don't see therapy as "political" and that they just treat "people" as opposed to seeing them as male or female. Feminists cogently argued that those who lack an explicit model for dealing with gender, power, and justice are inevitably enacting their implicit cultural model of gender inequality. Just as you cannot not communicate, you cannot not have a model for gender equity and power.

Extending this part of the feminist critique, I argued that therapists who claim to be value free and morally neutral are probably acting from the mainstream American cultural ethic of individual self-interest. In a capitalist society, pursuing personal goals as the highest end, as opposed to communal goals, is as normal as breathing air. When therapists focus narrowly on the question "What do you need to do for you?," they are masquerading as culture-free and morally neutral. It is a moral stance about the centrality of self-interest in human relations.

Once we realize that we are always dealing with moral issues in therapy, we can learn to deal with them well rather than poorly or unconsciously. Once we stop running from moral terms such as "fair," we can help couples process their division of labor not only in terms of a good bargaining process but also in terms of an equitable outcome for both parties. Sometimes this can mean systematically following up on the moral language of one of the partners when he or she raises it in therapy, as when someone says that their division of responsibilities for childcare is not fair. Other times it means introducing moral language when the moral domain is implicit in a conflict. An example is the case of a wife who was framing her requests for her husband's greater parenting responsibility (in working with the healthcare system on behalf of their chronically ill child) only in terms of him being more sensitive to her needs when she felt overwhelmed.

When I introduced the question of whether the current role arrange-
ment was fair, the conversation shifted from whether the husband was
"sensitive" enough to whether he was "carrying his weight in the
family." As a very large man, he was impressed enough by the challenge of this metaphor to get into motion and agreeing to handle all the
insurance hassles, an agreement that he followed through on. I have
found that many men respond better to the challenge of being fair, a
good team member who does his fair share, than just to the traditional
challenge of being more caring and sensitive.

I am suggesting that there is an organic connection between feminist-informed therapy and the broader model of moral consultation
that I have articulated in my work. The flow moves from a primary
focus on injustice to women to a general framework in which injustice, and other moral concerns, can be explored in all relationships
inside and outside the family–and in the community. In this broader
model, women's injustice to men and to other women can be the focus
of moral consultation, in addition to men's and society's injustice to
women. On the other hand, feminist-informed moral consultation
avoids the trap of equating all moral actions–for example, men's
physical abuse of women and women's physical abuse of men–and it
keeps in mind how micro-family behaviors are shaped by larger social
forces of inequality.

At the same time, a broader focus on moral accountability assures
that women are not excused for destructive behavior because they are
oppressed, a stance that infantalizes women by not seeing them as
moral agents responsible for their own actions. A blind spot for any
liberationist movement is the tendency to assign moral responsibility
to the members of the oppressor group and excuse moral lapses in
members of the oppressed group. John Red Horse, an American Indian family scholar and a founder of the American Indian Movement,
once said that in the 1960s he never saw a drunk Indian, only an
oppressed Indian. Now he sees oppressed Indians some of whom are
also drunk and responsible for getting sober and fighting the personal
and community problem of alcoholism.

Another connection between feminist therapy and a broader moral
consultation model lies in the domain of public action. A feminist-informed moral consultation model cannot focus only on the family. It
must examine three arenas neglected in most therapy models: the
influence of larger social forces on the problems of family life, the

ways in which men's and women's opportunities in the public domain influence their behavior in the family, and the role of women and men as citizens to name and take action on social and community problems. My own recent work, under the umbrella of the Families and Democracy Project, has focused on a model for thinking about families as citizens engaging in collective action in their communities (Doherty, 2000; Doherty & Beaton, 2000).

Everything I have written thus far has implications for training from the first day of graduate school, when we begin to define the "real" therapy issues versus the secondary concerns. When moral issues such as justice and community are left off the table at the beginning of training, they will always be add-ons. I believe we have to introduce the moral and community domains from the outset. I will end with more specific comments about the importance of developing skills in doing moral consultation.

I have found that it not difficult for students and trainees to grasp, at an intellectual level, the principles I have described here. Grappling with them personally and existentially, of course, takes more work. What is often missing is the development of the specific skills needed to do this work well. I sometimes refer to the "A or Z" approach that many therapists, including trainees, take to moral consultation. "A" means keeping your mouth shut and dealing with moral issues only in clinical terms or not at all. "Z" means telling people they are wrong and what they should be doing instead. In *Soul Searching,* I tried to lay out a more nuanced way of using moral discourse in therapy, one focusing on a continuum from validating and asking questions to identifying dilemmas and raising concerns, and finally to making direct challenges. Most moral consultation occurs at the less intense end of the continuum, but a skilled therapist can become more intense if necessary.

Students need these kinds of skills to go along with their moral, feminist, and clinical sensibilities. Here is a story of a student who got into trouble with her supervisor. She was seeing a woman in therapy who presented with a bizarre story. The client, her husband, and a woman who was their mutual best friend were enjoying a hot tub. The wife went inside to get soft drinks. When she returned, she found her husband and the other woman having sex in the hot tub. The wife was very upset, but her husband, over a period of days and weeks, kept telling her that she was the problem because of a lack of understanding of "how these things can happen." You see, she was repressed sexually and making too big a deal of this minor occurrence. After two sessions of individual therapy (the husband would not come to therapy because she was the problem, not him), during which the student therapist took a neutral stance (after all, the husband's story is just as valid as the wife's), the student could not stand it any more. She blurted out, "Do you think what he did was RIGHT?" The client was jolted out of her mystification and responded immediately with a resounding "NO! It was not right!" She regained her senses and began to face the problems in her marriage to this man. But the student later was confronted by her supervisor about taking a "moralistic" stance and bringing her "personal" values into therapy.

I'm afraid that there are still a lot of supervisors like this student's. But I suggested to the student that that her contribution to getting into trouble was that she "blurted" instead of having a thought-through, modulated response. She had good moral sensibilities, in my view, but could have eased into the moral issue, still helped her client, and perhaps stayed on the good side of her supervisors. (Example of a question: "Do you ever think about what your husband did in moral terms, about whether it was right or wrong?") The supervisor might still have had a problem with this, but I told the student that supervisors are almost guaranteed to challenge "blurting" behavior by trainees.

In sum, the challenge in training for feminist-informed moral consultation is to combine consciousness, cultural criticism, moral sensitivity, community awareness, and good practical skills to make it all work in the heat of the therapeutic crucible where healing and change occur. No small challenge, but an exciting way to integrate one's full personhood with the work of therapy, instead of checking one's moral life at the office door.

REFERENCES

Doherty, W. J. (1995). *Soul Searching: Why Psychotherapy Must Promote Moral Responsibility.* New York: Basic Books.

Doherty, W. J. (in press). Family science and family citizenship: Towards a model of community partnership with families. *Family Relations.* Vol. 49(3), July 2000, 319-325.

Doherty, W. J., & Beaton, J. M. (Sum 2000, 149-161). Family therapists, community, and civic renewal. *Family Process.*

When a Family Therapist Goes Pop

David MacPhee
Toni Schindler Zimmerman
Shelley A. Haddock

M. T. Joiner is eager to see the first clients of his budding family therapy career. He diligently prepared for this milestone in his training program by reading all of the in-vogue books on relationships: *Men Are from Mars, Women Are from Venus, The Rules,* and *How to Satisfy a Woman,* among others. Just in case a parenting issue came up in a session, he read James Dobson's *Dare to Discipline.*

Mr. and Mrs. Smith are seeing M. T. because they have been arguing about a number of issues, particularly how work and family responsibilities are apportioned. Gloria thinks that Jim should be doing more of the housework and should be more emotionally available to their daughter. Jim thinks that Gloria is too wrapped up in her job as a writer.

We join the session in progress . . .

Gloria: All I said was, "Could you take out the trash?"

David MacPhee is a Full Professor in the Human Development & Family Studies Department, Colorado State University, Fort Collins, CO 80523.

Toni Schindler Zimmerman is Director of the Marriage & Family Therapy Program and Associate Professor in the Human Development & Family Studies Department, Colorado State University.

Shelley A. Haddock is an Instructor and Clinical Supervisor, Marriage & Family Therapy Program, Department of Human Development & Family Studies, Colorado State University.

[Haworth co-indexing entry note]: "When a Therapist Goes Pop." MacPhee, David, Toni Schindler Zimmerman, and Shelley A. Haddock. Co-published simultaneously in *Journal of Feminist Family Therapy* (The Haworth Press, Inc.) Vol. 12, No. 2/3, 2001, pp. 157-161; and: *Integrating Gender and Culture in Family Therapy Training* (ed: Toni Schindler Zimmerman) The Haworth Press, Inc., 2001, pp. 157-161. Single or multiple copies of this article are available for a fee from The Haworth Document Delivery Service [1-800-342-9678, 9:00 a.m. - 5:00 p.m. (EST). E-mail address: getinfo@haworthpressinc.com].

M. T.: That explains a lot. You see, a leading expert, John Gray, says that women shouldn't be too demanding and should be cautious to use proper wording when making requests.[1] One of the secrets to asking a man for support is to say: "*Would* you take out the trash?," not "*Could* you take out the trash?"

Gloria: What? So you're saying that if only I said "would" instead of "could" that Jim would get off his lazy butt and do five minutes of chores?

M. T.: Well, there is a little bit more to it than that. But, saying "would" instead of "could" really is important so that you don't insult him or turn him off.[1] There is a real danger of pushing for change on Jim's part because it sends the message that he is "broken." [1] As John Gray says, the secret to empowering a man is never to try to change him or improve him.[1]

Gloria: Are you nuts?? What are we doing in therapy if Jim's not contributing his share to housework and childcare is just peachy? How do you expect this relationship to get any better? I'm supposed to just resign myself to doing it all?

Jim: Now, wait a minute . . . .

M. T.: I'm not really saying things can't improve, but it may help if you first focus on appreciating the favors that Jim already does for you, like fixing things around the house.[1] Then, I would recommend that–for three months–you practice asking correctly for those things that Jim already does for you.[1] Once you've got that down, you would be ready to risk asking Jim do to more–as long as you can graciously accept his declines.[1]

Jim: Now, wait a minute. Do you think men are so fragile that they can't handle a request?

M.T.:   I'm just saying that if Gloria can change . . . .

Gloria: So you're saying that all of the burden is on me to fix this marriage?

M. T.: Not entirely. There are some things that Jim can do, too. (Turning to Jim) For example, when Gloria becomes really upset for no reason[1]–like right now, for instance–she might get volatile and irrational. John Gray calls it "going to the well." At these times, one helpful strategy is for you to appear like you are listening.[1] It helps defuse things.

Jim: What do you mean–*appear* to be listening?

M. T.: For example, hang in there for awhile, like maybe five minutes of being a good listener. Look in her direction. Zip it up; don't say anything. Nod your head. Make Venusian noises like, "uh huh" or "Oh, really!"[1]

Jim: Sort of like a Sensitive New Age Guy on the outside but same old Privileged White Male on the inside?

Gloria: (Looking stunned) You must be joking.

M. T.: No, really. John Gray says that Martians get more sex if they can get their wives talking. What better way to get Venus' juices flowing than to be a good listener?[1]

Gloria: Tell you what, I've had about enough of this b.s.

M. T.: Honest! And these experts also say that another secret to rekindling your passion is to put your best face forward. You know, wear make up (even when you go jogging), tint your hair.[2] Maybe you'd have more passion if you got a nose job or paid more attention to appearance. [2]

Jim: I like the way Gloria looks . . . I just wish we had more time together–she's always working.

Gloria: Well, I would have more time with you if you'd do your share of the housework and childcare. I never get any recognition at home for being good at my career. I mean, here I am, this well-known author, and Jim sees me as a maid and escort service.

M. T.: Tsk, *big* mistake. In the book, *The Rules*, the authors say that men need to take charge. The worst thing you can do, Gloria, is to overwhelm him with your career triumphs.[2] Try to let him shine. He needs to take the lead, just like in ballroom dancing, or you'll fall over your feet.[1]

Gloria: (Sarcastically) Okay, I'm starting to get the picture. So instead of me being from Venus and him being from Mars, I'm supposed to be this minor asteroid orbiting around Jim's sun, right? Protect his fragile male ego, huh?

M. T.: (A little worried) You don't need to get so hostile. I'm just telling you what the experts recommend. You need to respect these inherent differences between men and women.[1] Let me give you another example. When a man is stressed, he needs to withdraw from relationships and go to his "cave." When he comes home, he wants to relax and unwind by quietly reading the news. He doesn't want to talk about what's bothering him. If he is really stressed, he needs to do something challenging like climb a mountain.[1]

Jim: Speak for yourself! This cave sounds like it would make things worse.

M. T.: John Gray says it's important for men to go to their cave. Otherwise, when she opens up and shares more intimate feelings, it may actually trigger your instinctual need to pull away.[1] John Gray likens it to a rubber band–men's alarm bells go off when women try to get close and they don't get enough time in their cave. Gloria, you can't really expect Jim to help out around the house when he needs to retreat to his cave to recover from a hard day's work. You need to be real careful about knocking on the cave door to ask for help because the dragon inside might burn you.[1]

Gloria: That's it! You go to your damn cave! We're out of here!

Later, on his drive home, M. T. ruminated about the session. Why was it such an utter disaster? His supervisor hadn't prepared him for the possibility that a client would storm out of a session. Why had Gloria seemed so angry and resistant but Jim so confused and insulted?

For solace, he tuned into Dr. Laura Schlessinger's radio program. A miracle had happened; she was confessing the 11th Stupid Thing That She Had Done: Put Down Feminists. [3] She finally realized that she may not even be in the position to have a radio show as an independent entrepreneur if her foremothers hadn't fought for women's rights. In hindsight, she saw that by putting down feminists (and the many others she puts down, like working moms and same-sex marriages . . .), she may actually be hurting relationships and families.

With a jolt, M. T. realized that he too might be hurting families. He decided to turn off Dr. Laura (and Rush Limbaugh and . . .) and begin reading professional *and* popular literature that had been *recommended* to him by the feminist supervisors in his training program. He tuned into National Public Radio, and drove straight to the bookstore.[4]

NOTES

1. Gray, J. (1992). *Men Are from Mars, Women Are from Venus: A Practical Guide for Improving Communication and Getting What You Want in Your Relationships.* New York: Harper Collins.

2. Fein, E., & Schneider, S. (1996). *The Rules: Time Tested Secrets for Capturing the Heart of Mr. Right.* Warner.

3. Schlessinger, L. C. (1995). *Ten Stupid Things Women Do to Mess Up Their Lives.* New York: Harper.

4. Zimmerman, T.S., Holm, K., and Starrels, M. (in press). A feminist analysis of self-help bestsellers for improving relationships: A decade review. *Journal of Marriage and Family Therapy.*

A Movie Review
of Will, Cole and Kate

Frank Pittman

Popular media provides situations and scenarios that illustrate
wide-spread themes, problems, and perspectives in our culture.
In examing these situations and scenarios, one is able to evaluate
larger social metaphors. Additionally, these larger social metaphors shape and inform the ways in which we think about our
lives and relationships.

Frank Pittman has used popular mediums, primarily movies
and plays, as tools in training and therapy and to illustrate con-
tempory issues. In utilizing popular media, Pittman has been able
to tap into larger social metaphors that inform all of us: therapists, clients, and trainees.

–Toni Schindler Zimmerman

We need plays, movies, operas and the like so we can watch other
people's lives going on and learn how to do it right and how to do it
wrong. We need to watch life on stage because it is not polite to stare

Frank S. Pittman, MD, is a psychiatrist and family therapist in private practice in
Atlanta. He is the author of four books, and, since 1983, the movie columnist for the
Family Therapy Networker.

Address correspondence to: Suite 543, 960 Johnson Ferry Road, NE, Atlanta, GA
30342-1624.

[Haworth co-indexing entry note]: "A Movie Review of Will, Cole and Kate." Pittman, Frank. Co-published simultaneously in *Journal of Feminist Family Therapy* (The Haworth Press, Inc.) Vol. 12, No. 2/3, 2001,
pp. 163-169; and: *Integrating Gender and Culture in Family Therapy Training* (ed: Toni Schindler Zimmerman) The Haworth Press, Inc., 2001, pp. 163-169. Single or multiple copies of this article are available for a
fee from The Haworth Document Delivery Service [1-800-342-9678, 9:00 a.m. - 5:00 p.m. (EST). E-mail
address: getinfo@haworthpressinc.com].

163

at real people leading real lives. The theater, and for the past century the movies, offer us our best chance, short of actually being a therapist, to stare and snoop at other people's lives.

But the experience of sitting in the audience and watching other people act out life's experiences and dilemmas is not the end of the process. The experience is not complete until the review is written and read. Criticism permits us to communicate with one another what we see in our shared experience of other people's lives and what we thus find provoked and illuminated within ourselves.

Harold Bloom, chronicler of the *Western Canon*, credits Shakespeare with *The Invention of the Human*, creating characters who have powers of their own and are not merely puppets in theological or, for that matter, sociological or psychological morality tales, batted about by various types of gods and devils. Instead Shakespeare, in the English renaissance of Good Queen Bess, created characters who could make life choices, reflect upon them and even soliloquize, learning and empowering themselves through self-examination and self-analysis. Shakespeare's characters change, not just in response to the things that other people do to them, but because of their own assessment of the choices they make.

Shakespeare's men are more fully human than any characters who had gone before. Hamlet, Falstaff, Prince Hal and Lear bleed, sweat and cry. That astonishing quartet notwithstanding, Shakespeare's women characters, i.e., Juliet, Cleopatra, Lady Macbeth, Gertrude, Viola, Portia, Rosalind, and Lear's daughters, could be, like Shakespeare's Queen, as powerful and complex as his men. Only a few, perhaps Desdemona and Ophelia, are too cowed by their love for abusive madmen to control their own fates.

The first of his great women characters is Katherina, the eponymous Shrew who is in need of "taming." Will's model was surely his Queen, who refused to marry but kept a stable of suitors and from time to time beheaded one of them (as her father had done her mother.) *The Taming of the Shrew* is a busy comedy, with disguises, mistaken identities and tiresome time fillers. Its only interest is in the central relationship between a man and a woman and, above all, a woman who, like his Queen, is determined not to marry.

In *Taming*, an arrogant Veronese blowhard named Petruchio has come to wive it wealthily in Padua and chooses as his booty the notoriously ill-tempered but well-endoweried termagant Katherina, who is depressively motherless and scorned by the father who adores her simperingly obedient sister Bianca. Kate announces, as she throws pots and pans, that "I hate men."

Everyone in Padua fears Katherina, except Petruchio, who is too cockily insensitive to know the meaning of the word fear. Petruchio's fearlessness catches her fancy. Even as she continues to bop him over the head with flower pots, she notices whether they hit the mark or not. She submits to a marriage to him, when she clearly has it within her power to refuse the coercion. And she is appalled and humiliated when he seems first to jilt her and then to demonstrate his control of her by dragging her out of her wedding reception. He carries his battling bride to his villa and starves her, declaring that none of the food is good enough for her, while throwing all the plates and pots around the room. He matches her storminess, but claims the most loving intent.

Petruchio sets out "to kill a wife with kindness." Kate storms and hits and kicks and throws things–the techniques that enabled her to terrorize her father's house and all of Padua, but they have no effect here. Petruchio can be as stormy as Kate herself, though he is careful not to resort to violence. Petruchio's approach somewhat resembles that of Annie Sullivan in taming Helen Keller in *The Miracle Worker.*

After several more acts of their battling, Kate catches on to how the game is played and proves a champion at it. In the last scene Petruchio and Katherina return to Padua and Petruchio is able to win a wager by demonstrating his bride's tameness. She takes the stage for half a page sounding for all the world like Phyllis Shafly and Marabel Morgan as she floridly apologizes for women who are not so subservient, or at least so wise and secure as to know when to appear subservient: "I am sorry women are so simple to offer war where they should kneel for peace." Petruchio shouts, "Why there's a wench. Come on and kiss me Kate." To the other wedding guests it might appear that Petruchio has won the power struggle, but to the audience it is clear that Kate has learned to play a more complex game and is full partner to a delicate balance. These domestic warriors may be the happiest Shakespearean couple short of the Macbeths.

I've seen the last scene played in different ways. Kate can recite her lecture with venomous sarcasm, acknowledging defeat but announcing a plot for revenge. Or she can do it conspiratorially, either by conspiring with Petruchio to help him best his fellows or by conspiring with the other women to bond in their contempt for men who would be doltish enough to think the final speech was being given straight.

In the spectacular and lively 1966 Zeffirelli film, Elizabeth Taylor and Richard Burton, fresh from *Who's Afraid of Virginia Woolf?*, are the battling couple and Taylor gives the last speech straight. Taylor's Kate falls in love with Burton's blustering and clearly vulnerable Petruchio as soon as she sees his boldness, is further enamored by the energy he throws into the relationship, and will do anything for him, except let him relax. She delivers the final speech humbly and lovingly, but with great strength and authority. Shakespeare, whoever and whatever he was, was not a romantic and I don't think he would have been satisfied with this sappily offensive conclusion. Kate must not sue for peace until she is affirmed as an equal partner.

No one has been quite so unromantic as songwriter Cole Porter in sophisticatedly acknowledging the pleasure, the pain and, above all, the impermanence of romantic love. He had a field day (and his greatest success) with *Taming of the Shrew* in 1948's *Kiss Me Kate*. Sam and Bella Spewack wrote the book, and turned Shakespeare's story into a play within a play, as a battling divorced couple, Fred Graham and Lilli Vanessi, come reluctantly together to play the well cast leads of *Taming of the Shrew* and to spar both on and off the stage. Lilli has a Hollywood career, a rich, and powerful fiancé, and a load of resentment about Fred's betrayals of their marriage and her love, while Fred has an inventory of failed ambitions and a brainless, tap dancing girlfriend who plays the more agreeable sister Bianca. Lilli and Fred are big egos who just like to show off.

Porter wrote both the irritatingly catchy music (it won't get out of your head or your feet after it's supposed to be over) and the magically clever and unendingly cynical lyrics, stuffed with double entendre, including "Why Can't You Behave?," "I'm Always True to You Darling in My Fashion," "Where Is the Life of Late I Led" and "Too Darn Hot." A pair of gangsters (don't ask) stop the show with "Brush Up Your Shakespeare." Porter's rhymes are outrageous, including "I hate men! I can't even stand them now and then," "I'd even give up coffee for Sanka, even Sanka, Bianca, for you" and "If you think his behavior is heinous, kick him right in the Coriolanus."

From the beginning, *Kiss Me Kate* was a bit of a shocker. At the end of Act One, after Kate has kicked, hit, bit and broken flowerpots over the head of Petruchio, and has stepped out of character in order to punish him for his latest dalliance, he unscriptedly throws her over his knee and spanks her. It is startling, and unShakespearean, but much in the spirit of the ever so slightly misogynist Cole Porter, who saw no evidence that men had the upper hand with women. (We may hear Cole Porter sung as love songs by Ella Fitzgerald, with that honeyed voice, impeccable diction, controlled emotions, and total respect. But Porter had a bite and a sting to his music. He was gay and married to a rich older woman; he was, by this time in his life, an invalid in constant pain; and he had had little but failures for quite a while. His bitterness and powerlessness are inseparable from his sophistication.)

Kiss Me Kate was a huge success on Broadway in 1948 (the year also of *Death of a Salesman* and *South Pacific*.) Five years later it was a movie with the absurdly pretty soprano Katherine Grayson, who could warble in ranges only dogs could hear, the big, leering, but ever-swaggering baritone Howard Keel and, as the ingenue, long-stemmed tap dancer Ann Miller, who gets to spin with, among others, a juvenile Bob Fosse. The film has many pleasures, but was filmed in 3-D and has the cast throwing things at the audience from time to time. The pacing for the non-musical moments is off. Grayson never understood comedy, Keel never understood subtlety, and Miller is merely loud and twitchy when her feet are standing still. The ending is dreadful. The tiny Kate does not sing her apology for her gender, but recites a bit of it and then puts herself in Keel's enormous hands. He carries her around like a doll as the curtain falls. I can not imagine that Shakespeare wanted Petruchio to abuse or dominate Kate or for Kate to surrender to him.

Kiss Me Kate has finally gotten a full scale revival on Broadway and is once again a huge hit, with minimal reshuffling and without any softening of the script to make it less offensive to the delicacies of current gender sensibilities (as was done recently with *Annie Get Your Gun* and its portrayal of Native Americans.) With a wonderfully versatile realistic backstage set, an aptly silly Paduvan set, and a cast of dancers, it moves briskly and is surely the liveliest, fastest evening of theater in memory. The stars are from *Ragtime*, energetic Marin Mazzie as Kate and dashing, blustering Brian Stokes Mitchell as Petruchio. Mazzie has a great emotional range, an appealing presence, and intermittent control over her unshakeable power. Mitchell has a beautiful baritone and cuts an appealing figure. He's slim, boyish and vulnerable; it is hard to find any menace in him and his efforts to tame his shrew don't feel threatening to anyone except himself. Lilli is in no danger from this guy and she knows it.

Those who dedicate themselves to finding abuse in relationships can certainly find it in either *The Taming of the Shrew* or *Kiss Me Kate*. Abuse requires a power differential and while Kate, in her day, has to fight for her power, Lilli does not. On almost any level, Lilli is the more powerful member of the team (she's a movie star, he's just a flailing, posturing stage wannabe) and she has an even more powerful partner waiting in the wings (in this version her fiancé is a Douglas MacArthurish general, currently running for President). Lilli is by far the louder, the more insulting, the more violent. She's also the one who is aware of the intricacies and pitfalls of the relationship. And Fred is the one who is trying to make it work. She punishes him for the rest of the play for spanking her after her assault on him in Act One, and thereby gets him under good enough control to risk taking him back. (Of course, her militaristic fiancé is even more patriarchal than Fred and presents a real, rather than metaphoric threat to marital equality.)

When, in the last scene, Lilli comes back to Fred and plays out her "women are so simple" scene, she seems to be acknowledging her awareness of his vulnerability and his great need for her. She is protecting his ego. And she is cutting the deal that they will treat one another with great respect, as strong allies must. At the end of her speech, she winks at the rest of us and gets down on her knees to Fred. Fred, not seeing the wink, gets down on his knees too, and supplicates himself even more to her. They compete to see who can be most humbly committed to the other.

Lilli's reversal did not come about because Lilli finally understood Kate, the difference between her situation and Kate's, and the nature of relationships between men and women. Instead it came about because she understood and loved Fred, and his adorable deficiencies. The in love state is generally considered a justification for essentially any self-sacrificial or idiotic course of action. When people tell me they are doing what they are doing because of in loveness, it hits me the same as if they had told me the voices told them to do it. I'd sure prefer for people to test it out, think it out and work it out.

Love may be enough for Lilli and Fred, whose power isn't threatened by it. It is not so easy for Kate and Petruchio. While Petruchio has little at stake (he doesn't really need Kate or her money, hasn't really noticed her as a person, and in marrying her at all is merely doing something akin to marital sky diving), Kate is the only character about whom we can be concerned. She's not very nice and is far more abusive than Petruchio, but she has more at stake. Most women, in those days, did not rule the world, and while marriage brought them the closest they could come to equality with a man, they had a hard time controlling their marital choices or their domestic situation, except by threatening to make a man's life hell. Kate's shrewishness has kept her from being married off as a piece of property. It has the same function as Sleeping Beauty's bramble thicket or Brunnhilde's magic fire: it keeps all but the bravest suitors away. Unfortunately, it is an exhausting posture to maintain, and creates intense self-loathing.

Kate's hero (and, in his willingness to endure the indignities of tussling with her, Petruchio is indeed her hero and ours) must recognize that she can inflict pain upon him if the relationship slips away from a bearable degree of equality. Kate knows her power comes from her freedom to be unpleasant. Once Petruchio knows that, she's relatively safe. Kate and Petruchio win once they know that each has a stinger. In domestic battles, whether in the 16th century or today, either both partners win or both lose.

Kate and Petruchio have learned that. While Lilli sweetly and protectively "submits" to the pathetic Fred, who responds by groveling at her feet, it must be the newly empowered Kate who gives that great, liberating wink to the audience. She and Petruchio have cut a deal to respectfully and lovingly fear one another, but Kate has not given up one iota of her sting–and Petruchio knows it. I think she tamed him pretty well and can now relax and enjoy the spoils of her victory. I think he understands that. It all seems O.K. to me. Now, if I could only stop my toes from tapping.

Experiencing Feminist
Family Therapy Supervision

Anne Prouty

SUMMARY. Although feminists have been writing about and practicing feminist family therapy for over twenty years, writing about feminist family therapy supervision has been limited to a few in-depth personal designs and Avis' (1986) Delphi study. This article reports on a portion of the findings of a larger study of feminist supervision. The sixteen participants described their therapist-supervisor relationship to be the heart of their supervision experience, the center point from which the supervision derived meaning. When asked if they thought they focused on anything that they would call feminist, supervisors and therapists described issues that fell into the following areas: gender, power, diversity and emotion. These results are reviewed within the context of the feminist family therapy supervision literature and with suggestions for their use. *[Article copies available for a fee from The Haworth Document Delivery Service: 1-800-342-9678. E-mail address:<getinfo@ haworthpressinc.com>Website:<http://www.HaworthPress.com> © 2001 by The Haworth Press, Inc. All rights reserved.]*

KEYWORDS. Feminist family therapy, clinical supervision, gender, power, diversity, emotion, supervision relationship

---

Anne Prouty, PhD, is Assistant Professor, Family Therapy Center, Virginia Tech, Blacksburg, VA 24061-0515. The author extends her respect and appreciation to the sixteen participants; the feminist interpretive team: Dr. Karen B. Helmeke and Ms. Mary Beth Stibbins; and her doctoral dissertation committee, especially Dr. Janie Long. The author enjoyed working together immensely. The author would also like to thank Dr. Judy Myers-Avis for inspiration, and for help with the preliminary methodology for this study.

[Haworth co-indexing entry note]: "Experiencing Feminist Family Therapy Supervision." Prouty, Anne. Co-published simultaneously in *Journal of Feminist Family Therapy* (The Haworth Press, Inc.) Vol. 12, No. 4, 2001, pp. 171-203; and: *Integrating Gender and Culture in Family Therapy Training* (ed: Toni Schindler Zimmerman) The Haworth Press, Inc., 2001, pp. 171-203. Single or multiple copies of this article are available for a fee from The Haworth Document Delivery Service [1-800-342-9678, 9:00 a.m. - 5:00 p.m. (EST). E-mail address: getinfo@haworthpressinc.com].

171

EXPERIENCING FEMINIST FAMILY
THERAPY SUPERVISION

Feminists (Avis, 1987; Goldner, 1991; Goodrich, Rampage, Ellman & Halstead, 1988; Hare-Mustin, 1978,1987; Hare-Mustin & Merecek, 1986; Libow, 1986; Roberts, 1991; and Storm, 1991), have been critiquing and reconstructing family therapy practice and training for almost 25 years. Ault-Riche (1988), Avis and Braverman (1994), and Wheeler, Avis, Miller and Chaney (1986) have proposed strong theoretical models of feminist informed family therapy supervision, based on their extensive experience providing therapy and training clinicians. However, we have yet to establish a formal research base. What does feminist family therapy supervision look like in practice? How are our feminisms (Avis, 1987) lived by clinicians, trainers and supervisors? How is feminist supervision experienced by the therapists with whom we work? In an effort to begin to fill that gap in our literature, I undertook a preliminary study of feminist supervision.

LITERATURE REVIEW

Feminist Supervision Theory in Family Therapy

In order to try to minimize my preconceived notions about what the participants would say, I kept the formal literature review until after I had interpreted the results of the study. Keeping in mind that I deliberately did not review the literature until after gathering my data–but that it had been read by many of the participants–let us briefly review the main points of three foundational models of feminist supervision. I review them in the order in which they were published, as that is the way the participant supervisors probably read them. To forgo redundancy, I've chosen to keep a review of a majority of the writing about feminist family therapy training and supervision literature for the discussion section.

In 1986, Wheeler and her colleagues published their article "Rethinking Family Therapy Training and Supervision: A Feminist Model." So new and important was their work that they revised and republished the work again in 1989. A new vision had come for marriage and family therapy (MFT) supervision. Their model emphasized using a feminist lens and living one's feminist values within our work as trainers. The personal had become the political within MFT. They proposed that the supervisor's *attitude* was a key component, in that she or he must take a positive and non-oppressive view of women and understand women's different experiences of gender and power. They suggested that supervisors' understandings should be expressed verbally and by example within the training. Wheeler and her colleagues said feminist supervision would minimize hierarchy through the use of such tools as contracting, shared evaluation, and the use of uncomplicated language. Social analysis would be used to clarify and politicize therapeutic issues, so as to connect what was going on in therapy to societal norms and prejudices. Their feminist supervision also included training therapists to provide feminist family therapy, which emphasized therapists' acquisition of feminist conceptual and executive skills. These skills fell into three categories: (a) skills for developing and maintaining a working alliance between the family and the therapist; (b) skills for defining the problem; and (c) skills for facilitating change. All three categories emphasized the roles of gender and power within relationships, families, and therapy, and taught the therapist to attend to these issues.

Two years later, in 1988, Ault-Riche published her article "Teaching an Integrated Model of Family Therapy: Women as Students, Women as Supervisors." Her model of supervision proposed a "continuum of emphasis on gender issues" (p. 175) that trained therapists to work with explicit and implicit interventions within an integrated model that included behavioral, emotional and cognitive therapies. Ault-Riche also talked about supervisors' internalized sexism and the need to examine their own experiences with sexist socializing forces. As a method of identifying and working with internalized sexism, she provided family of origin and personal evaluative exercises for supervisors. Ault-Riche was also one of the first feminists in family therapy to talk about the supervisor's experiences with sexism and other issues of discrimination in the work place, and about interpersonal challenges for women in positions of authority. Ault-Riche provided feminist family therapy with an apprenticeship model, as she emphasized the importance of supervisors modeling how to be competent, sensitive, and compassionate feminist family therapy professionals.

In that same year Goodrich and her colleagues (1988) published their book, *Feminist Family Therapy: A Casebook*, in which they outlined requisites for feminist training of MFT. They emphasized a feminist informed training context that would include women in authority positions, opportunities for therapists to learn about feminist theories, and promotion of self-examination around gender roles. Within supervision itself, they emphasized respect as reflected in the supervisor's clarity, support of the therapist's individual growth, willingness to hear different opinions, and for collaboration. They also stated the importance of supervisors attending to sexual politics, not only within the training context but also within the supervision relationship.

Previous Research of Feminist Family Therapy Supervision

Prior to the present project, there had been only one study of feminist family therapy supervision. In 1986, Avis performed a Delphi study to obtain the opinions of prominent feminist family therapists about what feminist family therapy training and supervision should include. Her panel of experts identified major teaching methods, supervisory processes, and reading resources relevant to the training and supervision of a feminist-informed approach to family therapy. In addition, Avis examined differences between feminist-informed and more traditional supervisory relationships, and identified family therapy training methods considered feminist. Most important to the present research, Avis' (1986) panel agreed that feminist supervision involved constantly questioning assumptions, considering alternatives, openly discussing sexist remarks, talking about attitudes concerning healthy family functioning, and making issues of power explicit. The panel proposed that feminist supervisors shared and modeled their feminist awareness, minimized competitiveness among trainees, addressed personal and political issues, and helped trainees learn about themselves without turning supervision into therapy. Finally, the panel thought that feminist supervisors helped therapists to develop their own style and techniques based on their strengths.

Avis' (1986) groundbreaking study told us what feminist family therapists thought feminist supervision *should* be. However, years later, there had been no studies describing what feminist family therapy supervisors *actually did*. This gap in the literature was the impetus for my study of feminist family therapy supervision.

METHODS

I adopted a collaborative, qualitative research process in order to minimize potential power differentials between the participants and the researcher. Based on the experiences reported by the participants, my feminist interpretive team and I built a model of feminist supervision that was consistent with feminist ideals and empirically rooted in the data. Grounded theory provided a framework for data collection and analysis (Glaser & Strauss, 1967; Strauss, 1987; Strauss & Corbin, 1990). Equally important, grounded theory supported my feminist values of: (a) giving voice to feminists about their ideas; (b) gathering knowledge from several different perspectives, including those with less power; and (c) reducing the power of a single researcher and increasing the power of the study (via multiple perspectives) through collaboration with the participants and a team of feminist colleagues.

Participants

I used criterion selective sampling (Rafuls & Moon, 1996) to contact people by telephone who identified themselves as feminists and who were also AAMFT approved supervisors, then I recruited one current therapist who was currently being supervised by each supervisor. Supervisors were contacted from coast to coast all over the United States and in a few places in Canada. Hereafter, I will use "participants" to refer collectively to both supervisors and therapists. In the end, there were eight supervision sites, which each included one supervisor and one therapist. Although the supervisors worked in various professional settings, five therapists were from a master's program practicum, one was in a private practice, one in a post-master's practicum, and one in a doctoral practicum. All participants' identities were kept confidential.

The therapists averaged 3.1 years (range 1-7) and the supervisors averaged 13.8 years (range 1-22) in MFT practice. There were seven female supervisors, one male supervisor, five female therapists, and three male therapists. Supervisors had been AAMFT approved for an average of 6.2 years, ranging from 6 months to 12 years. The ages of the therapists ranged from 23 to 55 and the supervisors' ranged from 33 to 47. Some therapists had experience doing other types of psychotherapy prior to their MFT training. Two of the therapists had new family therapy approved supervisor or supervisor-in-training credentials–which they both said provided them with a more informed perspective than they might otherwise have had. Although attempts were made to recruit Canadians and participants of color, the sample was limited to those who returned my calls, agreed to participate, and were currently supervising at least one therapist. The participants in this study were all United States citizens, were currently residing in six different states (in the western, mid-western, north atlantic, and south eastern regions of the country), and all were white–although they reported proximal ancestors from countries in Asia and Europe, and self-identified themselves as Jewish, Christian, or Agnostic.

Quality Assurance. To enhance the quality of the data and the credibility of the study, the data were triangulated at three levels to increase the internal validity, confirmability, and dependability (Denzin, 1978; Marshall & Rossman, 1989; Patton, 1990; Strauss & Corbin, 1990). First, I used three theoretical perspectives (phenomenology, symbolic interactionism, and systems theory) from which to ask the interview questions and interpret the data. Second, I obtained data from three sources: interviews of both the supervisor and the therapist, and videotapes of a supervision session when available. Third, I utilized three perspectives to interpret the data: the participants, a feminist interpretive team, and my own. The feminist interpretive team consisted of two colleagues who were feminist family therapists, trained in supervision, one of whom had served as the pilot study's supervisor. The participants and the feminist interpretive team served as a cross-check of my coding and interpretation, minimizing hierarchy and adding to the richness of the coding and interpretive processes. Internal validity (Seidman, 1991) was displayed by the consistency of the responses between therapists and supervisors, between different supervision sites, and between the interviews and the videotapes.

Data Collection and Data Management

Data Collection. All interviews were conducted face-to-face, consisted of open ended questions, and ranged from 45 to 110 minutes–the later interviews lasting longer. Each interview lasted until the participant indicated that s/he felt s/he had described completely her/his experience of supervision. The researcher told participants that they would receive a copy of their coded transcripts and would have the opportunity to make changes, clarifications and additions. The opening question of each interview was, for supervisors, "tell me about your supervision"; or, for therapists, "tell me about your supervision with [supervisor's name]." Subsequent interview questions followed-up on what past participants had talked about (themes generated from coding and preliminary interpretation between interviews), and I pursued ideas brought up in the current interview. In this way, grounded theory, like similar inductive theory building methods, allowed for each site's interviews to build upon the previous site's. By the end of the twelfth interview, I was not hearing any new themes nor was I hearing contradictions to current themes. However, I decided to include two more sites in order to verify data saturation. In addition to the interviews, I asked for a videotape of a typical supervision session. Four sites provided a videotape of the dyad's supervision session at the time of the interviews. In addition to the tapes used as data, one site offered to make a tape after the interview, and one offered a videotape of a session with another therapist. I did not accept either of these videotapes as they did not fit the informed concent protocol. The other two sites said they had not had time to make a videotape of supervision. No obvious differences existed between the sites that provided videotapes and those that did not. The participants at the four sites whose tapes I accepted were asked during their interviews to identify any similarities or differences between the videotaped session and a typical supervision session.

Data Analysis

Coding. Because I had audiotaped the interviews, I was able to transcribe the interviews and videotapes verbatim. Following grounded theory methodology, I used open and axial coding methods. I then sent a copy of the coded transcripts to each participant for her/his review. All participants returned approved transcripts, and seven made some type of change to the codes, sometimes making explanatory notes in the margins. At various stages of the process, transcripts were then sent to the two people who made up the feminist interpretive team, who each eventually read a total of twelve out of the sixteen transcripts and made many suggestions about the coding and future interpretation.

Interpretation. Like coding, preliminary interpretation was done in between each interview so that each interview could inform the next. Consequently, the data collection informed the emerging theory that in turn instructed the data collection. This constant comparative method of data interpretation allowed themes to emerge from the data (Glaser,

1978; 1992) that could be investigated in subsequent interviews and videotapes. Preliminary themes were tested in subsequent interviews by pursuing them if participants mentioned them or by carefully asking a participant an open ended question about the topic.

After all of the interviews were complete, the interpreted data were again sent to the interpretive team for review and suggestions. I incorporated the team's ideas and constructed a model of feminist supervision grounded in the experiences of the participants as reflected by the data. The *Supervision Relationship* and *Feminist Ideas* were *two* of the four themes of feminist supervision described by the participants.

RESULTS

Participants' stories and videotapes revealed that the supervisor-therapist relationship and feminist ideas were two major components of feminist supervision (Figure 1). Although the separation of the results and their discussion is an arbitrary one, for clarity's sake I have chosen to present the two themes, the supervision relationship and feminist ideas utilized in supervision, with a brief contextualization of the participants' explanations as I understood them. I have saved discussion of similar ideas found within the feminist family therapy literature for the discussion section.

The Supervisor-Therapist Relationship

The most subtle, yet most pervasive and powerful, aspect of feminist supervision was the importance–almost sanctity–that the supervisors

FIGURE 1. Feminist Supervision Relationship

Supervision Relationship

commitment
challenge
availability
talk about relationship
respect

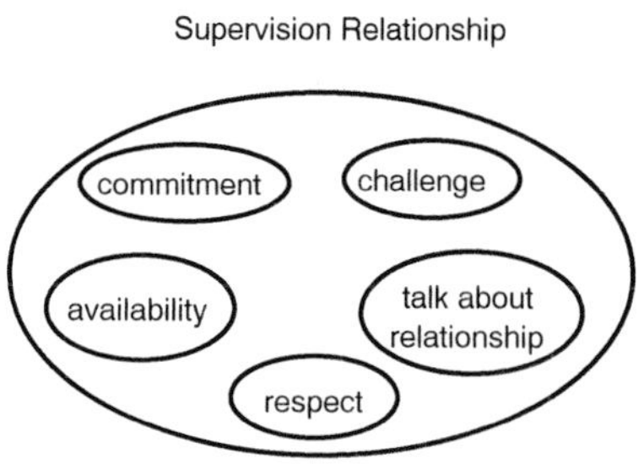

placed on developing the supervision relationship. As one supervisor described it:

> For me, it's about *being fully present in the relationship.* Which is about me being a feminist. What's most important to me is that I've given my all. That I've done the best that I can in supervision to help that person to become a better therapist.

Most of the supervisors talked about the *quality* of the relationship as being the supervisor's responsibility, and that valuing and nurturing the supervision relationship was an important aspect of living their feminism. The participants described several important things the supervisors used to develop and maintain the supervision relationship: commitment, availability, challenges, respect, and talking about the relationship.

Commitment. Participants, especially the supervisors, emphasized the importance of the therapists knowing that the supervisor was placing a priority on this relationship, not just their clinical business together. Being a feminist and living their feminist values included being very thoughtful and committed to their relationships and doing what was necessary to develop, maintain and grow those relationships –including their relationship with the therapists with whom they were working. As a supervisor related:

> All of my supervision is about being in relationship with my supervisee and to me that's real feminist informed in that I think about my relationships, my commitment to connection and caring. And that means that the most important commitment that I have . . . [is] . . . a very feminist commitment.

This commitment was reflected at many levels of supervision: as being committed to the therapists as people and as developing therapists, to the clients, and to the process of supervision. In other words, this commitment involved more than just being physically present; it was about being emotionally–even to some spiritually–present during supervision.

The therapists talked about commitment in several ways. Some described it as knowing the supervisor was there for them, others as feeling like the supervisor was their team or their dependable guide.

> She assured me that she's there, no matter what. She may be critical, but she's very committed. So that made it work for me.

> So I think it makes it more genuine, more real, more full. I think that's the way it impacts our relationship. She wants you to be in there, grappling with her.

In later interviews the researcher investigated if commitment existed from the beginning or developed with the relationship. As one supervisor put it: "I think it's an experiential thing that grows." Several supervisors also said they expected the therapist to be committed to the relationship. However, they qualified this by saying the amount of the therapist's responsibility for the relationship was dependent upon their developmental level, because more experienced therapists were able to be more responsible for the relationship process.

Respect. Respect was the second most talked about aspect of the supervision relationship. The participants talked about respect as necessary for both the supervision to be feminist, and for the professional growth of the therapist. One supervisor described it in this way:

> For me the basis of supervision is, as well as the basis of doing therapy, is respect for the people with whom I work.

Another supervisor talked about her growing respect for the therapist as an indicator of how well supervision in general, and the supervision relationship in particular, were progressing:

> I can think in my head about the process of supervision, how I change and how the supervisee changes. I think when it's good supervision I develop a deeper respect for the supervisee. When that happens I know supervision is working.

The therapists talked about respect just as readily as the supervisors, without being asked about it. Only in about half of the sites did the therapist report discussing mutual respect in supervision. Therefore, when I asked: "What does respect look like?" or "How did you know it existed within your relationship?" One therapist described: "For me I've just been very accepted for who I am. And all of us for who we are and where we are. I feel that we all get respected." And another said: "I think we both have a lot of respect for each other and a lot of awareness for each other."

Availability. Supervisors were physically present for supervision, whether it was for a scheduled supervision meeting, watching therapy or available for questions. One therapist reported:

She's real approachable. If I have a question I've felt free to call her at home, I've felt free to call her at her office. If I pop in on a Friday afternoon to watch tapes she invariably stops in and checks to see what's going on. She always makes sure at the end of the night when all of the interns are back writing notes, she always stops in to make sure we're okay with things, that we don't need to process something that came up that's disturbing us.

The concept of increasing the quality of the supervisor-therapist relationship represented both the physical presence of the supervisor and the approachability of the supervisor as a person. Therapists talked more about the latter than the supervisors. The supervisors were not asked what they did to be perceived as personally approachable but they did provide several methods for physical availability. As one supervisor described: "Being around, being available before, between, after supervision. I think that's one [thing] people would say, that I'm very accessible and very available." Some of these methods included: arriving early and staying late after clinical sessions, scheduling meetings to talk about cases and the relationship, and open office hours.

Challenge. Challenge was an aspect of feminist supervision that was described as part of the supervisors' relationships with therapists, but it was not directly related to therapy cases. The participants reported that an important aspect of the relationship included the supervisor challenging the therapist in a way that she/he still felt supported and stimulated. Supervisors also talked about the importance of setting up a learning environment, and encouraging the therapist to develop new skills, abilities–to become competent by risking failure. As one supervisor put it: "My role in supervision is to help [therapist's name] be the very best therapist she can be . . . My role is to create an environment in which she can risk."

Participants talked about supervisors challenging therapists about theory, process issues and their personal biases. But again, the key to challenge was *how* it was done. It was done in a way that the therapist knew the supervisor was there for her, present in the relationship to help her become the best therapist she could be. Sometimes challenging had to do with a therapist's personal biases, as one supervisor described:

I would continue to find out whether the supervisee believed it [personal bias] was getting in his or her way. If he or she didn't believe that is was, and I was still convinced that it was, I'd probably just leave it and then bring it up again until either I was convinced otherwise or he or she felt like they wanted to look at it.

At other times challenging reflected the use of the self-of-the-supervisor as a model, or challenging the therapist's ideas about feminism. As one therapist described an instance of both of these challenges:

And another thing too, her way of validating what I think and putting her own stuff out there, being a really strong woman and doing that, constantly challenging me. She's really made me think. Like she challenged me one day on the possibility of there being a patriarchy that wasn't harmful. And so in my coming to be a feminist, sometimes I'm rigid, that patriarchy is the most horrible thing and I want to eradicate it, and the minute I see it I want to attack it. So, she's really trying to let it develop in a more healthy way.

It appeared that an important part of the supervisor challenging the therapist was establishing trust that the supervisor had the best interests of the therapist in mind. But perhaps most important, establishment of trust and being supportive was neither passive or just about giving complements. Challenging the therapist was reflective of a deeper ability to join with the therapist in order to help them push their limits.

Talking About the Relationship. The final technique for establishing the supervisor-therapist relationship was to talk about the relationship itself. This encompassed talking about the positive aspects and difficulties of the supervisor-therapist relationship and all the growing in between. For some relationships it was on an as-needed basis, as this therapist described: "I think the agreement was, whether that it was explicitly said or that it was just that I know [supervisor's name], that you just talk about the relationship or any struggles that you have along the way." And another who reported: "She'll say things like: 'I didn't want you to feel like I was interfering in the session; when I asked to come in were you okay with that? How was that for you?' So, it's real open communication."

For other supervisors, they scheduled times throughout the semester or every so many sessions to spend time checking-in about the relationship. During these check-ins the supervisor would ask about the perspective of the therapist and express her own experiences regarding their work together and their relationship.

Feminist Ideas

The participants affirmed feminist ideas (Figure 2) were an important part of making supervision feminist. The participants reported that feminist ideas saturated their experience of feminist supervision, as one therapist put it:

> You name it, we're talking about it and I see it in the [therapy] room and I address those things in the room. And I wouldn't have [noticed them] if those themes weren't constantly brought up and constantly talked about.

Participants described experiencing a combination of several formats in which feminist ideas were included in supervision. These included, but were not limited to, live supervision call-ins, self-of-the-therapist groups, and discussions during therapy session breaks, case reports, and while watching videotapes of therapy–even training tapes. Feminist supervisors did not limit their supervision to only one format.

Some participants explained that even though feminist ideas were important, they could be included without being the focus of the supervision discussions. Therefore, feminist ideas were included to varying degrees in all of the feminist supervision described by the participants and many (gender, power and diversity) of the feminist ideas were found on all four videotaped supervision sessions.

Feminist ideas coalesced into five categories: socialization, gender, power, diversity, and emotion. The first category, socialization, was a word used by several of the participants and described the importance of the influence of larger systems such as culture and society, wherein

FIGURE 2. Feminist Ideas

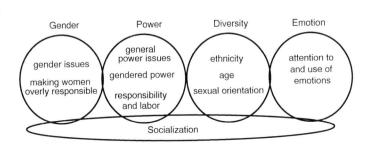

the political affected the personal. Socialization was different than the other four themes in that it seemed to influence the other four to a greater degree, and as such was a meta-theme. In other words, peoples' socialization constructed what they believed about gender, power, diversity and emotion.

Socialization. Participants, especially supervisors, explained that understanding human socialization was an important prerequisite to recognizing and working with other feminist ideas. Supervisors helped therapists to identify socializing forces that influenced them in the past and continued to influence them in the present. As one supervisor put it:

> Feminist supervision, like feminist anything else, pays attention to the way our experience is structured. The way in which it differs based on all kinds of societal structures. Gender, but not just gender, other systems of oppression also. So really trying to see people in context and to understand thoroughly the context that people are in.

Supervisors also helped therapist learn to identify socializing forces that influenced their clients' views of reality both around feminist ideas and in general. Identification of socializing forces was said to be a basic step in the therapist's learning to identify and use feminist ideas. As one supervisor described: "I feel like it's empowering for supervisees as well as clients to talk about broader issues that they're just a part of." Another supervisor linked the ability to recognize people's context to understanding larger interpersonal and socio-historical patterns: "Another would be the making the political-personal kind of piece. That is unusual for me to supervise a case and not talk about the sociological issues or political issues."

Supervisors also explained that learning to recognize socialization, and all feminist ideas, is a life-long journey. They explained that being a feminist is about constantly learning about one's own biases and perspectives, as well as other's experiences and perspectives. To that end, they talked about feminist supervision as making clear that being a feminist requires constant learning and conscientious work. As one supervisor put it: "The other thing is I really try to set up this sense that all of us are socialized in such a way that makes us have to work hard at feminist thinking. I like to talk to students about that."

Gender. Although the concept of socialization was a pervasive feminist idea, the most talked about of the five feminist ideas was gender.

Every participant mentioned this concept repeatedly. And as one supervisor reported: "I can't think of anything that's important to me that doesn't have some sort of implications, or that shouldn't stand some kind of analysis through a gender lens." Participants talked about gender within two areas: gender issues and making women responsible.

Gender issues included ideas related to roles, relationships and interpersonal styles that were experienced or constructed according to a person's gender. One of the most talked about roles was that of parenting. As one supervisor described the intersection of gender issues and parenting: "Also, ways in which parenting is different for mothers than it is for fathers . . . the ways in which we construct mothering and fathering . . . that really informs my thinking so I talk about it all the time in supervision."

Part of learning to recognize ways in which gender impacted lives was to teach the therapist to notice how people used words. As one supervisor described:

> I think part of my role as a feminist supervisor is to cue students to words or language, even subtle language, that reinforces traditional gender positions that devalue women and the female point of view.

Five participants talked about "making women overly responsible" as a therapeutic issue related to gender, and described it as related to, but separate from, gender roles. "Making women overly responsible" focused more on the therapeutic process. One supervisor described: "I think first and foremost, it's helping them look at gender imbalances. To look a the politics of the relationship through that lens so that they don't contribute to gender inequities." And as another supervisor conveyed:

> I'm aware of the tendency to blame women. I'm aware of the tendency to give women more homework assignments for change. I'm aware of the tendency to step lightly around him and confront her hard. I'm aware of the tendency to feel fortunate he's here so let's not lose him.

As I'll discuss later, even though women-blaming was an old and ardent topic within the feminist literature, only two supervisors and two therapists reported that they identified, talked about, or made interventions around the social phenomenon of making women overly responsible. And it should be noted that of these five participants, two were from the same site. Even after pursuing the topic in later interviews, it was not mentioned as a therapeutic process issue. However, the five people who did talk about making women overly responsible in therapy were adamant that it was still a problem and needed attention as an important topic of feminist supervision.

Power. One of the open ended questions I asked the therapists was: "Does [supervisor's name] ever talk about anything in particular that you would label as feminist?" Most answered with "gender," then "power," but once in a while they would say "power" first. As did this therapist: "Power. [supervisor's name] is constantly talking about power. Who has it and how is it being used, and is it overt, is it covert, is it known, is it unknown."

The feminist idea of power was more dissected than was gender. The participants reported several aspects of power that included: power issues, gendered power, and responsibility/labor within relationships. Power, as a feminist idea, represented the importance of identifying the role and effects of power in the therapists' relationships and in clients' lives. The participants talked about power as a generalized idea, and then more specifically as gendered power (power traditionally distributed because of gender), and as power distributed or less accessible to a person as a result of responsibility and labor.

Everyone talked about issues of power. However, even when asked, most often people did not break down power into types but several provided examples. They described paying attention to power between people that created some type of hierarchy, or used systemic descriptions such as: "I think it's important to look for other kinds of coercion," and gave a case example. Participants also talked about how learning to recognize power was fundamental to supervision because it enabled therapists to recognize and work with clients around important family therapy issues like violence and abuse.

All participants talked about paying attention to ways in which people experienced power differences according to gender. Because participants emphasized so clearly that power was the core of this experience, but that it only existed because of gender, these ideas emerged as a theme separate from gender and more differentiated than generic power issues. As one supervisor described it:

Helping people to understand that men and women see the world differently. We see the world differently *and* there's a hierarchy. And if you leave out that *and there's a hierarchy* piece, you're leaving out a major piece of feminism.

I also observed participants talking about gendered power on one of the supervision videotapes. In one clip, the therapist was talking with the supervisor about a couple's sexual frustration, and feelings of anger and alienation. The therapist proposed a pursuer-withdrawer cycle influenced by established gender roles and expectations. The supervisor then contributed to the hypothesis about the couple's dynamics by attaching the concept of power to the gender issues: "My guess is that if it starts off with a power struggle around dinner and then the sexual joking starts; my guess is that their chances for any kind of intimacy are dwindling by the end of the night."

Participants also reported that they paid attention to gendered power between therapists. For example, two participants noticed that within female-male co-therapy teams, men had a tendency to talk more than women. These participants reported that the supervisor had encouraged the male to use his voice less and the woman to use her voice more often. Participants also related stories about therapy, for example, when clients looked to one of the therapists in the female-male co-therapy team more than the other. One supervisor suggested that the idea of connecting power to gender was not familiar to all therapists. She also talked about having patience and respect with therapists, "It's been my experience that it's not malignant [when the therapist doesn't notice gendered power right away]. It's just they never noticed."

The third type of power that participants talked about fell into the category I called "responsibility and labor." This area represented the topics that the participants described when power was a part of familial functions such as emotional labor, household labor, child care, finances and family scheduling. Several participants said they thought these issues were often overlooked by both therapists and clients as real work, and that they represented types of power within relationships and families. As one supervisor described, [It's important to teach them how to pay] "attention to power in relationships. So that I ask the therapists I'm working with about power. Who's taking care of the kids? Who brings in the money? Who has the power? Who washes the dishes?" And a therapist remembered, "Another theme that is really common with . . . [supervisor's name] . . . is labor within the relationship. Household labor, child care labor, emotional labor, things of that sort." Participants went on to talk about the feminist supervisors helping therapists work with these important issues, beyond just noticing them. For example, when the family structure was too rigid, a supervisor said she would work on "helping the therapist or the family to think about other ways of sharing responsibilities in a family."

Responsibility and labor represent feminist topics whose importance and complexity I have found are sometimes difficult to understand and relate, but the participants described them eloquently. The above quotations do not relay participants' fervor for this area of feminist ideas. The therapist in the second quotation offered to get up from his chair and draw me pictures. This didn't happen in any of the other themes. I think this area was so important because it represented the application of abstract ideas to real peoples' lives, and the areas in which many therapeutic changes were focused. As one therapist put it: "I try to say something in every session, I try to address it in some way."

Diversity. The fourth feminist idea was diversity, and included three areas: ethnicity, age and sexual orientation. Whereas the concepts of gender and power were about deconstruction of people's ideas, diversity was about flexibility, acceptance and tolerance. Supervision was geared toward helping therapists become not only more knowledgeable about persons different from themselves, but also to help therapists to become more flexible around these differences. All of the categories of diversity were often linked to the other feminist ideas of gender and power within supervision.

By far the largest type of diversity talked about was ethnicity, and the participants talked about race and religion being the most important aspects of ethnicity. As a therapist reported: "She's very aware of issues surrounding religion in terms of different roles and belief systems." Supervisors also tried to help the therapist to ask about and imagine their client's experiences, and the many aspects of their identity in general, and how it related to their problem and their options. One supervisor provided an example via paraphrasing a supervision conversation from earlier that day:

> We talk[ed] about, "How do you think this person being black contributes to their experience?" "How would it be different if they weren't black?" "How would it be for you if a man said that?"

The participants also talked about other aspects of their training: reinforcing, amplifying, or clarifying diversity in supervision. This was one area that some of the participants mentioned the supervisors continuous construction of the training environment as supporting their emphasis on celebrating human diversity. For example, they referred to the importance of other parts of the therapist training. "Part of the [training] program is about recognizing those biases and working through them . . . taking the ethnicity course and struggling through that." They also talked about bringing diversity issues into the physical space in which the supervision took place, like the art on the walls of the therapy clinic. Although the clinical reasons for the decorating had originally focused on the therapy, participants reported that supervision benefited as well. As one supervisor described: "The way the therapy rooms are set up, the art on the walls celebrates diversity."

Age was another part of diversity. In addition to helping therapists to think of how age affected people's experiences, problems, and options, supervisors helped therapists identify and talk about how the dynamics of age affected their therapy. Some of the examples of situations where age had been a factor were: younger therapists and older clients, co-therapists of different age cohorts, and age differences between members in clients' families. An example from one supervisor was: "I see it with supervisees [working together] who are older and younger [than the average of their cohort], in terms of helping them value everybody's voice. Especially if they have no personal experiences with older people."

Sexual orientation was the fourth and final type of diversity emphasized by the participants. Supervisors and therapists talked about the importance of being respectful with clients around issues related to sexual orientation, such as heterosexual bias, coming-out, and legal issues. Sexual orientation and acceptance of different sexual orientations were mentioned as they occurred in client dynamics, self-of-the-therapist dynamics, and in the dynamics between co-therapists. As one supervisor was listing the different aspects of diversity she said, "Another would be the acceptance of diversity. However a couple are defined, whether that's gay and lesbian, however they define that."

Emotion. Feminist supervisors emphasized the importance of helping the therapist to elicit, validate and effectively deal with emotion as a part of being competent therapists. This feminist idea represented teaching therapists to be skilled with working with emotions in the therapy room. As a therapist recounted:

> She's always bringing up that theme [emotion] when we're doing couple work. She wants me to talk to one of the clients who isn't being congruent before they can talk to their significant other. To sort of work with them on congruence before, which is really being empowered I think, before they talk to the other person and just give to it and not be fully present and not be talking about their fear or whatever emotion is underlying the laughing or the anxiety.

In addition to helping therapists work with emotion in the therapy room, feminist supervisors also helped the therapists to learn to value their own emotional reactions, and to be emotionally and verbally congruent in therapy. As one therapist expressed, "She does a good job about wanting to know how we're feeling in the session, to help us through those types of things." And as another offered, "[If it hadn't been feminist supervision] I think it would have been very theoretical without the feeling, and without the emotional challenges." These, and other stories from therapists, suggest that therapists valued the balance of cognitive and emotional ways of knowing in their therapy, and felt that the additional concentration on their emotional competency was an important part of their training.

DISCUSSION

One of the difficulties I encountered in comparing these results with previous MFT feminist family therapy supervision literature was that it was sometimes unclear if a work was about feminist MFT supervision. I understand that including attention to issues that are important to feminists such as race, gender and sexual orientation are not the sole purview of feminist writers. Also, several MFTs who have identified themselves as feminists have subsequently written about the supervision process in general terms, without calling it feminist-informed supervision. Perhaps the recognition of this problem will help us all to be more clear in our writing about how feminism informs our work. On the other hand, many feminist family therapists would say that our goal is to have our ideas and values mainstreamed and utilized by all.

However, for theoretical clarity, only writings wherein the authors defined their work as being specifically about feminist family therapy supervision were included.

Reflection on the Supervision Relationship and the Literature

From the perspectives of the participants in this study, there is a strong emphasis on the importance of the supervisor-therapist relationship in feminist family therapy supervision. They talked about several aspects of the supervisor-therapist relationship: encouraging respect in the relationship; being committed and available to therapists; challenging therapists in a way that they felt supported and stimulated; and talking about the relationship itself. It is also important to note that participants delineated the supervision relationship as being a separate entity from the supervision contract (Prouty, Thomas, Johnson, & Long, 1998), the latter of which was more focused on the logistics of supervision. Indeed, the participants reported that what they described as their supervision relationship was more about being present in the moment and for each other over time. It was about being committed and being available, and it enabled the supervisor to challenge the therapist *because* supervision existed *within the context* of this relationship.

Avis' (1986) panel suggested feminist supervision would be made up of relationships that were personal and supportive. The feminists supervisors in this study reported that it was important to *be caring* and making sure that the *care was felt* by the therapist. It is also probable that the supervisors' commitment to the supervision relationship contributed to what therapists described as a safe atmosphere something essential to the discussion of gender and self-of-the-therapist issues in clinical training (Helmeke, 1994; Wheeler et al., 1986). Wheeler and her colleagues (1986) discussed the necessity of a woman supervisor using her power within the relationship to empower the therapist–through relaying her knowledge and challenging the therapist to expand her own knowledge and skill. Likewise, Goodrich and her colleagues (1988) said that an inherent aspect of being respectful in the supervision process was to identify therapists' competencies, affirm improvements, and support individuality. As the therapists in this study described, part of why they could hear criticisms, challenges and learn from hierarchical supervision (Prouty et al., 1998) was that all of these existed in the context of a supervision relationship built on caring, safety and respect.

In the participants' feminist supervision relationships, a value was placed on developing the relationship, and with that, developing a mutual respect for each other as people and for their professional abilities. Supervisors placed a premium on treating therapists well, hoping that therapists would in turn treat each other and clients with esteem, and that they themselves would be respected in return. What was interesting to me, was that the therapists reported that they felt the respect was mutual, but the supervisors were hesitant to assume that the therapists felt admiration for them. The supervisors were unwilling to speak for the therapists because, as they explained, they assumed the *hierarchy* within the relationship clouded their ability to be absolutely sure about the true feelings of the therapist. This was an example of supervisors' sensitivity to the *inevitable and necessary* hierarchy of the supervision relationship. I suspect that this simply represents the difference between theorizing about respect, and the real life supervision process–one never truly knows another's experience.

The participants' emphasis on respect was also a point stressed within the feminist family therapy literature. Goodrich et al. (1988) and Wheeler et al. (1986) described feminist systemic supervision as building relationships grounded in trust and respect; indeed, the latter was said to be essential to the process of making supervision feminist according to Goodrich and her colleagues (1988). An aspect of the supervisor-therapist relationship found in this study that was not reflected in earlier writings was the importance of the supervisor's availability. This was not talked about in the supervision process literature and seems to be an important part of the supervision relationship that has been overlooked. Perhaps it is an element of supervision that is taken for granted because supervision is often a scheduled relationship. What the participants seemed to be emphasizing was that access to the supervisor was key to developing a meaningful relationship. There is more to it than just scheduling time together to talk about therapy.

In addition to being available to the therapist, the participants also reported that they spent time talking about their relationship, not just the logistics of supervision, but about their supervision relationship itself. For as therapists, it may seem like common sense that an important aspect of nurturing any relationship is paying attention to it.

Within the feminist MFT supervision literature, Wheeler et al. (1989) suggested periodic check-ins during training to provide mutual feedback. However, this is the only reference to the need for feminist family therapy supervisors to actually talk with therapists, and it was not exactly clear to me what they were suggesting they talk about during the check-ins. The supervisors in this study believed conscientious reflection to be important to the feminist supervision process because paying attention to relationships was reflective of their feminist value of nurturing and growing relationships. Like availability, this seemed to be an obvious area of supervision that has been overlooked in the literature and is one of the keys to developing a meaningful and useful supervision relationship.

Reflection on Feminist Ideas in the Literature

The emphasis on gender, power and diversity discussed by the participants in this study were all found in the feminist family therapy supervision literature, as were the interconnections between the three areas. This is probably due to the fact that all of the supervisors and most of the therapists had read much of the feminist MFT literature. For example, several referred to Wheeler et al.'s (1986) model in their interviews. Munson (1987) proposed the need for both supervisors and therapists to have adequate information about feminist issues in order to minimize confusion, frustration, and defensiveness. Several of the therapists in the present study mentioned they had had a course on gender in family therapy or on feminist family therapy. I would expect that familiarity, whether or not therapists agreed with the concepts, made the emphasis on feminist ideas in supervision more clear and less of a surprise.

Socialization and the emphasis of society's influence on constructing gender and bestowing power are prominent themes in the feminist family therapy literature. Hare-Mustin (1978) brought it to the attention of family therapy with her critique of systems theory for its failure to place events within the sociopolitical context. Although feminist family therapists initially emphasized the socialization of people around gender and gender roles, the focus has broadened to include other sociocultural effects of people's experience of gender (Goodwin, 1993). As a part of this broader focus, Wheeler et al.'s (1986) model for feminist training and supervision suggested that feminist systemic supervisors emphasize social analysis when training therapists, in order to teach them how to make broader political connections for themselves as well as for their clients. On the practical side, several feminist family therapists have provided suggestions and exercises to help therapists and supervisors to identify socializing forces (Ault-Riche, 1988; Avis and Braverman, 1994; Roberts, 1991; Storm, 1991). For example, Roberts' (1991) exercise helps supervisors guide therapists in an examination of the messages they have learned–including those from their families and other personal relationships. Although feminist family therapists have been promoting the importance of socialization, no studies were found investigating its presence or effects in feminist family therapy supervision. However, Avis' (1986) panel predicted feminist supervision would pay attention to larger contextual issues, social, and financial issues as they affected women and families. They reported that feminist supervisors would address personal and political issues. Their prediction was accurate. The current study suggests that talking about social and political contexts is preliminary to becoming more sensitive to feminist ideas and incorporating them into one's work. Perhaps it is akin to noticing the forest in order to learn how to distinguish between and appreciate the trees.

Given the amount of writing on gender and the fact that gender is at the heart of many types of feminism, I was not surprised that the participants said that gender was the most commonly mentioned feminist idea. Looking to the feminist family therapy literature, Avis' (1986) panel of feminists predicted that gender would be an important theme of feminist supervision. They described it as one of the three most important areas in feminist training along with the issues of power and equality. They also suggested gender be a part of therapists' curricula along with other gender related topics: the psychology of women, sex roles, and social and financial issues affecting women and families. The panel also described feminist supervisors as being willing to openly discuss sexist remarks.

Likewise, several feminist family therapy writings focused on gender within the supervision experience (Good, Gilbert, & Sher, 1990; Nelson, 1991; Roberts, 1991; Storm, 1991). Helmeke (1994) proposed that a safe atmosphere was primary to the discussion of gender in training programs. She suggested that students be assured that their views on gender would be heard in a respectful way and attention be paid by the supervisor to unequal power dynamics among therapists. She provided three approaches for supervisors to promote a safe environment. People should first be curious about each others' ideas, then try to take on others' perspectives while maintaining their own, and lastly, people try to stay non-reactive. She proposed that supervisors should lead the discussion and encourage the three approaches to the discussion of gender.

Similarly, Avis (1987) suggested that gender issues which arise within the supervision process should be addressed whether they be between the supervisor and the therapist, the therapist and the family, or therapists with each other. Nelson (1991) suggested that supervisors pay attention to their conceptions about gender. She proposed that supervisors examine and challenge what they thought were gendered roles and behaviors. As discussed above, Roberts (1991) developed exercises to help clinicians examine their ideas about gender, and several theorists (Avis & Braverman, 1994; Roberts, 1991; Storm, 1991) advocated that the supervisor use circular questioning to elicit sexist assumptions from their supervisees. Ault-Riche (1988) proposed training women as supervisors with a model that would help them identify their sexism and attitudes toward women in authority. And more recently, Avis and Braverman (1994) provided a way of integrating feminist and narrative ideas into training and supervision to examine the construction of the meaning of gender for both therapists and supervisors.

To some extent feminism and the analysis of the effects of gender sometimes seem to be synonymous. However, the participants talked about gender and gendered power as being separate, different, and important as were the different types of social power and the effects of a person either having power or not having power–especially in the area of family violence. (Please see Prouty et al., 1998, for a more thorough discussion of how the participants talked about dealing with family violence in supervision.)

Examining the topics of gendered power that these feminist supervisors emphasized, blaming women for family problems and making women more responsible for change than men–in life and in therapy–is an old topic from the original feminist critiques of family theory and family therapy theory (Gilligan, 1982; Goodrich, Rampage, Ellman & Halstead, 1988; Hare-Mustin, 1978; Hare-Mustin & Marecek, 1990; Miller, 1986; 1991) and a revisited topic within the feminist family therapy training literature (Werner-Wilson, Price, Zimmerman, & Murphy, 1997). On a related issue, Wheeler and her colleagues (1989) said it is necessary for feminist supervisors to encourage female therapists not to take on too much responsibility for their clients. They briefly discussed this as a common part of female socialization and as being detrimental to the therapy process and the client's growth. Avis' (1986) panel of feminists predicted that power would be one of the three most important feminist topics for feminist supervisors. They believed in making issues of power explicit in supervision and in therapy. They believed in identifying issues of power with clients, between therapists, and between the supervisor and the therapist. Similarly, the area about which several participants were most passionate was the need to recognize responsibility and labor, especially emotional responsibility and labor, within families. This was the area most likely to be accompanied by arm waving, raised voices, and in one case a friendly offer to draw me a picture. They were intent on making me understand: work must be recognized, and the emotional work in many relationships must be valued and included in this tally. There were several feminist writings (Baber & Allen, 1992; Goodrich, 1991; Goodrich et al., 1988) that explored the different elements within the area of responsibility and labor in feminist family *therapy* but only Goodrich et al. applied their ideas to feminist supervision. They forewarned us about how important it is for feminist MFT supervisors "to explore the division of labor, power, and rewards in the family as it is affected by gender bias and stereotyping" (p. 31). Indeed, they viewed the division of labor as an extension of gender stereotyping. Although the participants in this study didn't seem to contradict this perspective, they spoke about it more often within their discussion of the analysis of power dynamics within relationships, families, and society in general. In many areas, this being one, the intersection of power and gender expectations seemed inherent–passed down through generations of socially prescribed expectations. I also expect that, given more pointed questions, I would have heard more overlap among the issues of power and other aspects of diversity (age, sexual orientation and ethnicity). This is an area about which more research and theoretical writings are needed to explicate feminist systemic supervision–not only *what* do we see with regard to labor and rewards, but *how* do we as feminists teach therapists to do something different.

The third idea identified by the participants as feminist was a broad one: issues of human diversity. Both within the literature and within the participants' responses race was discussed more than religion.

However, when the participants were asked about additional aspects of diversity they all responded with religion, and sometimes with sexual orientation and age. All of the participants in this study talked about the importance of discussing diversity of the clients, between the clients and the therapists, between co-therapists, and between the supervisor and the therapists. Two supervisors related stories around the difficulties of these discussions and the need to challenge therapists' personal biases around diversity. All of the supervisors attempted to have group discussions around diversity, and all agreed that they resorted to one-on-one discussions only during live supervision or when they believed it was more helpful for the struggling therapist. One important aspect of these discussions was that supervisors all talked about encouraging the therapists to challenge them (the supervisor) on their own personal biases and ignorance. This was probably related to the use of balancing power within the supervision relationship.

There is a long history of feminist MFT writing emphasizing the clinical importance of examining diversity. Several feminist theorists (Ault-Riche, 1988; Hare-Mustin, 1987; Goldner, 1991; Goodrich et al., 1988; McCannell, 1986; Roberts, 1991; Storm, 1991; Wheeler et al., 1989) believe that therapists must examine their own biases and learn about the culture of others, often referring to the growing work about cultural sensitivity in the general MFT literature (for example, Boyd-Franklin, 1989; Falicov, 1983; 1988; Lopez & Hernandez, 1987; Martinez, 1994; McGoldrick, Pearce & Giordano, 1996).

Rampage (1991) proposed that cultural stories may hinder clinicians from understanding their story apart from either the predominant culture or their personal culture's narratives. She emphasized the importance of listening to the client's perspective before reinterpreting or helping the client to create new stories. Similarly, Kliman (1994) asserted those persons whose voices and stories have not been heard require a therapist familiar with their culture. Hare-Mustin and Merecek (1986; 1990) and Kliman (1994) proposed training therapists to examine clients' power according to their gender, race, class, and age. Using their framework the supervisor and therapist could discuss how therapeutic models or interventions might be experienced or what might be their outcomes given the client's identity and experiences. Kliman's inclusion of age seemed to be almost unique, even though the participants reported age to be an aspect of diversity within the context of feminist family therapy training and supervision models.

With the baby-boom generation maturing and entering senior citizen status, geriatric family therapy is an increasingly important facet that can no longer be ignored. However, even within the sample of this study, age was mentioned far less than ethnicity and sexual orientation. It seems that more family therapy curricula and publications need to include topics of importance to seniors and their relationships.

Feminists have written about sexual orientation, especially working with lesbian couples, in the feminist family *therapy* literature (for example, Goodrich et al., 1988; Goodrich, Ellman, Rampage, & Halstead, 1990; Laird, 1993), and at present there is an increasing number of conceptual publications about the relationship between sexual orientation and general family therapy training (Gautney, 1994; Long, 1994; 1996; 1997; Long, Lindsey, Manders, Dotson, & Wilson, 1993). However, this work was not identified as being about *feminist* MFT supervision. Therefore, although these contributions are important we cannot know if the supervision might look different if made overtly feminist. Talking with the participants in this study, only two of the therapists said that they had read any of the literature about attending to heterosexual bias or working with other issues related to sexual orientation in family therapy.

Although all participants mentioned the importance of sensitivity and respect related to sexual diversity as being feminist, sexual orientation seems to have received limited attention in the feminist supervision and training literature. Thus, I wonder if therapists are getting the covert message that, like age and physical ability/disability (an area not mentioned by participants), sexual orientation is not as important as ethnicity and gender in attending to human diversity from their feminist supervisors. If these are not our values, and the issues of age, ability, and sexual orientation are indeed as important as gender and ethnicity, then we need to attend to them more clearly in our writing and research about *feminist* training and supervision in family therapy.

The fourth feminist idea identified by the participants was the teaching of the importance of emotion, and emotional ways of knowing. I found no research on emotionally focused supervision, feminist or otherwise. However, feminist therapy values emotion, so it makes sense that feminist systemic supervisors do also. Within the feminist MFT training literature, Wheeler and her colleagues (1986) talked about the importance of the supervisor encouraging the therapists to use both cognitive and emotional skills in an atmosphere that valued the therapist's strengths and competencies. They suggested that feminist supervisors encourage thera-pists' expression of feelings, warmth, and empathy. They also stressed the importance of supervisors validating therapists' emotions and helping use emotional ways of processing circumstances.

CONCLUSIONS

In order to know who we are we must first look inside ourselves. Similarly, feminist MFT supervisors emphasized their supervision was *an extension of who they were: feminists.* They lived their feminism in their supervision (Prouty, 1996). Feminist MFT supervision valued construct-ing and nurturing the supervisor-therapist relationship and noticing and utilizing feminist ideas in their clinical systemic supervision. It is also important to remember that the two aspects of feminist family therapy supervision reviewed in this article, the supervisor-therapist relationship and the feminist ideas emphasized within supervision, were two impor-tant pieces of a larger picture (Prouty, 1996) and were based in a history of diverse American feminist values and perspectives.

Although I felt it was not appropriate to use as a backdrop for this study's results, feminists writing in our sister field of feminist psychol-ogy supervision have provided many excellent writings that could inform our clinical training of MFTs. Some of these works have ex-tended difficult dialogues further than we have in family therapy, in the feminist discourses about ethnicity (for example, Porter, 1994; Porter & Yahne, 1994; Vasquez, 1999; Vasquez, & Eldridge, 1994) and sexual orientation (for example, Brown, 1989; Morrow, 1998; 2000) in psychotherapy training. In addition to expanding our writing, I would encourage more feminist MFTs to attend and extend invitations for feminist mental health professional meetings (for example, the Association for Women in Psychology's annual conference) where many important discussions occur about feminist therapy, pedagogy, mentorship and supervision. Perhaps if we can feel more physically like a community of feminist supervisors our practice, research, and writing can continue to be enriched by each other's ideas and experiences.

I hope feminist family therapy supervisors and feminist supervisors from other mental health disciplines will review my findings, these experiences of supervisors and therapists, and work with them, talk about them, challenge them and above all add to them. We need more research and more writing about feminist clinical supervision, training and teaching in MFT. We also need research and writing about how our feminism and our experiences of human diversity and spirituality inform our work–our lived experience, our relationships with the people whom we train and are trained and mentored by. For example, I hope future research can include the perspectives of feminist systemic supervisors of color, non-Americans, and more of those who train outside the context of academia. Also, research is needed about the struggles and challenges of providing supervision that is feminist. Diversity of perspectives can only add to the richness of our understanding and our supervision. For many people, like myself, the reading and the doing of this research provide invaluable training and mentorship in learning how to incorporate our feminist values into work very dear to our hearts.

REFERENCES

Ault-Riche, M. (1988). Teaching an integrated model of family therapy: Women as students, women as supervisors. *Journal of Psychotherapy and the Family, 3*(4), 175-192.

Avis, J. (1986). *Training and Supervision in Feminist-Informed Family Therapy: A Delphi Study.* Unpublished doctoral dissertation. Purdue University, West Lafayette, Indiana.

Avis, J. (1987). Deepening awareness: A private study guide to feminism and family therapy. *Journal of Psychotherapy and the Family, 3*(4), 15-45.

Avis, J. M., & Braverman, L. (1994, October). *Integrating Feminist and Narrative Ideas into Training and Supervision.* Paper presented at the meeting of the American Association of Marriage and Family Therapy, Chicago, IL.

Baber, K., & Allen, K. (1992). *Women and Families: Feminist Reconstructions.* New York: Guilford.

Boyd-Franklin, N. (1989). *Black families in therapy.* New York: Guilford.

Brown, L. (1989). New voices, new visions: Toward a lesbian/gay paradigm for psychology. *Psychology of Women Quarterly, 13,* 445-458.

Denzin, N. (1978). *Sociological Methods: A Sourcebook.* (2nd ed.). New York: McGraw-Hill.

Falicov, C. (1983). *Cultural Perspectives in Family Therapy.* Rockville, MD: Aspen Publications.

Falicov, C. (1988). Learning to think culturally in family therapy training. In H. Liddle, D. Breunlin & R. Schwartz (Eds.), *Handbook of Family Therapy Training and Supervision* (pp. 335-357). New York: Guilford.

Gautney, K. (1994). What if they ask me if I'm married? A supervisee's view. *Supervision Bulletin, 7,* 3-7.

Gilligan, C. (1982). *In a Different Voice.* Cambridge, MA: Harvard University Press.

Glaser, B. (1978). *Theoretical sensitivity: Advances in the Methodology of Grounded Theory.* Mill Valley, CA: Sociology Press.

Glaser, B. (1992). *Basics of Grounded Theory Analysis.* Mill Valley, CA: Sociology Press.

Glaser, B., & Strauss, A. (1967). *The Discovery of Grounded Theory.* New York: Aldine de Gruyter.

Goldner, V. (1991). Feminism and systemic practice: Two critical traditions in transition. *Journal of Family Therapy, 13,* 95-104.

Good, G., Gilbert, L., & Scher, M. (1990). Gender aware therapy: A synthesis of feminist therapy and knowledge about gender. *Journal of Counseling and Development, 68,* 376-380.

Goodrich, T. (1991). Women, power, and family therapy: What's wrong with this picture? In T. J. Goodrich (Ed.), *Women and Power: Perspectives for Family Therapy* (pp. 3-35). New York: W. W. Norton.

Goodrich, T., Ellman, B., Rampage, C., & Halstead, K. (1990). The lesbian couple. In M. Mirkin (Ed.), *The Social and Political Contexts of Family Therapy.* Allyn and Bacon: Boston.

Goodrich, T., Rampage, C., Ellman, B., & Halstead, K. (1988). *Feminist Family Therapy: A Casebook.* New York: W. W. Norton.

Goodwin, B. (1993). Psychotherapy supervision: Training therapists to recognize family violence. In M. Hansen & M. Harway (Eds.), *Battering and Family Therapy: A Feminist Perspective* (pp. 119-133). Newbury Park, CA: Sage.

Hare-Mustin, R. (1978). A feminist approach to family therapy. *Family Process, 17,* 181-194.

Hare-Mustin, R. (1987). The problem of gender in family therapy theory. *Family Process, 26,* 15-27.

Hare-Mustin, R., & Merecek, J. (1986). Autonomy and gender: Some questions for therapists. *Psychotherapy, 23,* 205-212.

Hare-Mustin, R., & Merecek, J. (1990). Gender and the meaning of difference: Postmodernism and psychology. In R. T. Hare-Mustin & J. Marecek (Eds.), *Making a Difference: Psychology and the Construction of Gender* (pp. 22-64). New Haven, CT: Yale University Press.

Helmeke, K. (1994). Fostering a safe atmosphere: A first step in discussing gender in family therapy training programs. *Contemporary Family Therapy, 16,* 503-519.

Kliman, J. (1994). The interweaving of gender, class, and race in family therapy. In M. Mirkin (Ed.). *Women in Context: Toward a Reconstruction of Psychotherapy.* New York: The Guilford Press.

Laird, J. (1993). Lesbian and gay families. In F. Walsh (Ed.), *Normal Family Processes* (2nd ed., pp. 282-328). New York: Guilford.

Libow, J. (1986). Training family therapists as feminists. In M. Ault-Riche (Ed.), *Women and Family Therapy* (pp. 16-24). Rockville, MD: Aspen.

Long, J. (1994). MFT supervision of gay, lesbian and bisexual clients: Are supervisors still in the dark? *Supervision Bulletin, 7,* 1,6.

Long, J. (1996). Working with lesbians, gays, and bisexuals: Addressing heterosexism in supervision. *Family Process, 35,* 377-388.

Long, J. (1997). Sexual orientation: Implications for the supervisory process. In T. Todd & C. Storm (Eds.), *The complete systemic supervisor: Context, Philosophy and Pragmatics.* Allyn and Bacon: Boston.

Long, J., Lindsey, E., Manders, J., Dotson, D., & Wilson, R. (1993, October). *Train-*

ing MFTS to Work with Gay and Lesbian Couples and Families. Workshop presented at the meeting of the American Association for Marriage and Family Therapy, Anaheim, CA.

Lopez, S., & Hernandez, P. (1987). When culture is considered in the evaluation and treatment of Hispanic patients. *Psychotherapy, 24,* 120-126.

Marshall, C., & Rossman, G. (1989). *Designing Qualitative Research.* Newbury Park, CA: Sage.

Martinez, K. (1994). Cultural sensitivity in family therapy gone awry. *Hispanic Journal of Behavioral Science, 16,* 75-89.

McCannell, K. (1986). Family politics, family policy, and family practice: A feminist perspective. *Canadian Journal of Community Mental Health, 5* (2), 61-71.

McGoldrick, M., Pearce, J., & Giordano, J. (Eds.). (1996). *Ethnicity and Family Therapy* (2nd ed). New York: Guilford.

Miller, J. (1986). *Toward a New Psychology of Women* (2nd ed.) Boston: Beacon.

Miller, J. (1991). Women and power: Reflections ten years later. In T. J. Goodrich (Ed.), *Women and Power: Perspectives for Family Therapy* (pp. 36-47). New York: W. W. Norton.

Morrow, S. (1998). Toward a new paradigm in counseling psychology training and education. *The Counseling Psychologist, 26,* 797-808.

Morrow, S. (2000). First do no harm: Therapist issues in psychotherapy with lesbian, gay and bisexual clients. In R. Perez & K. DeBord (Eds.), *Handbook of Counseling and Psychotherapy with Lesbian, Gay, and Bisexual Clients.* (pp. 137-156). Washington, D.C.: American Psychological Association.

Munson, C. (1987). Sex roles and power relationships in supervision. *Professional Psychology: Research and Practice, 18,* 236-243.

Nelson, T. (1991). Gender in family therapy supervision. *Contemporary Family Therapy, 13,* 357-369.

Patton, M. (1990). *Qualitative Evaluation and Research Methods.* Newbury Park, CA: Sage.

Porter, N. (1994). Empowering supervisees to empower others: A culturally responsive supervision model. *Hispanic Journal of Behavioral Sciences, 16,* 43-56.

Porter, N., & Yahne, C. (1994). Feminist ethics and advocacy in the training of family therapists. In M Snyder (Ed.), *Ethical Issues in Feminist Family Therapy* (pp. 29-47). Binghamton, NY: The Haworth Press, Inc.

Prouty, A. (1996/1997). A grounded theory of feminist supervision: A qualitative study. (Doctoral dissertation, Purdue University, 1996). *Dissertation Abstracts International, 58 (3-B),* 1543.

Prouty, A., Thomas, V., Johnson, S., & Long, J. (in press). Feminist supervision methods. *Journal of Marital and Family Therapy.*

Rafuls, S., & Moon, S. (1996). Grounded theory methodology in family therapy research. In D. Sprenkle and S. Moon (Eds.), *Research Methods in Family Therapy* (pp. 64-80). New York: Guilford.

Rampage, C. (1991). Personal authority and women's self stories. In T. J. Goodrich (Ed.), *Women and power: Perspectives for Family Therapy* (pp. 109-122). New York: W. W. Norton.

Roberts, J. (1991). Sugar and spice, toads and mice: Gender issues in family therapy training. *Journal of Marital and Family Therapy, 17,* 121-131.

Seidman, I. (1991). *Interviewing as Qualitative Research: A Guide for Researchers in Education and the Social Sciences.* New York: Teachers College Press.

Storm, C. (1991). Placing gender in the heart of MFT masters programs: Teaching a gender sensitive systemic view. *Journal of Marital and Family Therapy, 17,* 45-52.

Strauss, A. (1987). *Qualitative Analysis for Social Scientists.* New York: Cambridge University Press.

Strauss, E., & Corbin, J. (1990). *Basics of Qualitative Research: Grounded Theory Procedures and Techniques.* Newbury Park, CA: Sage.

Vasquez, M. (1999). Trainee impairment: A response from a feminist/multicultural retired trainer. *Counseling Psychologist, 27,* 687-692.

Vasquez, M., & Eldridge, N. (1994). Bringing ethics alive: Training practitioners about gender, ethnicity and sexual orientation issues. *Women & Therapy, 15,* 1-16.

Werner-Wilson, R., Price, S., Zimmerman, T., & Murphy, M. (1997). Client gender as a process variable in marriage and family therapy: Are women clients interrupted more than men clients? *Journal of Family Psychotherapy, 11,* 373-377.

Wheeler, D., Avis, J., Miller, L., & Chaney, S. (1986). Rethinking family therapy education and supervision: A feminist model. *Journal of Psychotherapy and the Family, 1,* 53-72.

Wheeler, D., Avis, J., Miller, L., & Chaney, S. (1989). Rethinking family therapy training and supervision: A feminist model. In M. McGoldrick, C. Anderson & F. Walsh (Eds.), *Women in Families: A Framework for Family Therapy* (pp. 135-151). New York: W. W. Norton.

Therapy with Families in Poverty: Application of Feminist Family Therapy Principles

Scott J. Ziemba

SUMMARY. Issues of economic marginalization have been largely neglected in training of family therapists. However, attention to the effects of economic instability on family and individual well-being is important in preparing clinicians to address the needs and goals of families in poverty. This paper has been designed as an attempt to apply principles of feminist family therapy to therapeutic work with low-income families. Specifically, 7 principles commonly included in the practice of feminist family therapy are given special consideration. Practical applications of each principle are discussed for developing a model of class-conscious therapy. It is argued that feminist family therapy can serve as a framework for providing effective and respectful therapy to families in poverty. *[Article copies available for a fee from The Haworth Document Delivery Service: 1-800-342-9678. E-mail address: <getinfo@haworthpressinc.com> Website: <http://www.HaworthPress.com> © 2001 by The Haworth Press, Inc. All rights reserved.]*

Scott J. Ziemba, MS, is a recent graduate of the Marriage and Family Therapy Program, Department of Human Development and Family Studies, Colorado State University, Fort Collins, CO 80523-1570 (E-mail: scottziemba@hotmail.com). The author would like to dedicate this manuscript to the memory of his mother, Linda Mary Ziemba, the biggest feminist influence of his life.

The author would also like to sincerely thank Shelley A. Haddock, MS, and Toni S. Zimmerman, PhD, for their invaluable creative influence, motivational energy, and editorial mentoring.

[Haworth co-indexing entry note]: "Therapy with Families in Poverty: Application of Feminist Family Therapy Principles." Ziemba, Scott J. Co-published simultaneously in *Journal of Feminist Family Therapy* (The Haworth Press, Inc.) Vol. 12, No. 4, 2001, pp. 205-237; and: *Integrating Gender and Culture in Family Therapy Training* (ed: Toni Schindler Zimmerman) The Haworth Press, Inc., 2001, pp. 205-237. Single or multiple copies of this article are available for a fee from The Haworth Document Delivery Service [1-800-342-9678, 9:00 a.m. - 5:00 p.m. (EST). E-mail address: getinfo@haworthpressinc.com].

KEYWORDS. Poverty, feminism, feminist family therapy, training

During the past decade, a concerted effort has been made by feminist scholars to integrate issues of culture, social class, and social justice into family therapy training (e.g., Almeida, Woods, Messineo, & Font, 1998; Boyd-Franklin, 1993; Boyd-Franklin & Shenouda, 1990; Falicov, 1995, 1998; Hopps & Pinderhughes, 1999; McGoldrick, 1998; McGoldrick et al., 1999). However, while long considered by feminists as an issue of social justice, poverty has received little attention in submissions published by this journal. In fact, in the eleven volumes published from its inception in 1989 through the completion of 1999, only 2 of 160 (1.25%) articles appearing in the *Journal of Feminist Family Therapy* have explicitly focused on issues of poverty and family therapy (Atwood & Genovese, 1997; Walker, Eric, Pivnick, & Drucker, 1991). Unfortunately, this shortcoming in the literature leaves student clinicians, family therapists, and clinical supervisors with relatively little guidance in providing services to families in poverty (Aponte, 1991; Rabin, 1989). In this regard, more could be done by the field to carry on the tradition begun by Salvador Minuchin, who devoted a portion of his early work to helping low-income families from New York City (Minuchin, Montalvo, Guerney, Rosman, & Schumer, 1967).

This discussion is intended as a step toward reintroducing issues of poverty and economic marginalization into marriage and family therapy training. Specifically, the main emphasis will be to integrate considerations of poverty into a model of feminist family therapy. To this end, the goal is to accomplish three tasks. First, I will briefly outline a series of arguments in favor of integrating poverty into family therapy training. Second, I will attempt to provide a working definition of feminist family therapy by discussing seven principles commonly found in the literature. Third, these principles will be considered in the context of therapeutic work with families in poverty. In discussing these principles, feminist family therapy will be examined as a framework for providing effective, respectful, and class-conscious therapy to families living in poverty.

THE IMPORTANCE OF INTEGRATING POVERTY INTO FAMILY THERAPY TRAINING

The lack of attention given to families in poverty by marriage and family therapy perhaps begs the question, "Why are issues of poverty relevant in family therapy training?" First, current research in social and family science has demonstrated the negative impact of poverty on individuals and families who must contend with financial disadvantage as a daily fact of life. Coping with the conditions of poverty and economic instability is a significant source of stress that can have detrimental effects on the individual, marital dyad, and family system over time (Aponte, 1991, 1994; Costello, Messer, Bird, Cohen, & Reinherz, 1998; McLoyd, 1990, 1998; McLoyd, Jayaratne, Ceballo, & Borquez, 1994). The challenge for clients is to cope with the conditions of poverty and secure basic survival needs, while simultaneously attempting to maintain family cohesion and individual well-being. Given the pervasive and deleterious influences of poverty, this task is clearly not a simple one for many clients. In light of these challenges, many families in poverty could potentially benefit from therapeutic interventions designed to target the family system. An appreciation for these detrimental influences is critical in developing therapists who are sensitive to issues of poverty and prepared to assist low-income families in the development of effective coping strategies.

Second, consideration of social class and poverty is also relevant for family therapists in light of the increasing number of women and children facing financial difficulties. On average, women in the United States have higher rates of poverty than men (Hendley & Bilimoria, 1999). This phenomenon has been referred to as "the feminization of poverty" (Atwood & Genovese, 1997; Avis, 1989; Goldner, 1985). Specifically, single mothers, divorcees, and widows are often hardest hit by difficult financial straits, with some estimates claiming that as many as 50 percent of these women live in poverty (Montemurri, 1998). However, the impact of poverty is not felt by these women alone. Economic hardships experienced by women also influence their children. A recent government report estimates that over half of all families receiving food stamps were headed by a single parent (Gunderson, LeBlanc, & Kuhn, 1999), that parent typically being a mother. Also of significant concern is the fact that the fastest growing homeless population in the United States is composed of women and children (Boettcher, 1999). Given these statistics, considerations of poverty and economic deprivation are of critical concern for family therapists waging the war to preserve the well-being of women, children, and families in this country.

Third, integrating issues of poverty into family therapy training is critical for developing a greater appreciation for the influence of culture on family dynamics. Culture encompasses more than ethnicity, including other contextual factors, such as religion, political ideology, sexual orientation, and socioeconomic status (Falicov, 1995, 1998). This multidimensional approach to defining culture allows for a more complete understanding of the ecological niche occupied by a family. To this end, it is vital for therapists to develop adequate cultural competence, while refraining from simultaneously perpetuating stereotypical evaluations that disregard the individual perspectives and stories clients carry into therapy (Falicov, 1998). Attending to multiple contextual factors allows therapists to design interventions that are relevant given a family's unique structure, cultural narrative, values, ideologies, and experiences. This can be especially important in combating the cultural and social stereotypes often used to describe low-income families in therapy and the disrespectful treatment many families encounter when accessing the mental health system (Inclan & Ferran, 1990; Saba & Rodgers, 1989). Tailoring therapy to fit the cultural and ecological niche occupied by a particular family allows the process to be more respectful of family idiosyncrasies (Falicov, 1995, 1998). From this perspective, appreciating the dynamics operating in a family confronting poverty is one element in increasing cultural sensitivity among family therapists.

Fourth, consideration of poverty and its effects on family functioning is even more significant in the context of recent economic trends. There is evidence that the American economy is becoming increasingly stratified, creating a significant gap between the proverbial "haves" and "have nots" (Inclan & Ferran, 1990). Concern is growing over a disintegrating middle class and an accumulating number of families facing economic hardship. These trends are alarming for two main reasons. First, continuation of these patterns will likely leave a growing proportion of American families to contend with the stress and struggles associated with poverty. Second, economic stratification is also producing a subgroup of low-income families who are neither "poor enough" to qualify for Medicaid benefits nor financially capable of purchasing health insurance for themselves. These families often find themselves in an extremely difficult position when accessing the mental health care system. Granted, *pro bono* mental health services are a potentially valuable asset to these families, when available. However, when denied such services and lacking the financial resources to seek treatment through a private practice therapist, these families are often relegated to lengthy waiting lists at community mental health agencies. Often these agencies are understaffed (Friedman & Levine-Holdowsky, 1997) and, when providing Medicaid services, legally obligated to give those clients first priority. In this context, it is not uncommon for clients seeking care to often wait several weeks for a first appointment (Bateman, 1993; Northam, 1996; Rosenheck & Lam, 1997). If unaddressed, these economic trends are likely to create a growing number of families facing a mental health care crisis and a growing number of families having difficulty obtaining services.

Fifth, urban low-income families typically fail to access services that are available to them at community-based mental health care agencies (Friedman & Levine-Holdowsky, 1997; Schnitzer, 1996). To account for this pattern of underutilization, barriers to service access have been identified in client-therapist interactions, such as negative relationships (Kazdin, Holland, & Crowley, 1997; Saba & Rodgers, 1989), treatment that is disrespectful, indifferent, and irrelevant (Hunter, Getty, Kemsley, & Skelly, 1991; Murrell, Smith, Gill, & Oxley, 1996), economic and/or racial discrimination and stigmatization by care providers (Feinson & Popper, 1995; Funkhouser & Moser, 1990; Meyerson & Herman, 1987), and care that is rarely integrated between multiple service providers (Calloway & Morrissey, 1998). Underutilization of mental health care services is particularly troubling given the impact that poverty can have on family functioning. Without receiving intervention sensitive to their needs, families in poverty may find themselves seemingly trapped in a vicious cycle of poverty, stress, and crisis. Awareness of barriers to service utilization and experiences of low-income families with the mental health care system can be a meaningful first step toward providing care that is accessible, beneficial, and respectful to these families.

Finally, the lack of training material applying family therapy techniques to issues faced by families in poverty may have detrimental effects on the social perspectives clinicians bring to therapy. For example, Schnitzer (1996) has critiqued the field of psychiatry for largely neglecting poverty and social class issues in formal clinical training. Without the sensitivity and attention to social justice fostered by such training, this author found that students, instructors, and supervisors tend to create a professional culture that shares stereotypical beliefs about families in poverty. Specifically, these stories characterized low-income clients as lacking the responsibility necessary to follow through with treatment, the cognitive capacity to understand therapy, and the moral integrity to care about family well-being (Schnitzer, 1996). These generalizations about clients in poverty have the potential of producing negative interactions between clients and therapist, such as those discussed previously. Failing to address poverty issues, the experiences of families living in financial hardship, and the stresses associated with economic deprivation can lead to clinical training that ill-prepares therapists for work with families in poverty. Due to this lack of preparatory training, it appears that therapists fail to consider how economic factors may influence client behavior and the overall course of treatment. Interestingly, a similar argument has also been used to justify the inclusion of gender issues into family therapy training (Avis, 1989). Beginning to understand dimensions of poverty can equip therapists with a social class lens through which to filter interactions with low-income clients, a tool invaluable in creating a class-conscious therapeutic environment.

PRINCIPLES OF FEMINIST FAMILY THERAPY

For over two decades feminist scholars have committed themselves to exposing the deficiencies, inconsistencies, and explicit and implicit sexism present in the theoretical underpinnings of marriage and family therapy (Ault-Riche, 1986; Bograd, 1987, Dermer, Hemesath, & Russell, 1998; Goldner, 1985, 1988; Hare-Mustin, 1978; James & MacKinnon, 1986; MacKinnon & Miller, 1987; Treacher, 1988). From these critiques, a growing body of literature has emerged helping to define the practice of feminist family therapy.

Rather than being a distinct theoretical approach, feminist family therapy is instead considered a conceptual lens or social philosophical perspective through which to view relationships. In this sense, a feminist perspective is one that can be integrated into virtually any therapeutic model. In fact, efforts have been made to synthesize feminist critiques and various therapeutic approaches (Hill, 1992; Lee, 1997; Terry, 1992). When considered in a historical context, systemic models of family therapy and feminist scholarship have evolved a great deal since the late 1970s (Goldner, 1991), giving rise to a greater awareness of gender issues and social justice among marriage and family therapists.

In an effort to capute a sense of this evolution, I have drawn from a series of articles, spanning a period from 1978 through the present, that define the practice of feminist family therapy (Ault-Riche, 1986; Avis, 1989; Bograd, 1986; Chaney & Piercy, 1988; Dankowski, Penn, Carlson, & Hecker, 1998; Fish, 1989; Goldner, 1985; Haddock, Zimmerman, & MacPhee, 2000; Hare-Mustin, 1978; James & McIntyre, 1983, 1989; Leslie & Clossick, 1992; Rabin, 1989; Simola, 1992; Taggart, 1985; Wheeler, Avis, Miller, & Chaney, 1989; Whipple, 1996). From this reading, seven common principles emerged, each receiving mention in no fewer than 5 of the previously mentioned articles. When taken together, these principles provide the starting point for constructing a working definition of feminist family therapy. The seven principles of feminist family therapy that will receive consideration are: (1) attention to the family's social context; (2) gender as a topic of therapy; (3) encouraging egalitarian couples; (4) empowerment; (5) nonhierarchical therapeutic relationship; (6) therapist non-neutrality; and (7) attention to both individual and family well-being.

In the following section an effort will be made to briefly apply each of these principles to therapy with low-income families. However, before doing so, mention will be given to cultural and social class issues important to consider when applying feminist family therapy principles. While the scope of this paper will not allow for a detailed definition of each of these principles, the reader is directed to the above citations for a more comprehensive explanation of these basic concepts.

FEMINIST FAMILY THERAPY AND LOW-INCOME FAMILIES

While feminist scholarship has long focused on issues of social justice, it has been critiqued as a political and social philosophy created by and in the interest of predominantly middle-class, Euro-American women (hooks, 1981; Kanuha, 1990). With its primary emphasis on sexism, feminism has often failed to consider other forms of oppression faced by nonmiddle-class women (e.g., racism, classism, and heterosexism). These critiques have raised questions as to the relevance of mainstream feminist philosophy for all women. As such,

Kanuha (1990) has articulately argued in favor of an integrated approach to feminism that incorporates greater sensitivity to race, social class, and sexual orientation in its social and political agenda. In response to this call, this paper is an effort toward developing a more integrated approach to feminist family therapy, one that has potential applicability for families in poverty.

However, it is also important to acknowledge that poverty is not a monolithic influence that affects all families in the same manner (Boyd-Franklin, 1993). In fact, there is great diversity among low-income families, diversity that cuts across age, ethnic, religious, and political groups. It could be argued that greater diversity exists among families in poverty than any other social class purely on the basis of ethnicity. Members of ethnic minority groups are disproportionately represented among those facing economic deprivation. While it is beyond the scope of this discussion to focus on these multiple dimensions, it is critical to not underestimate how the considerations mentioned in this paper may interface with ethnicity, nationality, and other characteristics that define a family's ecological niche (Falicov, 1995, 1998). As issues of poverty and social class become prominent considerations for marriage and family therapists, it is hoped that future research will attempt to raise awareness of the dynamic interactions between a family's socioeconomic status and their multidimensional cultural identity.

In this effort to integrate principles of feminist family therapy into work with families in poverty, it is imperative to include mention of Denny's (1986) work. This paper offers a four-part critique that questions the applicability of feminist family therapy for women in poverty. First, as with feminist social philosophy, emphasis on gender discrimination as the fundamental form of social oppression inadvertently ignores the racial, political, and economic oppression faced by many women in poverty. Second, it is important to appreciate that the ideal world for a woman in poverty may include different definitions of justice and success than those espoused by a therapist from a middle-class, feminist perspective. Third, it is crucial to understand the reality of women in poverty, considering a woman's psychological distress as a reasonable response to a maddening world characterized by racial and economic discrimination. Finally, feminist therapists must not fail to consider how their low-income, female clients have been gender socialized, as these women may have been taught to be powerful and assertive in certain facets of family life. These areas of strength have been traditionally overlooked in the literature, leaving it unsafe to assume that women in poverty need the same degree of empowerment training as their middle-class counterparts. Without incorporating these considerations into therapy, Denny (1986) cautions that feminist family therapy is in danger of unintentionally subjecting women in poverty to the same type of ignorance and inadvertent oppression that traditional forms of psychotherapy have to all women.

In the context of these critiques, this paper will offer a synthesis applying principles of feminist family therapy to work with families in poverty. Each of the seven principles mentioned above will be considered individually in terms of its potential applicability for therapeutic interventions with low-income families. In considering these recommendations, it will be argued that a feminist approach to family therapy can be effective with families in poverty. It is hoped that therapists and clinical supervisors can profit from this training material by incorporating greater awareness and sensitivity to issues of economic marginalization in therapeutic work with clients in poverty.

Attention to the Family's Social Context

The first and perhaps most frequently mentioned principle of feminist family therapy involves an attention to the family's social context. Feminist scholars have repeatedly challenged the assumption of traditional systems theory that family therapy can be separated from the social, political, and economic context in which women and families exist (Chaney & Piercy, 1988; Fish, 1989; Haddock et al., 2000; James & McIntyre, 1989). From this expanded systems perspective, the development and maintenance of family problems is largely attributable to the oppressive nature of the social environment. In fact, it has been cogently argued that inclusion of the broader social context makes systems theory more truly systemic (Avis, 1989; Simola, 1992; Taggart, 1985). Considering the ecological context from which a family enters therapy increases the power of a systems approach to explain a family's social environment, understand a family's past and current situations, and intervene for a family's benefit (Bograd, 1986).

In training to conduct therapy with low-income families, it is important to understand the historical, social, and political factors that have contributed to the creation and continuation of poverty. To this end, Inclan and Ferran (1990) offer a brief sociological account, tracking the development of urban poverty in the United States across a period spanning from World War II through the early 1970s. From this broader perspective, Aponte (1994) describes the struggles of low-income families as a direct result of failures of the American economy. These views of urban poverty appreciate that economic disadvantage is a phenomenon attributable to social forces that reach beyond the family system, factors that often leave families feeling hopeless to produce change. Yet, while appreciating the historical, social, and political origins of poverty is critical for developing a greater understanding of clients' lives, the challenge remains to develop a non-blaming view of these clients while simultaneously remaining optimistic that they have the power to change their family dynamics in the face of stress caused by oppressive social forces.

While appreciating the social factors that have shaped urban poverty, it is also crucial to not overlook the experiences of these families in the here-and-now. It is not uncommon for families in poverty to face limited access to basic resources, confront a host of personal and familial stressors, conceptualize life as an endless series of crises, and require multiple forms of social service. As such, many low-income families enter therapy while also seeking assistance from an array of community agencies. As previously mentioned, the recommendations offered by these care providers are rarely coordinated or integrated, a situation that can leave these families facing treatment advice that is often confusing, contradictory, and disorganized (Minuchin et al., 1998). In addition, many families in poverty feel socially isolated due to a profound distrust of their community, a neighborhood with which they may have had very few positive experiences. As such, these families are often left without a community support network to cope with the multiple stressors associated with poverty (Kaplan & Girard, 1994). Further, in a culture that emphasizes the accumulation of wealth as a measure of success, many families in poverty struggle to maintain a positive image of themselves. It is not uncommon for these families to view their own lives as worthless in relation to the dominant culture of capitalistic affluence (Kaplan & Girard, 1994). Surrounded by what can be perceived as an overwhelming amount of negative energy, these families often lose faith in their own strengths and enter therapy feeling defeated. In the context of poverty's multiple stressors, Minuchin et al. (1998) encourage professionals to approach therapy with a low-income family from the perspective of "a mural rather than a close-up" (p. 34), echoing previous work that has also argued in favor of interventions that consider multiple factors operating within the family and its social environment (Aponte, 1974, 1976, 1986, 1994; Boyd-Franklin, 1989; Boyd-Franklin & Shenouda, 1990; Hartman & Laird, 1983; Walker et al., 1991).

In designing comprehensive interventions for families in poverty, several authors have endorsed programs based upon a social-ecological model (Illback, 1994; Mueller & Patton, 1995; Sharlin & Shamai, 1995; Shayne & Kaplan, 1991; Walker et al., 1991; Walker & Small, 1991). These programs typically offer multilevel interventions that include family therapy, case management, multi-family support, community advocacy, securing basic survival needs, and facilitating financial assistance. Such comprehensive intervention programs are guided by a mission to offer a coordinated and holistic system of care (Mueller & Patton, 1995). In the process, the hope is to offer families encountering multiple treatment issues a respectful environment designed to meet their needs and instill a sense of belonging and social support. As such, attending to a family's social context is not only vital during treatment assessment, but also in creation of intervention programs. By incorporating a sociopolitical awareness into therapy, a feminist approach can be particularly well-suited to work with families in poverty.

Gender as a Topic of Therapy

Another defining element of feminist family therapy is the explicit inclusion of gender as a topic of therapy. To this end, feminist therapists commonly explore the origins of gender beliefs, discuss the effects of gender stereotypes, and often point out the connection between gender ideologies and the larger cultural context in which a family lives (Whipple, 1996). In doing so, a conscious effort is made to examine ways in which gendered behavior manifests itself in the family (James & McIntyre, 1989). Within this context, the goal is threefold: to challenge rigid and restrictive gender stereotypes, to allow for more flexible and adaptive belief systems to develop in the place of traditional ones, and to provide affirmation for the experiences of women in a patriarchal society (Rabin, 1989; Simola, 1992). However, when working with families in poverty, gender and economic status often interact to create complex family dynamics. As such, exploring gender in isolation from other social factors may create therapeutic interventions that fail to consider the lived experiences of families in poverty.

Exploring gender as a topic offers the opportunity to consider cultural, social, economic, and political pressures that women in poverty face on a daily basis. Feminist scholars have long argued in favor of an equal division of paid and domestic labor among men and women and in favor of allowing women the option to seek paid employment outside of the home. However, many women in low-income families face significant financial pressure to work. Such a conversation will likely have little relevance for a woman who may not and potentially never has considered paid employment to be an option. Yet, including gender as a topic of therapy provides an opportunity to explore the intersection of gender and social class and the conflicting social pressures that lie therein.

For example, after becoming recently widowed, Roxanne, age 42, considered her employment necessary for family survival. She worked full-time as a grocery stocker and also waited tables part-time at a local restaurant. Without having completed high school, Roxanne felt as if her employment opportunities were limited, a situation she found particularly distressing given her increasing frustrations with work. She was upset that she often worked 60 hours per week under strenuous work conditions, yet still could not fully provide for her family financially nor afford the meager insurance benefits available through the grocery store. In addition, she had yet to reach 12 months of employment at either job, the point at which she would begin accumulating paid wellness days and personal leave time from work. Roxanne complained that work kept her away from her family for large parts of the day and that it was often difficult to feel involved with her children due to difficulties coordinating her work schedules. At the same time, she also felt a great deal of pressure to stay at home with her two sons, ages 10 and 13, as the neighborhood had recently seen an increase in crime, drug trafficking, and gang activity. She originally sought family therapy because the police had caught her eldest son shoplifting on three occasions in the past six months. In an individual session, she discussed the often overwhelming guilt she experienced over being unable to provide close supervision for her children and offer greater protection from the negative influences present in the community. However, she felt trapped in a bind, because she was also unwilling to consider sacrificing either of her jobs. She reported that doing so would leave the family little option other than to apply for welfare benefits. This was not a viable option either, given the personal humiliation associated with seeking public assistance and the negative messages she had received from society, media, local community leaders, and her traditional Italian-American family about welfare mothers.

As such, Roxanne clearly articulated the tension she felt from conflicting gender and economic pressures. These pressures pulled her in different directions in the name of providing the best for her family. In the process, Roxanne found herself carrying a burden of guilt, discouragement, and powerless about her family situation. During individual sessions, a portion of treatment was devoted to providing support, validation, and affirmation for Roxanne's internal struggles and discussing the messages transmitted by our culture about working mothers' inability to be good parents. Further, discussions also focused on devising strategies for making the time with her children meaningful, exploring creative options for employment and childcare, the possibility of bringing her children to the restaurant on some evenings, and strategies for translating gains from her individual sessions into family sessions. In accomplishing these goals, it was also necessary to become familiar with the services available in the larger community and assist Roxanne in accessing the local social service network agency, resources on resume building and job hunting, and support services available through her Catholic church.

It is also important to appreciate the social position occupied by women in poverty. By virtue of being female and in financial hardship, low-income women are often the victims of dual discrimination–one on the basis of gender, the other on the basis of economics. Further, due to the correlation between poverty and ethnicity, women from low-income families are also the victims of a third layer of social oppression, racial discrimination. These layers of oppression have been powerful in the denigration and dehumanization of "welfare mothers" and in the reduction of welfare benefits ushered in by the passage of the Personal Responsibility and Work Opportunity Reconciliation Act of 1996 (Sidel, 2000). It is critical to not overlook the intrapsychic and interpersonal dynamics that stem from these multiple layers of social marginalization. These effects remain invisible in therapy without consideration of the social context and its influence on a female client. As such, exploring gender in concert with economic and other forms of oppression is critical in helping therapists appreciate the pressures these women must cope with. In addition, it is also helpful to reframe a female client's current situation as an expected response within an oppressive social environment (Denny, 1986).

Addressing gender as a topic of therapy also offers the opportunity to explore cultural, social, economic, and political pressures that men in poverty face on a regular basis. Men are often defined by themselves and others on the basis of their ability to provide economic and material sustenance for their families. Due to the social pressures and confining gender roles placed on them, men are often expected to fulfill the role of primary breadwinner (Fish, 1989). Yet, when facing poverty and economic struggles, many come to view themselves as failing in their duties of manhood and acutely experience the guilt associated with those feelings of failure (Rabin, 1989). While being socialized as instrumental providers, men are often discouraged from participating in the affective dimensions of family life, further limiting the role they occupy in the family. In this sense, it is important to investigate with men the detrimental effects of male socialization and how those cultural messages influence their definitions of themselves. When appropriate, encouraging men to adopt a greater parental role in the family may help to counteract the negative feelings associated with not being the family's sole economic provider. From experience, I have found it helpful to frame this as a contribution to overall family well-being that goes beyond the value of dollars and cents, but is rather like an investment in the future of the family. Such a role has been powerful in giving male clients a sense of contributing to family success in ways other than those they are accustomed to. However, given the powerful nature of gender socialization and the tendency for men to be reluctant customers of family therapy, this is often a long process requiring a firm belief that small, measurable changes can have larger effects over time.

Encouraging Egalitarian Couples

Another key principle of feminist family therapy involves encouraging egalitarian couple relationships. Feminist therapists are attuned to power differentials in intimate relationships, primarily in the interest of rebalancing power between women and men (Rabin, 1989; Wheeler et al., 1989; Whipple, 1996). In essence, egalitarian relationships are based upon mutual respect, reciprocal support, domestic task sharing, equal opportunity to define and set rules for the relationship, shared access to material resources, and joint decision making (Goldner, 1985; Haddock et al., 2000; Rosenbluth, Steil, & Whitcomb, 1998). In the name of gender equity and social justice, feminist therapists attempt to facilitate the creation of a safe home environment where partners can share influence over family affairs and provide mutual support in managing the everyday tasks and stresses of family life. Thus, in a respectful manner, feminist therapists encourage couples to strive toward a relationship in which both partners assume equal control and responsibility for marital and family well-being.

Helping couples in poverty achieve relationship equality can be particularly valuable as a means of coping with the difficult circumstances that typically surround financial instability. Egalitarian couples often enjoy a sense of deep friendship with one another, share increased intimacy, and benefit from mutual support (Schwartz, 1994). On a general level, support between equal partners is critical for two main reasons. First, by virtue of their commitment to fairness, egalitarian partners are likely to offer each other instrumental support in the struggle to provide for their family's basic needs. Couples in poverty often have little choice but to work incredibly hard to supply the time, financial resources, and energy necessary to maintain family operations. However, helping couples to do so in the context of an equal relationship can increase dyadic cohesiveness, promote greater teamwork between partners, and encourage partners to help each other as well as the family. Second, egalitarian couples are also better prepared to offer each other emotional support and nurturance in the face of extreme personal trials. Providing this support may be a challenge for couples when both partners are under a great deal of stress. However, in many cases few people understand the family's circumstances better than a close partner. It may be helpful to frame this mutual support as a united struggle against oppression or a united struggle for the benefit of each other and the family. Doing so prevents the experience from further taxing the emotional reserves of either partner or becoming a competition between partners to determine who is suffering from a greater amount of stress.

By way of a case example, Shirley and Michael originally entered marital therapy seeking relief for Shirley from the depressive symptoms she had been experiencing for approximately six months. In the initial evaluation, they revealed that Shirley was largely responsible for the household labor, childcare, and management of the family's finances. Even though both of them worked full-time outside of the home, Michael's role was to provide assistance when household tasks became too cumbersome for Shirley to handle herself. However, this assistance would not come without a price, as Shirley reported that it was not uncommon for Michael to leave her feeling guilty for having to ask. In the course of therapy, Shirley and Michael came to see how the distribution of marital power and Michael's emotional tactics were associated with Shirley's symptoms. Over the course of several sessions, this couple began to implement strategies for equally sharing responsibility for the family. In the process, Michael commented on how he felt they had rediscovered each other as friends, partners, and confidants. They both agreed that these qualities were significant strengths, particularly since they lived hundreds of miles from either of their families and found very little social support as an African-American couple living in a rough Euro-American neighborhood. Further, they also came to understand their partnership as an allegiance against "the cloud of stress" that seemed to darken their lives. They both admitted that their jobs were physically grueling and that work took a lot out of them. In fact, they found that it was a relief to have a teammate in the struggle, rather than an antagonist. Further, in the course of their conversations, they realized that they shared many of the same concerns for their family. Particularly, they worried about their children's education and social opportunities in a predominately Euro-American school, how to afford medical supplies for their diabetic son, and what to do in the face of rumors that Michael's company will soon be considering massive layoffs. Without coming to see each other as equal partners, it is likely that this couple would not have found each other to be such a significant source of support.

However, in this discussion of egalitarian relationships, it is also important to entertain a few words of caution. First, while from a feminist perspective patriarchal oppression of women is of paramount importance, therapists should take care not to overlook the greater context of oppression in which their low-income, female clients live. Focusing exclusively on sexism may prove irrelevant or even offensive to women in poverty who are also contending with racial, political, and/or economic oppression (Denny, 1986). In fact, some clients' experiences of sexism pale in comparison to these other forms of social marginalization. Second, encouraging egalitarian relationships may be a delicate issue in the context of power dynamics operating between the family and the larger social context. As previously mentioned, men who feel as if they are failing to provide economic resources for their families often experience profound feelings of inadequacy, inferiority, and shame in their masculine role. Asking a man in such a position to prematurely relinquish power to his partner will further augment his feelings of social inadequacy and powerlessness. In doing so, a therapist may produce a defensive reaction, by which he attempts to assert greater control over the relationship. In certain circumstances, this is the only element of the man's life over which he feels any control. The potential of losing this control may be perceived as a threat to his manhood. As such, a therapist may inadvertently produce greater inequality within the family and marital systems. Clearly, timing and delivery of such an intervention can be critical in protecting female clients from further control and, in the most extreme cases, abuse. Third, in the interface of poverty and culture, it is important to appreciate the cultural heritage a family carries into therapy. While not necessarily offering endorsement, it is important to maintain respect for families that value a patriarchal structure. In these situations, it can be difficult for feminist therapists to find a balance between honestly disclosing their personal and professional values and entertaining multiple views of reality. To this end, it is advisable to overtly discuss different approaches to relationships, while also maintaining an ethical commitment to challenge client value systems and help clients explore the range of viable alternatives for their lives. Yet, in the context of these considerations, exercising caution, care, and good judgment in encouraging egalitarian relationships will prevent therapy from becoming both disrespectful and potentially harmful to female clients.

Empowerment

Another principle commonly discussed in the feminist family therapy literature is that of client empowerment. A feminist approach encourages clients to explore the various alternatives available in their lives and to make beneficial lifestyle decisions even when running contrary to societal expectations (Wheeler et al., 1989; Whipple, 1996). Inadvertently asking a low-income family to adapt or assimilate to the norms of the dominant middle-class culture, may, in some instances, be asking them to sacrifice a source of personal and familial strength. Further, in assisting clients to consider alternative solutions to problems, feminist therapists help clients develop skills for self-sufficiency that have tremendous value outside of therapy. Rather than facilitating a family's dependence on a therapist, the goal is to help families recognize their sources of strength and develop tools that will allow them to navigate a course through an otherwise oppressive social system.

While helping clients to break free from restrictive roles outside of therapy may benefit family well-being, it may be equally as important to also liberate clients from oppressive roles operating in the therapy room. Traditional family therapy has been criticized on grounds that it does not fit the experiences of families in poverty. It has been argued that psychotherapy includes inadvertent biases that value verbal skills, understanding and expressing emotions, and a willingness to engage in open and intimate self-disclosure with a relative stranger (Faunce, 1990). By and large, this is a Euro-American, middle-class model of therapy that may not feel appropriate for clients who prescribe to a different set of cultural norms (Faunce, 1990). Asking clients to verbally express emotions and communicate about the most intimate aspects of their relationships may feel oppressive to clients who are uncomfortable approaching problems from such a perspective. In these cases, a behavioral, solution focused, or experiential approach can prove more effective in addressing a family's needs. Therapeutic flexibility that allows low-income clients freedom to solve problems in a way that suits their style helps the process to be more sensitive and effective for these families.

While encouraging client empowerment, it is important to recognize the inherent challenges in achieving this goal with clients from low-income communities. By lacking access to financial resources, these families also lack access to a significant source of power in American society. In the face of this challenge, helping clients develop a sense of their own strength and self-efficacy requires creativity on the part of the clients, therapists, and the agency providing services. Furthermore, interventions must be tailored to a family's economic situation. Applying techniques normally used with a middle-class family may be unrealistic for a family in poverty to follow through on (which incidentally is often interpreted as a form of client resistance) or may demonstrate insensitivity for the family's economic struggles. For example, suggesting that a family in poverty enroll their children in another school because of overcrowded classrooms and substandard teachers is not be a realistic option when both spouses earn little more than minimum wage, are employed with companies that offer little job security, share one unreliable car, and work long shifts on the opposite side of town. In situations like these, therapists must work in conjunction with case managers and other community service providers to meet a family's practical, material needs. Often these needs become obstacles to meeting therapeutic ends. In addition, creating unorthodox interventions may be necessary, such as neighborhood family support groups, teaching groups of clients to formulate grant proposals for funds that would meet their needs, approaching community colleges to donate adult teaching time, helping clients form their own food, clothing, and toy drives, family car pools, child care co-operatives, organizing clients to ask local high schools and/or colleges to donate used textbooks for a client library, and asking successful clients or families to return to the agency to offer peer support. In fact, this latter example has become a vital portion of narrative therapy. In a process referred to as the "definitional ceremony," former clients are invited into therapy to offer acknowledgment for a current client's struggles against a problem and authentication of the counter-plot that client is in the process of creating for his or her life story (White, 2000). In doing so, the stories of people's lives become linked around shared themes, purposes, and values in a form of community-wide change (White, 2000). While limited financial resources are often an obstacle to promoting client empowerment, creative problem solving by clients, therapists, and agency administrators may be necessary to overcome this barrier.

Furthermore, when facing multiple service needs, families in poverty often rely on the social service system to provide them with needed resources. This can be a dangerous outcome for clients who are not shown tools for interacting with the system on their own behalf. The potential exists for these families to become dependent on a paternalistic system that only has limited understanding of their experiences. As such, the goal is to empower clients as advocates for their own interests. Therapists can facilitate self-advocacy by providing a safe environment in which to model and develop skills that will allow clients to take a proactive approach with the social service system. With the goal of empowerment in mind, therapists and case managers can assist clients to access medical, food assistance, employment, housing, childcare, and transportation services in a way that can produce future success, even after termination. By valuing empowerment, feminist approaches to family interventions can help clients take a more active role in meeting multiple service needs and avoid undue reliance on the social service system in the future.

Nonhierarchical Therapeutic Relationship

Another principle of feminist family therapy involves a commitment to establishing nonhierarchical relationships with clients. With an awareness of power dynamics both inside and outside of the therapy room, it is important to recognize the implicit power differentials involved when a family seeks the help of a therapist. Due to the virtual inevitability of this client-therapist hierarchy, a feminist perspective encourages therapists to recognize this power differential and make efforts to minimize its presence in therapy (Chaney & Piercy, 1988; Haddock et al., 2000). Yet, families often enter therapy seeking the healing touch of an "expert." A critical consideration in conducting feminist family therapy is to resist the pressure of adopting an "expert role" (Wheeler et al., 1989). Adopting such a role often disempowers clients and inhibits growth that commonly accompanies efforts at therapeutic change. Further, clients also leave therapy without having learned techniques for finding their own solutions in the future, as clients potentially dependent on an overly-directive therapist. Resisting such a role is particularly challenging with families who have developed an expectation from past experience that the job of a service provider is to do something for them or to them, not with them (Minuchin et al., 1998).

However, despite these challenges, an overly directive approach can be extremely harmful to clients in poverty. Failing to work collaboratively with clients can produce a therapeutic experience that feels invasive and intrusive. Families in poverty often view such therapists as paternalistic and disrespectful to their experiences of financial hardship. Therapists adopting a directive stance may also breed contempt and resentment in their clients, particularly from those who are already suspicious of mental health professionals as representative of middle-class privilege and oppression. By adopting an "expert" stance, therapists also inadvertently undermine parental authority, disrupt family unity, and replicate society's messages that the family is incapable of solving problems through their own devices (Minuchin et al., 1998).

For example, I recently began meeting with Martha and her family for family therapy. She originally sought help for her 11-year-old son, Michael, who had been exhibiting angry and disrespectful outbursts over the previous nine months. As a single mother, she expressed concern and frustration over being unable to control Michael and cope with his continuing disobedience. During an initial session, Martha discussed the negative experiences she recently had with the family's previous therapist. She found this therapist to be stubborn, disrespectful, and judgmental. Upon exploring her description further, I found that Martha was frustrated with this therapist who continually caused her to feel like Michael's problems were her fault and who would not take the time to listen to her opinions on the problems at home. She expressed a desire to find a therapist who would listen, demonstrate a sincere interest in helping her family, and not be so quick to offer judgement about the problem. In communicating with the previous therapist about this family, he expressed reservations about the family's ability to change and found Martha to lack the intelligence and insight to benefit from family therapy. For those reasons, he felt it was his job to take a directive role and show the family how to best address their problems. In working with this African-American family, I did not want to make the same mistakes, but instead adopted a stance of curiosity. In the first five sessions, I found that Martha demonstrated a great deal of insight in response to my questions and even began noticing repetitious patterns of interactions between Michael and herself. This process has since slowly evolved, but having the patience to work *with* this family, rather than *on* this family, has begun to pay dividends. This collaborative approach to therapy has been effective for Martha in that she has been able to devise parenting strategies on her own and reports feeling more in control of her circumstances than when the family entered therapy. In line with previous research findings, these feelings of self-efficacy have appeared to help Martha cope with her son's misbehavior, handle stress more effectively, and demonstrate greater wisdom in her interactions with Michael (Jackson, 2000). By taking this collaborative approach, I have found that it has demonstrated greater respect for this family and allowed Martha the space to take an active part in the therapeutic process.

In order to foster a collaborative therapeutic relationship, therapists are suggested to frame their role as that of facilitator, rather than leader, a role that involves the family in the process of problem identification, goal setting, and treatment planning (Kaplan & Girard, 1994). Collaborative therapists communicate a profound faith in a family's assets and abilities (Aponte, 1994). This message can be particularly important for families in poverty, many of whom carry family narratives characterized by a seemingly endless series of intense crises. Finding a therapist who believes in them can offer a family hope that their current situation is not destined for despair. A collaborative stance also allows therapy to be more respectful, relevant, and acceptable for families in poverty (Bailey, 1987; Brandt, 1993). Further, non-hierarchical therapy is effective, in that it is often a non-judgmental and open environment for the resolution of differences between clients and therapist, prevents the therapist from being perceived as aloof and self-righteous, and provides an opportunity for the therapist to model communication, respect, and problem-resolution skills.

Therapist Non-Neutrality

Feminist family therapists recognize that therapeutic neutrality is a myth originally developed from the early traditions of psychoanalysis. In fact, from a feminist perspective, it is impossible to practice value-free therapy, as all therapists are creations of their unique social contexts (James & McIntyre, 1983; Simola, 1992). The question of whether or not values influence a therapist's approach is moot, for that is an unavoidable part of the therapeutic process. Values influence virtually any behavior that occurs in the therapy room, from what therapists say or do not say all the way to what type of clothing they wear. Instead, a more appropriate question asks *which* values influence a therapist's approach. It is important to recognize and remain conscious of these values, in order to understand the implicit messages being reinforced through the therapeutic process (Avis, 1989).

This lesson is critical, given the value placed on financial success in the American capitalist tradition. The Culture of Poverty and the Puritan Work Ethic are two value codes underlying many of the economic and political ideologies of the United States (Eitzen & Zinn, 2000; Inclan & Ferran, 1990). These doctrines have created a set of beliefs that characterize people in poverty as deserving of their circumstances due to inherent character deficiencies (Culture of Poverty) and due to a lack of hard work that would have allowed them to "pull themselves up by their bootstraps" (Puritan Work Ethic). These views have been powerful determinants of American cultural values and social policy for decades. It is critical for therapists working with families in poverty to reflect on how these messages may or may not have influenced their views of the world. Further, therapists are urged to critique these value codes from a systemic perspective and understand the logical flaws in these arguments. In fact, Aponte (1991; 1994) argues that values clarification is a critical step for developing therapists who are sensitive to the needs and experiences of families in poverty.

As family mental health professionals, one of the most important questions for family therapists to ask themselves can be "What is my definition of a 'healthy' family?" This question often explicitly or implicitly guides a great deal of what family therapists do. However, there are often circumstances in which the response a therapist might give differs from that given by a family in poverty. Without understanding the professional consequences of their answers to this question, therapists run the risk of imposing a definition of "normal family functioning" that is not necessarily the same as that of the families they treat. For example, a family facing both financial stress and relationship crises may be content with reducing family conflicts to once or twice a week, while their therapist may have a goal in mind that includes reduction of conflict to once per month, increased emotional intimacy between family members, and honest communication of innermost feelings. When therapists do not take the time to appreciate and respect a family's definition of a "healthy" family, they run the risk of alienating clients, communicating that their definition is somehow inadequate, and prolonging therapy longer than the family would like or can afford.

Due to a belief that therapists' values are ever present during the process, a feminist approach encourages overt expression of value systems to clients as a demonstration of respect (Leslie & Clossick, 1992). While recommended for work with middle-class clientele, disclosing values is also an effective tool when working with families in poverty. Carefully taking this step during the initial sessions can serve as a means for diffusing the implicit tension that exists between the value systems of the therapist and the client. By and large, a therapist holding a graduate degree will likely approach therapy from a different perspective than a family who is struggling financially. Even in those cases where values do not greatly differ, clients, therapist, or both will likely expect them to. When done in a respectful and collaborative manner, this discussion can remove the pressure from the therapist and family alike inferring each other's value system. This conversation also allows an opportunity for the therapist to explain his or her approach to therapy, be understood as a unique person with particular values, provide clients with a sense of where particular beliefs originate from, open a dialogue concerning these beliefs, and deconstruct any stereotypes the family has about therapists or therapy, in general.

However, disclosing personal and professional values must be done judiciously, particularly in a community-based agency setting. Disclosure of values has been advocated in order to provide clients with the opportunity to select another therapist when value systems are incongruent (Leslie & Clossick, 1992). Yet, in an agency setting, where staff is often limited, waiting lists can be lengthy, and clients typically do not have the power to originally select a therapist, families in poverty do not realistically have the option of changing clinicians. In this context, when presented in an inflexible and disrespectful manner, a therapist's value system may inadvertently become an instrument of client oppression. As such, families may feel as if they are facing limited options–either drop out of therapy and not receive the help they are seeking or remain with a therapist who does not necessarily agree with their perspectives. The responsibility for therapists is to honestly determine if their personal and professional assumptions allow them to provide ethical, sensitive, and responsible services for clients in poverty (Aponte, 1991). However, failing to find a perfect match between value perspectives does not necessarily preclude the possibility of providing effective family therapy. In this context, engaging in a respectful, collaborative decision-making process with clients concerning the future of the therapeutic relationship is beneficial in maintaining an open dialogue between client and therapist. Should clients decide to continue therapy, it is the responsibility of the therapist to reassure clients that therapy is a collaborative process that will help them explore various solutions for their problems, rather than an environment in which an "expert" will instruct them on what is best. Despite any values and research findings that the therapist brings to treatment suggestions, it is ultimately the family's prerogative to select the alternatives that are the most appropriate for their lives. This discussion will remove the mystery of the therapist's hidden agendas and place the power for making final decisions in the hands of the clients.

For example, an often controversial issue in family therapy and parent education programs concerns the use of corporal punishment. This topic is particularly relevant in work with low-income clients, given the higher prevalence of spanking in families that receive public assistance, have children living in poverty, or experience maternal unemployment (Giles-Sims, Straus, & Sugarman, 1995). While approaching my work from a feminist perspective, my personal and professional value systems will not allow me to advocate the use of corporal punishment. I have found it helpful to be direct with clients in discussing spanking as a potentially aggressive, power assertive, and demeaning form of child punishment. However, it is also important for clients to be aware that research on the outcomes of spanking has been largely inconclusive (Larzelere, 1996). In this context, evidence has emerged that spanking in African-American families does not typically produce the detrimental effects associated with spanking among Euro-American families (Deater-Deckard, Dodge, Bates, & Pettit, 1996). As such, the effects of corporal punishment appear to be mediated by a host of contextual factors, such as family ethnicity, neighborhood environment, developmental stage of the child, community norms, and overall level of affection in the home (Baumrind, 1996). In discussing this topic with parents, I typically attempt to accomplish three goals: (1) acknowledge parents as experts on what is best for their children, (2) be honest and respectful in presenting my professional values, and (3) educate parents through the use of recent research findings both for and against the use of spanking. I have found that simultaneously attending to these goals creates an open environment in which to engage parents in discussion about discipline strategies for their children.

Attention to Both Individual and Family Well-Being

The final principle to receive mention involves sensitivity on the part of therapists to both the individual well-being of each family member and the overall well-being of the family system. From this perspective, feminist therapists attempt to avoid subordinating personal needs, especially those of women, to the needs of the family (Bograd, 1986). The goal is to examine the special needs of individuals as well as the family (Chaney & Piercy, 1988), in order to help women resist gender socialization that has taught them to sacrifice their emotional well-being in support of other family members (Fish, 1989).

Encouraging self-care behavior in low-income clients can be particularly important in coping with poverty. The stress associated with
crowded living conditions, neighborhood crime, substandard education systems, local gang activity, finding or maintaining employment,
or coping with demanding labor can often be overwhelming for family
members living in urban poverty. When unchecked, this stress has
been associated with self-destructive behavior and psychological disturbance (Costello et al., 1998; Minuchin et al., 1998). When appropriate
for a family's circumstances, individual family members may benefit
from discovering personalized forms of self-care that can provide
relief from the stress of everyday life. Finding this relief can help to
energize family members and prepare them emotionally to contribute
to family well-being. In this sense, encouraging self-care helps to
gradually strengthen the family system, one member at a time. However, in designing interventions, consideration must be given to the
family's access to financial resources, transportation, and childcare.
These factors influence the type of self-care behavior that these family
members can realistically entertain. Again, recommending self-care
techniques in light of these factors requires a great deal of creativity on
the part of therapists and clients.

However, while promoting personal well-being, the needs of the
family must also remain central to the treatment plan. The stress
related to poverty not only affects individual family members, but also
has detrimental influences on the overall cohesiveness of the family
system. Research has demonstrated a relation between socioeconomic
disadvantage, parental and family exposure to acute and chronic stressors,
less nurturant and more punitive parenting practices, and detrimental
developmental trends in children (e.g., low school achievement, low
IQ scores, and low socioemotional functioning) (McLoyd, 1990, 1998;
McLoyd et al., 1994). Simply stated, the stress associated with poverty
tends to weaken the family's structure over time (Aponte, 1991;
1994). Given these outcomes, it may be uncomfortable to women and
their families for a therapist to overemphasize autonomy and self-interest when the primary goal of therapy is to develop and maintain
greater family unity (Denny, 1986). Even though they may be attending family therapy to resolve interpersonal conflicts, these families
still consider their kin network to be a significant source of social
support in an otherwise fragmented community. In order to design
interventions that are sensitive to a family's needs, it is important to

understand how they conceptualize their needs for both personal autonomy and for family cohesion. Doing so can help in striking a balance between encouraging individual self-care and promoting the overall well-being of the family.

CONCLUSION

While issues of social class and economic marginalization have been largely excluded from family therapy training, these considerations are important in preparing clinicians to address the needs and goals of families in poverty. Poverty has profound effects on personal well-being and family cohesiveness. These outcomes are particularly alarming in the context of recent economic trends that seem to indicate that more and more families are struggling to survive financially. There may also be reason to believe that ignoring these issues may leave therapists ill-prepared to provide sensitive and respectful mental health care. More subtly, this lack of training may also leave clinicians largely unaware of the implicit social class assumptions that drive their work with families in poverty. In overcoming these deficiencies in the training literature, this paper has been designed as an attempt to apply principles of feminist family therapy to therapeutic work with low-income families. While criticized as a philosophy created from a middle-class, Euro-American perspective, adapting principles of feminist family therapy has potential as a model for designing class-conscious family therapy.

While this paper has been intended as a step in the process, it is hoped that future work will consider the more specific nuances of providing family therapy for families in poverty and continue academic discourse on this topic. Doing so will help develop a foundation of knowledge from which therapists may begin to appreciate the complexities of this issue. To this end, future work may address therapeutic considerations relevant at the intersection between poverty and other dimensions of a family culture. These contextual dimensions may include, but are not necessarily limited to ethnicity, religious preference, sexual orientation, location of residence (i.e., urban, suburban, rural), political ideology, number of children, family constellation, and immigration status. Attempting to synthesize issues of poverty with other cultural factors will hopefully produce a greater appreciation for the way that economic marginalization and cultural diversity influence family therapy. In addition, further training material de-signed to help therapists to understand their own assumptions and value systems may prove beneficial in uncovering the inadvertent biases present in their therapeutic work. Values clarification resources may be particularly important given family therapy's origins, the dif-fering ideologies often held by clients and therapists, and the emotion-al and political beliefs that often surround discussions of poverty and social marginalization. It is also hoped that attempts will be made to apply various family therapy theories to work with families in poverty. Applying both theory and practice of specific therapeutic models may help provide therapists and clinical supervisors with guidance when approaching cases with low-income families. These efforts may be particularly valuable in light of the potential match between contem-porary family therapy's emphasis on brief, solution-oriented treatment and the lack of resources often faced by many families in poverty. Finally, it is also hoped that this question will be addressed through applied, clinical research. Employing survey, interview, and observa-tional methods may be valuable in determining the applicability of family therapy models to the experiences of families in poverty. Fu-ture research is needed in this area to increase therapists' clinical competency and reintroduce issues of poverty and social class into family therapy training. Doing so can only increase awareness in the field for the benefit of clients and therapists alike.

REFERENCES

Almeida, R., Woods, R., Messineo, T., Font, R. (1998). The cultural context model: An overview. In M. McGoldrick (Ed.), *Re-visioning Family Therapy: Race, Culture, and Gender in Clinical Practice* (pp. 414-431). New York, NY: The Guilford Press.

Aponte, H. J. (1974). Psychotherapy for the poor: An eco-structural approach to treatment. *Delaware Medical Journal, 46*(3), 134-144.

Aponte, H. J. (1976). The family-school interview: An eco-structural approach. *Family Process, 15,* 303-311.

Aponte, H. J. (1986). If I don't get simple, I cry. *Family Process, 25,* 531-548.

Aponte, H. J. (1991). Training on the person of the therapist for work with the poor and minorities. *Journal of Independent Social Work, 5*(3/4), 23-39.

Aponte, H. J. (1994). *Bread and Spirit: Therapy with the New Poor: Diversity of Race, Culture, and Values.* New York, NY: W. W. Norton and Co., Inc.

Atwood, J. D., & Genovese, F. (1997). The feminization of poverty: Issues and therapeutic concerns. *Journal of Feminist Family Therapy, 9*(2), 21-40.

Ault-Riche, M. (1986). A feminist critique of five schools of family therapy. *The Family Therapy Collections, 16,* 1-15.

Avis, J. M. (1989). Integrating gender into the family therapy curriculum. *Journal of Feminist Family Therapy, 1*(2), 3-26.

Bailey, D. B., Jr. (1987). Collaborative goal-setting with families: Resolving differences in values and priorities for services. *Topics in Early Childhood Special Education, 7*(2), 59-71.

Bateman, A. L. (1993). Barriers to mental health care access for the individual in crisis. Unpublished doctoral dissertation, University of Massachusetts, Amherst.

Baumrind, D. (1996). A blanket injunction against disciplinary use of spanking is not warranted by the data. *Pediatrics, 98*(4), 828-831.

Boettcher, K. (1999, August). Clinton's poverty tour an insult to millions. *The People, 109*(5), 3.

Bograd, M. (1986). A feminist examination of family therapy: What is women's place? *Women & Therapy, 5*(2/3), 95-106.

Bograd, M. (1987). Enmeshment, fusion, or relatedness? A conceptual analysis. *Journal of Psychotherapy and the Family, 3*(4), 65-80.

Boyd-Franklin, N. (1989). *Black Families in Therapy: A Multisystems Approach.* New York, NY: The Guilford Press.

Boyd-Franklin, N. (1993). Race, class, and poverty. In F. Walsh (Ed.), *Normal Family Processes* (pp. 361-376). New York, NY: The Guilford Press.

Boyd-Franklin, N., & Shenouda, N. T. (1990). A multisystems approach to the treatment of a Black, inner-city family with a schizophrenic mother. *American Journal of Orthopsychiatry, 60*(2), 186-195.

Brandt, P. (1993). Negotiation and problem-solving strategies: Collaboration between families and professionals. *Infants and Young Children, 5*(4), 78-84.

Calloway, M. O., & Morrissey, J. P. (1998). Overcoming service barriers for homeless persons with serious psychiatric disorders. *Psychiatric Services, 49*(12), 1568-1572.

Chaney, S. E., & Piercy, F. P. (1988). A feminist family therapist behavior checklist. *American Journal of Family Therapy, 16*(4), 305-318.

Costello, E. J., Messer, S. C., Bird, H. R., Cohen, P., & Reinherz, H. Z. (1998). The prevalence of serious emotional disturbance: A re-analysis of community studies. *Journal of Child and Family Studies, 7*(4), 411-432.

Dankoski, M. E., Penn, C. D., Carlson, T. D., & Hecker, L. L. (1998). What's in a name? A study of family therapists' use and acceptance of the feminist perspective. *American Journal of Family Therapy, 26*(2), 95-104.

Deater-Deckard, K., Dodge, K. A., Bates, J. E., & Pettit, G. S. (1996). Physical discipline among African American and European American mothers: Links to children's externalizing behaviors. *Developmental Psychology, 32*(6), 1065-1072.

Denny, P. A. (1986). Women and poverty: A challenge to the intellectual and therapeutic integrity of feminist therapy. *Women & Therapy, 5*(4), 51-63.

Dermer, S. B., Hemesath, C. W., & Russell, C. S. (1998). A feminist critique of solution-focused therapy. *American Journal of Family Therapy, 26*(3), 239-250.

Eitzen, D. S., & Zinn, M. B. (2000). The missing safety net and families: A progressive critique of the new welfare legislation. *Journal of Sociology and Social Welfare, 27*(1), 53-72.

Falicov, C. J. (1995). Training to think culturally: A multidimensional comparative framework. *Family Process, 34*(4), 373-388.

Falicov, C. J. (1998). *Latino families in therapy.* New York, NY: The Guilford Press.

Faunce, P. S. (1990). Women in poverty: Ethical dimensions in therapy. In H. Lerman, & N. Porter (Eds.), *Feminist Ethics in Psychotherapy* (pp. 185-194). New York, NY: Springer Publishing Co., Inc.

Feinson, M. C., & Popper, M. (1995). Does affordability affect mental health utilization? A United States-Israel comparison of older adults. *Social Science and Medicine, 40*(5), 669-678.

Fish, L. S. (1989). Comparing structural, strategic, and feminist-informed family therapies: Two Delphi studies. *American Journal of Family Therapy, 17*(4), 303-314.

Friedman, B. D., & Levine-Holdowsky, M. (1997). Overcoming barriers to homeless delivery services: A community response. *Journal of Social Distress and the Homeless, 6*(1), 13-28.

Funkhouser, S. W., & Moser, D. K. (1990). Is health care racist? *Advances in Nursing Science, 12*(2), 47-55.

Giles-Sims, J., Straus, M. A., & Sugarman, D. B. (1995). Child, maternal, and family characteristics associated with spanking. *Family Relations, 44,* 170-176.

Goldner, V. (1985). Feminism and family therapy. *Family Process, 24,* 31-47.

Goldner, V. (1988). Generation and gender: Normative and covert hierarchies. *Family Process, 27,* 17-31.

Goldner, V. (1991). Feminism and systemic practice: Two critical traditions in transition. *Journal of Strategic and Systemic Therapies, 10*(3/4), 118-126.

Gunderson, C., LeBlanc, M., & Kuhn, B. (1999). The changing food assistance landscape. In U.S. Department of Agriculture Economic Research Services, *USDA Agricultural Economic Report* (USDA Publication No. 773, pp. 1-28). Washington, DC: U.S. Department of Agriculture.

Haddock, S. A., Zimmerman, T. S., & MacPhee, D. (2000). The power equity guide: Attending to gender in family therapy. *Journal of Marital and Family Therapy, 26*(2), 153-170.

Hare-Mustin, R. T. (1978). A feminist approach to family therapy. *Family Process, 17,* 181-194.

Hartman, A., & Laird, J. (1983). *Family-centered social work practice.* New York, NY: Free Press.

Hendley, A. A., & Bilimoria, N. F. (1999). Policy paper: Minorities and social security: An analysis of racial and ethnic differences in the current program. *Social Security Bulletin, 62*(2), 59-64.

Hill, M. (1992). A feminist model for the use of paradoxical techniques in psychotherapy. *Professional Psychology: Research and Practice, 23*(4), 287-292.

hooks, b. (1981). *Ain't I a Woman: Black Women and Feminism.* Boston, MA: South End Press.

Hopps, J. G., & Pinderhughes, E. (1999). *Group Work with Overwhelmed Clients: How the Power of Groups Can Help People Transform Their Lives.* New York, NY: The Free Press.

Hunter, J. K., Getty, C., Kemsley, M., & Skelly, A. H. (1991). Barriers to providing health care to homeless persons: A survey of providers perceptions. *Health Values,* *15*(5), 3-11.

Illback, R. (1994). Poverty and the crisis in children's services: The need for services integration. *Journal of Clinical Child Psychology, 23,* 413-424.

Inclan, J., & Ferran, E. (1990). Poverty, politics, and family therapy: A role for systems theory. In M. P. Mirkin (Ed.), *The Social and Political Contexts of Family Therapy* (pp. 193-213). Boston, MA: Allyn & Bacon.

Jackson, A. P. (2000). Maternal self-efficacy and children's influence on stress and parenting among single Black mothers in poverty. *Journal of Family Issues, 21*(1), 3-16.

James, K., & MacKinnon, L. K. (1986). Theory and practice of structural family therapy: Illustration and critique. *Australian and New Zealand Journal of Family Therapy, 7*(4), 223-233.

James, K., & McIntyre, D. (1983). The reproduction of families: The social role of family therapy? *Journal of Marital and Family Therapy, 9*(2), 119-129.

James, K., & McIntyre, D. (1989). "A momentary gleam of enlightenment": Towards a model of feminist family therapy. *Journal of Feminist Family Therapy, 1*(3), 3-24.

Kanuha, V. (1990). The need for an integrated analysis of oppression in feminist therapy ethics. In H. Lerman, & N. Porter (Eds.), *Feminist Ethics in Psychotherapy* (pp. 24-35). New York, NY: Springer Publishing Co., Inc.

Kaplan, L., & Girard, J. L. (1994). *Strengthening High-Risk Families: A Handbook for Practitioners.* New York, NY: Lexington Books.

Kazdin, A. E., Holland, L., & Crowley, M. (1997). Family experience of barriers to treatment and premature termination from child therapy. *Journal of Consulting and Clinical Psychology, 65*(3), 453-463.

Larzelere, R. E. (1996). A review of the outcomes of parental use of nonabusive or customary physical punishment. *Pediatrics, 98*(4), 824-828.

Lee, J. (1997). Women re-authoring their lives through feminist narrative therapy. *Women & Therapy, 20*(3), 1-22.

Leslie, L. A., & Clossick, M. L. (1992). Changing set: Teaching family therapy from a feminist perspective. *Family Relations, 41,* 256-263.

MacKinnon, L. K., & Miller, D. (1987). The new epistemology and the Milan approach: Feminist and sociopolitical considerations. *Journal of Marital and Family Therapy, 13*(2), 139-155.

McGoldrick, M. (Ed.). (1998). *Re-Visioning Family Therapy: Race, Culture, and Gender in Clinical Practice.* New York, NY: The Guilford Press.

McGoldrick, M., Almeida, R., Preto, N. G., Bibb, A., Sutton, C., Hudak, J., & Hines, P. M. (1999). Efforts to incorporate social justice perspectives into a family therapy training program. *Journal of Marital and Family Therapy, 25*(2), 191-209.

McLoyd, V. C. (1990). The impact of economic hardship on Black families and children: Psychological distress, parenting, and socioemotional development. *Child Development, 61*(2), 311-346.

McLoyd, V. C. (1998). Socioeconomic disadvantage and child development. *American Psychologist, 53*(2), 185-204.

McLoyd, V. C., Jayaratne, T. E., Ceballo, R., & Borquez, J. (1994). Unemployment and work interruption among African-American single mothers: Effects on parenting and adolescent socioemotional functioning. *Child Development, 65,* 562-589.

Meyerson, A. T., & Herman, G. H. (1987). Systems resistance to the chronic patient. *New Directions for Mental Health Services, 33,* 21-33.

Minuchin, P., Colapinto, J., & Minuchin, S. (1998). *Working with Families of the Poor.* New York, NY: The Guilford Press.

Minuchin, S., Montalvo, B., Guerney, B., Jr., Rosman, B., & Schumer, F. (1967). *Families of the slums: An exploration of their structure and treatment.* New York, NY: Basic Books.

Montemurri, P. (1998, December 9). Local news: Out of poverty. *Detroit Free Press,* pp. B1-B2.

Mueller, M. R., & Patton, M. Q. (1995). Working with poor families: Lessons learned from practice. *Marriage & Family Review, 21*(1/2), 65-90.

Murrell, N. L., Smith, R., Gill, G., & Oxley, G. (1996). Racism and health care access: A dialogue with childbearing women. *Health Care for Women International, 17,* 149-159.

Northam, S. (1996). Access to health promotion, protection, and disease prevention among impoverished individuals. *Public Health Nursing, 13*(5), 353-364.

Rabin, C. (1989). Gender issues in the treatment of welfare couples: A feminist approach to marital therapy of the poor. *Contemporary Family Therapy, 11*(3), 169-188.

Rosenbluth, S. C., Steil, J. M., & Whitcomb, J. H. (1998). Marital equity: What does it mean? *Journal of Family Issues, 19*(3), 227-244.

Rosenheck, R., & Lam, J. A. (1997). Client and site characteristics as barriers to service use by homeless persons with serious mental illness. *Psychiatric Services, 48*(3), 387-390.

Saba, G. W., & Rodgers, D. V. (1989). Discrimination in urban family practice: Lessons from minority poor families. *Journal of Psychotherapy and the Family, 6*(1/2), 177-207.

Schnitzer, P. K. (1996). "They don't come in!" Stories told, lessons taught about poor families in therapy. *American Journal of Orthopsychiatry, 66*(4), 572-582.

Schwartz, P. (1994). *Peer Marriage: How Love Between Equals Really Works.* New York, NY: Free Press.

Sharlin, S. A., & Shamai, M. (1995). Interventions with families in extreme distress (FED). *Marriage & Family Review, 21*(1/2), 91-122.

Shayne, V. T., & Kaplan, B. J. (1991). Double victims: Poor women and AIDS. *Women & Health, 17*(1), 21-37.

Sidel, R. (2000). The enemy within: The demonization of poor women. *Journal of Sociology and Social Welfare, 27*(1), 73-84.

Simola, S. K. (1992). Differences among sexist, nonsexist, and feminist family therapies. *Professional Psychology: Research and Practice, 23*(5), 397-403.

Taggart, M. (1985). The feminist critique in epistemological perspective: Questions of context in family therapy. *Journal of Marital and Family Therapy, 11*(2), 113-126.

Terry, L. L. (1992). I want my old wife back: A case illustration of a four-stage approach to a feminist-informed strategic/systemic therapy. *Journal of Strategic and Systemic Therapies, 11*(4), 27-41.

Treacher, A. (1988). The Milan method: A preliminary critique. *Journal of Family Therapy, 10*(1), 1-8.

Walker, G., Eric, K., Pivnick, A., & Drucker, E. (1991). A descriptive outline of a program for cocaine-using mothers and their babies. *Journal of Feminist Family Therapy, 3*(3/4), 7-17.

Walker, G., & Small, S. (1991). AIDS, crack, poverty, and race in the African-American community: The need for an ecosystemic approach. *Journal of Independent Social Work, 5*(3/4), 69-91.

Wheeler, D., Avis, J. M., Miller, L. A., & Chaney, S. (1989). Rethinking family therapy training and supervision: A feminist model. In M. McGoldrick, C. M. Anderson, & F. Walsh (Eds.), *Women in Families: A Framework for Family Therapy* (pp. 135-151). New York, NY: W. W. Norton and Co., Inc.

Whipple, V. (1996). Developing an identity as a feminist family therapist: Implications for training. *Journal of Marital and Family Therapy, 22*(3), 381-396.

White, M. (2000, April). *Narrative Therapy: Re-Authoring Lives.* Paper presented at the conference of the Center for Collaborative Change and Colorado Center for Narrative Therapy, Denver, CO.

A Conversation
with Evan Imber-Black, PhD:
Progress and Challenges
in Integrating Gender and Culture
in Family Therapy Training

Shelley A. Haddock

Shelley: As you look back over the past couple of decades as the field began to recognize and integrate the organizing principles of gender and culture into our training activities, what are your reflections on this process?

Evan: I think the changes–especially with regard to gender–have been enormous. When I think back to when we first started looking at these issues, I remember that maybe 10% of the journal boards were comprised of women, and that almost no women were in key leadership positions. Since that time, the changes have been quite profound. These changes were accomplished by a good, old-fashioned political process where women got together, looked at what was happening, and said these things need to change. As a result of this political organizing, there were changes in how we

---

Shelley A. Haddock, MS, is affiliated with Colorado State University.

Address correspondence to: Shelley A. Haddock, MS, 119 Gifford Building, Colorado State University, Fort Collins, CO 80523.

[Haworth co-indexing entry note]: "A Conversation with Evan Imber-Black, PhD: Progress and Challenges in Integrating Gender and Culture in Family Therapy Training." Haddock, Shelley A. Co-published simultaneously in *Journal of Feminist Family Therapy* (The Haworth Press, Inc.) Vol. 12, No. 4, 2001, pp. 239-242; and: *Integrating Gender and Culture in Family Therapy Training* (ed: Toni Schindler Zimmerman) The Haworth Press, Inc., 2001, pp. 239-242. Single or multiple copies of this article are available for a fee from The Haworth Document Delivery Service [1-800-342-9678, 9:00 a.m. - 5:00 p.m. (EST). E-mail address: getinfo@haworthpressinc.com].

looked at theory, practice, the way papers were written, and how students were trained and supervised. With regard to training–at least in the training programs that I know about–there have been some very profound changes. That is not to say that it is all "hunky dory" everywhere. However, I think the message not only got across, but helped to transform the field from what it looked like 20 years ago.

Shelley: When you say that there have been profound changes in at least some of our training programs, what are you seeing?

Evan: I think gender and culture have been largely integrated into much of the training. Gender, however, has been more fully integrated than culture, especially with regards to race. I do not think the importance of gender and culture is a question like it was in the past. There are no longer the kind of debates that went on years ago about whether we should even be talking about such things. I think you see an understanding of the construct of gender and women's position in couples and families as very much a part of training. You see it when people are teaching trainees how to interview and intervene, and when they are helping students look at tapes. These topics are not taught as a separate course on gender or culture. Instead, they are part of every case right from the beginning–from the conceptualization of the presenting problem, to the genogram, to the kinds of questions that are asked. Again, however, I am speaking only about the training programs of which I am aware. I am sure there are places where this kind of integration is not happening. But, if I contrast the present with the early 80's, it is like night and day.

Shelley: In the early 80's, people were debating if gender and culture were even legitimate topics of conversation and now . . . .

Evan: That's right. There was a lot of fighting going on and a lot of craziness at the meetings. For instance, when I was chair of AFTA in the late 80's, I was blasted for inviting thirteen women and three men to be the key speakers and moderators. I was excoriated in print in the *AFTA Newsletter* by Frank Pittman. People did not believe me at the time, but I did not deliberately select more women than men. I deliberately set out to get the best people that I could to be the speakers for the topics of the meeting. But, in responding to some people's concerns, I did go back and count all of the presentations at all of the prior meetings, and then framed this as a mid-course correction. This experience led to more sensitivity about trying to achieve some gender balance in all of the plenaries and the election slates.

Shelley: Are there other comments or reflections that you would like to make as you look back over this time?

Evan: Just that I am very proud of us. I am proud of the whole group of mostly women and some good male allies. I feel proud of how we went about this process, and of how we stayed the course. There were some very painful times, with people getting publicly attacked and that sort of thing. And, I think we supported each other; we held together. I think that we then developed to a point where we could begin to look at our differences from one another, which is a very important development in this process. I think we have been largely successful.

Shelley: As a woman who is coming up a bit later, I am really grateful for all of the work that you and others did, because I know that the field is a very different place. I hope that these changes will not be taken for granted–that the hard work will be remembered and continued.

Evan: I'm really glad to hear you say that.

Shelley: When you reflect on the field now, particularly with regard to training, what do you see as some of the contemporary challenges or opportunities?

Evan: I think that continuing to look at race, class, and sexual orientation is our most important work and challenge. We need to understand that some of the "white, upper middle-class constructions of feminism" might not fit certain other cultures or ethnicities in quite the same way. We need to maintain multiple perspectives. Just as we brought women into positions of leadership in the field at large, we need to work to bring persons of color and gay and lesbian individuals into leadership positions. We have not done a sufficient job of opening the field, recruiting trainees, or mentoring people so that more and more of these leadership positions are filled by persons of color and gay and lesbian individuals.

Shelley: What do think are some of the important next steps in this work?

Evan: Some of these steps will involve affirmative action kinds of effort in both trainee and faculty recruitment and development. I think that this is the way it is going to happen. It will not happen if we just wait. It will take different organizations, training institutes, and academic institutions going through the very difficult work of truly embracing difference and diversity. This is very difficult work–sometimes very painful work–and it has to be done. It involves power sharing–giving up some power, which can be very painful. I think that men had difficulty with this process of power sharing years ago.

I also have a concern that we are not recruiting a sufficient number of men into the field. I think there are many possible reasons for this, but I think we need all of our diverse voices to really help families in the way that we need to.

Shelley: Evan, thank you for your thoughts on this topic, and for all of your hard work and significant contributions to the field over the years. The field has been and continues to be greatly enriched by your voice.

Reflections on Current Feminist Training in Family Therapy

Rhea V. Almeida
Miguel Hernandez

The authors of these reflections are situated in two different training contexts and as a result reflect some differences in context and training emphasis. Our reflections include observations and conversations with numerous other training sites as well. As two trainers of color with differences in gender, age, and culture, we also represent a particular standpoint with respect to social location. One of us is an Asian Indian woman. She is of color while her hair passes for white and the other a Latino man. He is light skinned, has hair that can pass for white, however, his language and country of origin resituate him at the margin. We both have class privilege and hold a social political perspective of identity and socialization, rather than one defined solely by gender. For the purposes of these reflections we have chosen to use the language of "women who are other" when describing women who are not from a dominant group. We use this descriptor in order to include many women, such as Arab women, for instance, who may not fit the category of "women of color" but are certainly "other" due to their culture and religion.

The concept of standpoint is an important one as it relates to these

Rhea V. Almeida is Founder/Director, Institute for Family Services, and faculty, Family Institute of New Jersey, Metuchen, NJ.

Miguel Hernandez is on the faulty at the Ackerman Institute for Family Therapy and at the Roberto Clemente Center, NYC.

[Haworth co-indexing entry note]: "Reflections on Current Feminist Training in Family Therapy." Almeida, Rhea V., and Miguel Hernandez. Co-published simultaneously in *Journal of Feminist Family Therapy* (The Haworth Press, Inc.) Vol. 12, No. 4, 2001, pp. 243-249; and: *Integrating Gender and Culture in Family Therapy Training* (ed: Toni Schindler Zimmerman) The Haworth Press, Inc., 2001, pp. 243-249. Single or multiple copies of this article are available for a fee from The Haworth Document Delivery Service [1-800-342-9678, 9:00 a.m. - 5:00 p.m. (EST). E-mail address: getinfo@haworthpressinc.com].

particular reflections as well as feminist family therapy training (FFTT). Defining one's standpoint or position in any micro/macro context provides some of the definitional boundaries. It conveys to the reader the origin of the narrated knowledge. Standpoint for us is the particular position we occupy both in the larger world, and within the family therapy training arena itself. While outsiders mostly, we still retain a passage to the inside as long as our movement is somewhat silent. When we begin to question the issues of privilege and oppression as they relate to the training context we are often forced to divert our attention towards the client systems, or towards more "relevant" matters. A familiar silencing strategy. Other times we are persuaded to believe that our agenda is different from that of the training institute, or that we just tend to focus too much on the politics of life, and not sufficiently on the personal/emotional realm of life. The realm, after all, that we, the outsider/therapist/trainers, know is the MOST significant to our clients is the realm of politics of power and oppression.

White male models of family therapy still dominate the legitimate training sphere with a few feminist insertions here and there. In our view there are currently NO family therapy training programs that we would call feminist. Unlike the voice of publication that has achieved notoriety through a separate journal, the role of feminism within the context of family therapy training centers is undefined, and consequently still marginal. Whether FFTT can consider itself legitimately institutionalized remains debatable, although the writings of particular feminist therapists (White women who still see feminism as a gender issue, ignoring class, race, culture, religion and history) have gathered a wide and acknowledging audience.

It is a good 10 years that our field has merged the White dominant feminist discourse with the Family Therapy discourse. It is a common belief that feminist ideas and structural contributions are relevant for all women regardless of their class, culture, race or religion. This perspective is exclusive towards all women who are "other" and no doubt reflects the very type of patterned domination that the movement attempted to disenfranchise and liberate. When feminism is defined by White, intellectual women, which the case in family therapy, it can only alter structure and expand choices for women with similar experience and background. The experience of women who are "other" is excluded from such a discourse–a discourse that supports the universality of gender experience. Furthermore, the FFTT discourse in its current collective endeavor is relevant only for women who have the power to define themselves as "feminist," and/or those who have the option to hear and think about these issues. This assumption of literacy only contains a small collective of knowledge bearers. The question that continues to be a moral dilemma in FFTT is "how to provide power to all women so as to create sources of self-determination and liberation that will ultimately transform their own definitions and thus create choices."

We want to reflect on two important roles: one is the role and power of FFTTs to language definitions of gender; and the other is the absence of genuine narratives of liberation–narratives that would embrace both transformations of empowerment and accountability.

Our definition of feminist family therapy is one that conceptually holds larger categories of women's experience, and thus includes complex and often competing notions of experience. From a standpoint of liberation FFTTs ought to embrace components of social action, with the reference point for change being larger than the nuclear family system. Sources for liberation and empowerment ought to originate within the culture/race of origin, rather than originating within the white therapeutic system and then being imposed upon the client system. Partnering with the therapeutic system in this way creates transformations that are rooted within the particular cultural/racial group. In maintaining a dominant paradigm most FFTTs fail to:

1. attend sufficiently to the role of masculinity/accountability;
2. challenge conservatism found within communities considered "other";
3. hold a mosaic of complexity, thereby reducing issues to gender and culture;
4. hold an expanded concept of time and thus create truly feminist models of delivery.

Since the liberation of women that is intrinsically tied to the accountability of men is NOT a dominant prescriptor it is most often left out of the analysis. Nowhere in the family therapy literature, and certainly only in a few contributions of FFTTs, is there sustained attention to the role of masculinity as it pertains to the liberation of women. It is the dominant prescription to theorize the liberation of women only within systems of empowerment excluding those of accountability. White women can be liberated outside of their familial/

community context as the entire culture consists of white men as holders/supporters of institutional power. White women are not isolated from their larger communities, even while they hold less power than their male counterparts. Women who are "other," in contrast, are systematically disenfranchised institutionally, and therefore more oppressed when the role of men in their communities is not attended to in a way that brings systems of accountability and empowerment into the therapy of liberation–into the therapy room.

There is another thorny dilemma in addressing the different women who are "other" that is missing in most Family Therapy programs discourse. That is the need to raise the difficult conversation regarding the conservatism that surrounds these communities and therapists from these same communities. This conservatism or "vigor for racial/ cultural pride" often authenticates the desire for male survival at the expense of female decimation. If FFTTs are both unaware of and unable to challenge these complex social and political forces, there will be a collusion that will most certainly disinherit any system of liberation that centers women with men.

Through a critique of consciousness there have been efforts to redefine this monolithic view of feminism and provide the field with an expanded view of women's experience. This definition of feminism requires that FFTTs authoring change for women in families be able to hold a mosaic view that would more likely contain complexities. Consider this presentation: a Jewish (Caucasian) man and Vietnamese (Asian) woman request marital therapy. Assessing the power distinctions within the interior of the couple's life–money, sex, children/ childcare, occupations–is something that most FFTTs can unflinchingly describe. However, constructing the power imbalances as defined by the social location of this couple is not familiar terrain for most FFTTs. Our definition of social location is the entire sociopolitical context of this family: both their perceptions of themselves and each other, as well as that of the larger culture's perceptions of them; their class distinctions; their general connection to work and a community. These larger social distinctions frame the couple's experience in numerous ways and therefore need to be part of the on-going construction of therapy.

An expanded concept of time is also central to intervening within a feminist perspective. The ordering of time and space in the dominant culture is used to attend to a single issue at any given moment. (It is the way we have to come to accept "segregation" as a normal way of life.) Time regulates and socializes with the pulse of a dominant spirit: White western linear constructions. By focusing on singular issues, "one at a time," within the interior of family life alone, the therapist makes the family's interior problem/s larger than their social context. When therapists (or managed care companies) designate a specific time frame (50 minutes or 6 weeks) to address specific problems, they create a structure that contradicts the multidimensionality of the family's lived experience. An example of how this might be countered is the flexible scheduling that we use at the Institute for Family Services. Within this framework, clients are able to attend a community meeting that starts at 6:00 p.m. and ends at 10:00 p.m. Multiple issues are addressed by a team of therapists and clients experience the freedom of knowing that that they do not have to pack their information into a limited time frame and that their social location is the backdrop to whatever solutions for change emerge.

Another large gap in the training as we see it is a lack of knowledge about "HOW" to implement at a micro level the experience of race, gender, culture and sexual orientation. While many feminist therapists have an intellectual understanding of these parallel discourses, they do not have a feminist model of family therapy to draw upon. This creates a reliance on the major, albeit male, models of family therapy, or a didactic/lecture form of intervention about the experiences of gender, race, culture and sexual orientation. A didactic approach with the couple described above would entail the FFTT speaking to both partners about patriarchy (detailing the two different forms of patriarchy within these two cultures) and the oppressive role of men in families. Didactic interventions privilege a particular level of literacy about gender and patriarchy. So the intention to address power imbalances within the family assumes a particular standpoint with respect to the woman in therapy. The assumption is that she would have a specific knowledge base that would facilitate her critique of consciousness as it relates to her particular dilemma. Absent are culturally/gendered narratives of liberation that might empower the woman and simultaneously offer the man new forms of masculinity.

With such a narrow training approach there are arguably two problems. One of the problems is what social learning theorists like Ogbu and Hale-Bensen have long articulated, that many individuals learn less effectively through cognitive delivery and more through other forms of exposure. These alternate channels of learning might be audiovisual mediums as well as other experiential modes. In particular, with families/couples/children who are "other," learning and change occurs in many different ways which may exclude cognitive process. Not providing alternative systems of intervention/learning creates a dominant prescription for change under the rubric of "feminism."

Another problem with a strictly didactic approach is what Freire (1992) describes as a lack of developed critical conscience. For example when the woman/man in the therapy room is asked to offer their analysis of gender within the culture (a stance often used to convey "respect" to the culture) the response will be within a range of gendered norms within their own communities. Oftentimes the woman might reflect a position of culture that notoriously elevates men and describes women's position from a traditional perspective. If the FFTT is not informed about the range of diversity around gendered norms within that particular culture, it becomes standard practice to accept the woman's definition and assume that the cultural restraints are homogenous within that group. This type of assumption, no matter how respectful the intent, is another form of racism and ultimately not reflective of a high moral conscience within that culture.

As FFTTs we ought to strive towards an acute understanding of the range of normative expression for women within all cultures. To illustrate, when an Islamic woman describes forced veiling (purdah) as part of her culture, we need to know that not all veiling is forced. We ought to familiarize ourselves with the discourse of Islam and feminism in order to redefine the pride system for the particular woman who sees no way out of her oppression and to create a collaborative system of intervention between the woman in the room, Islamic feminists, and the therapeutic context.

So while the relevance of culture and gender has penetrated most training contexts, FFTT remains suspended at the level of ethnicity and group stereotypes. That is why we proclaim at the outset that there are no FFTT programs that we would call feminist. FFTT is still stalled in forms of knowledge acquisition that insert conservative norms regarding difference, generalizes in-group characteristics, and does not further the scholarship on women's empowerment or men's accountability to that system of liberation.

As the authors of these reflections, we would like to address the fact that we have not paid sufficient attention to the ways in which the structure of family therapy training still remains isomorphic to dominant institutions.

Questions that need to be considered:

1. What kinds of conversations or structural maps exist for handling difficult situations around gender, race, and culture and power?
2. How is gender and diversity handled among faculty?
3. How do faculty deal with power and control of leadership vis-à-vis the members of the organization?
4. What are the boundaries for mentoring students who are "other"?
5. How are leaders considered "other" integrated into a particular training institute without being co-opted into the particular organization which maintains their "otherness"?
6. Are there models of collaboration that would sanction the building of scholarship between trainees who are "other" and feminist trainers?

REFERENCE

Freire, P. (1992). *Pedagogy of the Oppressed*. New York: Herder & Herder.

Index